CONJUGAL RITES

Conjugal Rites
Marriage and Marriage-like Relationships before the Law

Heather Brook

palgrave
macmillan

First published in 2007 by

PALGRAVE MACMILLAN™
175 Fifth Avenue, New York, N.Y. 10010 and
Houndmills, Basingstoke, Hampshire, England RG21 6XS.
Companies and representatives throughout the world.

PALGRAVE MACMILLAN is the global academic imprint of the Palgrave Macmillan division of St. Martin's Press, LLC and of Palgrave Macmillan Ltd. Macmillan® is a registered trademark in the United States, United Kingdom and other countries. Palgrave is a registered trademark in the European Union and other countries.

ISBN-13: 978-1-4039-7656-7
ISBN-10: 1-4039-7656-2

Library of Congress Cataloging-in-Publication Data
Brook, Heather.
    Conjugal rites : marriage and marriage-like relationships before the law / Heather Brook.
        p. cm.
    Includes bibliographical references and index.
    ISBN 1-4039-7656-2
    1. Domestic relations—History. 2. Marriage law-History. 3. Unmarried couples—Legal status, laws, etc.—History. 4. Cohabitation agreements—History. 5. Same-sex marriage—Law and legislation—History. I. Title.

    K670.B76 2007
    346.01'609-dc22   2007023136

A catalogue record of the book is available from the British Library.

Design by Scribe Inc.

First edition: December 2007

10 9 8 7 6 5 4 3 2 1

Printed in the United States of America.

Parts of Chapters 2 and 6 were published as "Just Married? Adversarial Divorce and the Conjugal Body Politic," *Feminism & Psychology*. Special Issue on Marriage (II), Volume 14 (1): 81–99, 2004; and "Stalemate: Rethinking the Politics of Marriage," *Feminist Theory* 3 (1): 45–56, 2002. Parts of Chapter 5 were originally published as "The Troubled Courtship of Gladys & Mick," *Australian Journal of Political Science* 32 (3): 419–36, 1997.

Transferred to Digital Printing in 2008

CONTENTS

ACKNOWLEDGMENTS

Since I have been thinking about the issues and ideas explored in this book for many years now, and since thinking is never as solitary as we might like to imagine, there are a number of people whose part in the process I wish to acknowledge.

Without patient support from Ella Georgiades, Joanna Mericle at Palgrave, and others, this project would have been more difficult and less satisfying. I am thankful, too, for the friendly guidance offered by Rosemi Mederos at Scribe.

Closer to home, I thank my colleagues and friends in Women's Studies and the Faculty of Social Sciences at Flinders University for providing research assistance and a collegial working environment. Thanks especially to Barbara Triffett, whose help over many years has been invaluable. I am also indebted to the faculty, graduate students, and visiting researchers of the Political Science Program at the Australian National University's Research School of Social Sciences between 1996 and 1999, and to Barry Hindess in particular.

For their crucial partnership in the complex dance of learning, teaching, and friendship, I extend hearty thanks to Kylie Wilson, Emma Wilkinson, Deb Whitelock, Veronika von Bujdoss, Barbara Sullivan, Hayley Smart-Welgus, Siti Aisyah, Irabinna Rigney, Tracy Riddiford, Sandie Price, Dee Michell, Deb King, Carol Johnson, Tania Innocenti, Belinda Hounslow, Mary Holmes, Barry Hindess, Mary Heath, Ali Elder, Shannon Dowling, Lisa Crago, and Chris Beasley.

For institutional support of a different kind, my gratitude goes to the strong, loving, inspired, and inspiring women in my family: Barbara Brook, Wendy Miller, Brooke Miller, and Tricia McLuckie. For being there for all of us, I thank Des Hollamby. The sisters I choose—Kate Sugars, Meredith Walsh, and Rebecca Stringer—are a

source of enormous pride and joy for me, and I thank each of you for
your good ears, love, wisdom, and wit. For their different orders of
knowledge and lessons in courage, I thank Lindsay Brook and
Martin Brook, both of whom I revive in memory every day. To the
constellation of families sustaining me throughout—the Millers,
McLuckies, Sugars, and Butlins—my warmest thanks.

For being gentle on my mind, for having broad shoulders and a
strong stomach, and for seeing the best in me even at my worst,
thanks beyond measure to Rod Butlin.

CHAPTER 1

INTRODUCTION:
PROPOSALS AND PROPOSITIONS

As a little girl, I received for my sixth or seventh birthday a bride doll. It was a beautiful thing—about a foot high, with blue eyes (which opened and shut), decked from head to toe in voluminous white nylon. Staging the "Wedding of the Year" at the foot of my bed, my bride doll swept down the aisle to meet Ted at the altar, while imaginary guests wept at the gorgeousness of it all. But after the ceremony, as I prepared the bride for what I precociously knew to be "her special night," my pleasure turned to frustration: there were no zips or clasps for removing the doll's outfit. She had been *sewn into* her wedding gown. This seemed to me to be a horror of the magnitude of magical dancing shoes stuck permanently to one's feet. The doll had but one role—one line—and her principal motivation was to avoid getting dirty. There could never be anything beyond the wedding for her—no honeymoon, no affairs, no divorce—just "Here Comes the Bride" rendered over and over on my trusty school recorder. All I could do with her was flip her veil in relentless iterations of the moment of her wedding.

With the repertoire of play limited by her costume, my new bride doll soon became boring. Once she'd married all the other toys, I subjected her to hairdressing with nail scissors and the application of felt-tipped make-up. Before long my beautiful bride doll was dirty and disheveled, and I stopped playing with her. She sat abandoned

on top of the wardrobe, a stained ornament to my imperfect devo-
tion, gathering the dust of her short-lived glory. There is probably a
moral in this story somewhere—if I had hankered after building
blocks rather than dolls, perhaps this would be a book about structural engineering and not marriage. But I doubt it. If I had been
given construction toys, I would probably have built props to be
used in the matrimonial careers of my toys. The moral, if there is
one, is that little girls begin to think about marriage from a very early
age. Some girls' thinking turns to romantic yearning, or longing to
be sewn into a bridal gown. Some of us, mercifully, grow up to be
feminists.

Writing in 1909, English feminist Cicely Hamilton suggested that
our curiosities tend to be aroused by the unusual and exotic.
Familiar things like marriage and the social situation of women, she
said, are so much an accepted part of our lives that we never stop to
think about them (Hamilton 1981, 19). I am not entirely convinced
that this is so. It is true that the marriage practices of white western
societies have not been an especially popular subject of mainstream
scholarship. But for me, at least, marriage has always seemed very
curious indeed. What's more, it seems that an enormous amount of
energy is expended in the maintenance of our interest in marriage.
On a grand scale, there is the pomp, circumstance, and media frenzy
of royal weddings, and the very big business of bridal industries. On
a more mundane level, there is the inevitable boost in soap opera rat-
ings when a wedding looms into the story line. Marriage is anything
but ignored—we are alerted to it at every turn, bombarded daily
with images and messages laden with its social significance. Movies,
magazines, chat shows, soap operas, talk radio, novels, pop songs,
newspaper announcements—the social noise surrounding marriage
is positively cacophonous.

Marriage is an integral aspect of most people's everyday lives, but
its effects are arguably more readily apparent for women. Marital status is an important indicator of identity for men and women; it is one
of the first things we seek to know about a person, second only to
occupation, perhaps. But for women, marriage sometimes *is* an
occupation. For women, marital status is a marker of identity and
interpellation. In all sorts of situations, and upon every form we are
asked to complete, women must nominate a preferred title: Miss
(single), Mrs. (married), or Ms. (not telling).[1] Perhaps Cicely
Hamilton was right, after all. It could well be that the most familiar

and mundane aspects of marriage are those to which we pay the least attention, despite the flurry of activity that surrounds them.

A deep and abiding curiosity to better understand what marriage is and, more importantly, what it does and how it works prompted my research for this book. This curiosity is manifest in several ways. Taking the long history of feminist analysis of marriage as my starting point, it seemed to me that feminist critiques of marriage had to a certain extent become exhausted. In most of the existing first- and early second-wave feminist literature, marriage is cast as a device shackling women in various ways. But in recent years, marriage seems to have lost much of its menace for feminists. This has occurred as society at large has become in many respects more tolerant of people's relationship choices; it is no longer so rebellious or subversive *not* to marry. We are marrying later and divorcing more frequently than ever before. The availability of "easy" divorce and the huge rise in the number of people choosing to live with their partners instead of (or before) marrying seems to constitute evidence of a substantial change in the organization of sexual-affective relationships. Marriage is no longer so *necessary* for women. Marriage could, in this sense at least, be viewed as the scene of a far-reaching feminist victory.

But despite shifts in its characterization as a feminist issue, marriage continues to figure in analyses of women's subordination. The sexual division of labor and sexual-domestic violence, for example, are still theorized as intimately bound up in the sexual politics of public/private dichotomies in which marriage assumes a paradigmatic role. In such analyses, it seems not to matter whether women marry or merely live with men. In either case, the organization of gendered power relations is predicated on an institutional model of marriage. Recent calls to allow gay and lesbian couples to marry raise new (but similar) problems. Some argue that same-sex marriage would subvert the heterosexist history of matrimony. Others insist that it would stamp an institutionally heterosexist imprint onto relationships that have, until now, been resistantly and critically queer. Perhaps the most fundamental aspect of my curiosity to understand marriage, then, hinges on its social-political significance. How does marriage *matter*? What differentiates marriage from merely marriage-*like* relationships?

Further, if marriage has been a scene of feminist resistance, its successes have been somewhat paradoxical. Feminists keen to limit the exploitation of "common-law" wives spearheaded campaigns for the legal regulation of de facto relationships. Yet in broadening the scope of matrimonial legislation to include de facto relationships, their potential as an avenue of marriage resistance seems to have been cordoned off. In the interests of extending justice to women in sexual-affective relationships, more women—even *resistantly* unmarried women—have been deemed "wives." In these and other ways, the effects of reforming women's experience of marriage can be seen to influence who we are—our identities, subjective capacities, and so on. It has become clear to many feminist theorists that there are links between marriage, heterosexuality, and women's political subjectivities, but their connectedness has remained stubbornly resistant to any clearly satisfactory delineation. This is a critical lacuna in feminist thought. While perhaps not sealing that lacuna, this book is situated squarely at its edges, developing a precise and particular understanding of how marriage and marriage-like relationships are governed.

Conjugal Rites, then, is a book about marriage and other intimate relationships—it is a book about conjugality and its various regulatory schemes. It is an interdisciplinary analysis whose raw materials include historical and contemporary social and legal discourses from the United Kingdom, the United States, Canada, Australia, and Aotearoa New Zealand: nations whose political systems, legal ancestry, and experience of conjugality are broadly similar. This book examines marriage but neither celebrates nor condemns it. I certainly do not claim to be "solving" the problem of marriage. On the contrary, I argue that adopting any of the competing stances for or against marriage is unhelpful and, in general, not terribly meaningful when what is meant by "marriage" shifts and changes. My guiding question, in fact, is concerned less with what is "wrong" with marriage, so much as why and how relationships are regulated through law and government in the first place. By this I do not mean to imply that my project is a search for origins. There has been some stimulating work on the social and political origins of marriage— Pateman (1988) and Engels (1902) being the most famous examples. But such speculation is, I believe, worrisome. Positing a historical blueprint for marriage risks reducing it to one (inevitably inadequate) model and attracts the inference that marriage is not many things to many people but operates everywhere as a uniform organizing principle. My research, then, asks not why marriage exists or where it came from, but rather how the government of marriage and marriage-like relationships has been rationalized, and points to some of the effects of such regulation.

In insisting that marriage is not merely private, *Conjugal Rites* develops a view somewhat similar to historian Nancy Cott's. In *Public Vows* (2000), Cott shows how marriage has operated as an institution of American public life. Cott's approach to the territory of marriage is geodetic: she maps the political movement of marriage as continental drift. *Conjugal Rites* begins where Cott leaves off; rather than fixing the continent of conjugality in a global positioning system, my analysis tours the territory itself. The borders and contours of marriage as well as cohabitation and other marriage-like relationships are explored, extending and detailing Cott's groundwork to map conjugality as a field in which personal and political power relations create a range of social effects.

In response to questions concerning why and how marriage is governed, each chapter of *Conjugal Rites* offers its own answer. The answers are different because the meanings and effects of marriage change depending on when, where, and whom its subjects are. The book begins by considering how conjugality as an arena of feminist inquiry has been understood until now. In feminist thought—and in a broader social sense—marriage symbolizes relations between the sexes. If we look at how marriage has been criticized over time, we see a number of historically specific "snapshots" of gender relations. Flicking through this social wedding album offers a context for how we might understand the contemporary sexual politics of conjugality. The main aim of this chapter, then, is to get a sense of where we stand at the start of the twenty-first century in relation to a social institution that presents itself as timeless. Pursuing questions raised here, Chapter 2 identifies several critical approaches to marriage analysis, explaining what is exciting, interesting, and troublesome about each before positing an alternative approach. Using elements of contemporary social theory which attend to gendered activity, embodiment, and the government of conduct, marriage can be reconceptualized as a dynamic arena of regulation. Everyone is familiar with feminism's most enduring slogan: "the personal is political." This chapter demonstrates that nothing is more personal and central to sexual politics than conjugality.

But what is marriage, anyway? Beyond its intense familiarity in everyday life, the legal shape of marriage has been determined by countless decisions concerning entry to and exit from its grasp. In

Chapters 3 and 4, the rules governing such decisions are investigated. In Chapter 3, rules and cases concerning the annulment of marriage are examined, and the boundaries of something that generally appears solid and straightforward are revealed to be much less certain and more permeable. What goes wrong when a wedding fails to accomplish a valid marriage? Mistakes can be made; some pairings are forbidden; some spouses are considered inherently "defective"; and some conditions vitiate the consent required to produce a valid marriage. Citing a number of controversial cases, Chapter 3 examines how marriage is established, paying particular attention to the historical requirement that a valid marriage must accomplish the union of one man and one woman. This aspect of marriage is currently under challenge on several fronts. Here, we will consider tests presented by transsexual spouses. In these and other questions of validity, the question of consummation is often crucial.

In Chapter 4, the seemingly magical operations produced by certain sex acts in the government of conjugality are exposed. Here I argue that just as gender (and its associated identifications of "man" and "woman") can be understood as performative, so too can sexual *activity*. The key effects of various sexual performatives associated with marriage are to establish, reinforce, or rupture conjugal unity. This chapter explores a number of sexual performatives historically linked to conjugality: consummation, adultery, and condonation (or "forgiving" sex). Are these sex acts related to "conjugal rights?" Do husbands and wives exercise them equally? In answering these questions, I turn to historical cases in which the personal and the political collide in intriguing and sometimes salacious ways. Can a virgin be guilty of adultery? Is a married woman's pregnancy during her husband's protracted absence prima facie evidence of adultery? Analyzing such cases and the rules that govern them demonstrates how heterosexual privilege has been constituted through the performative legal éclat of conjugal sex.

Although sex and sexualities are marriage's most obvious sphere of regulation, they are not the *only* relevant factors. Inscriptions of "race" have been overtly regulated through marriage, particularly in the historical prohibition of marriage between "mixed race" couples. Chapter 5 explores conjugality as a site at which sex/gender and "race" intersect in sometimes contradictory ways. The focus is on two cases that occurred at virtually the same time on two continents. The first of these is *Loving v. Virginia*. Until 1967, a number of U.S.

states continued to prohibit "mixed-race" marriage. The last pin to fall in overturning these bans was the Supreme Court decision in *Loving v. Virginia*. The decision is celebrated in the United States as establishing a right to marry, and is often cited as an analogous precedent for the legalization of same-sex marriage. Just as the state once objected to certain marriages on grounds that turned out to be specious, it is argued, so it now unfairly denies gay and lesbian couples the chance to enjoy married life together. An Australian case suggests that this analogy is dangerous. In the troubled courtship of Gladys Namagu and Mick Daly, marriage served as a model of racial and cultural assimilation. Its coherence depended, to a large extent, on vestiges of coverture linking white privilege and male privilege. Though narratives of interracial romance are sometimes presented as the triumph of forbidden love, Gladys Namagu was, in the end, less like Shakespeare's Juliet and more like Portia, who could neither choose the man she wanted nor reject those whom she wished to deny.

In Chapter 6, regulations governing divorce as an exit from marriage are considered. Beginning with the historical workings of fault-based divorce, various matrimonial offenses (or grounds for divorce) are explored, illuminating governmental operations that are at times remarkably subtle and interesting. Three categories of offense in fault-based divorce law are identified: offenses against public order, offenses against one's spouse, and offenses relating to absence or neglect. The matrimonial offense of "cruelty" and its relationship to the criminalization of domestic violence will be examined in some detail to illustrate how a strange fiction of chivalry permeated divorce laws and eventually led to their widespread corruption. This paved the way for fault-based or "adversarial" divorce to be superseded by new, no-fault provisions—which have since been blamed for rising divorce rates and all manner of social ills. Bearing in mind the continuing heritage of matrimonial offenses and recent calls from some quarters to reinstate the concept of fault, Chapter 6 explores the operation and effects of the broad movement from fault-based to "no-fault" divorce.

Chapter 7 deals with cohabitation. With the advent of no-fault divorce, marriage was figured as more companionate—as *consortium vitae* (or "life together") rather than union. For the purposes of determining its absence—that is, the "irreconcilable" nature of parties' differences—this "togetherness" had to be *normatively* defined.

This meant that the weight of marriage's performative utterances (that is, wedding vows) was reduced. What mattered now were norms rather than rules. For regulatory purposes, in many places, bona fide and de facto marriage became equivalent—both were to be measured against a number of identical norms. While it might be suggested that cohabitation mimics or simulates certified marriage, I argue that the reverse case is more convincing. This chapter analyzes what marriage means when it is normatively defined and pinpoints some remaining differences between marriage and de facto relationships.

The rise of *norm-based* conjugality prompts new questions: If certified marriage and de facto relationships perform "conjugality" identically and so justify equal treatment, why should similar standards of conjugality between same-sex partners be excluded from the regulatory arena? Should sex acts between same-sex couples be subject to the same sorts of sanctions as heterosex—whether in certified or de facto marriage? Chapter 8 explores these questions. A number of jurisdictions have moved to make same-sex unions lawful, while others have enacted legislation "defending" marriage's exclusively heterosexual purview. The controversy of these decisions has inspired a large (and still increasing) volume of scholarly and other publications. Rather than add to the pile of scholarship on the rights and privileges of marriage, Chapter 8 reconsiders the sexist and heterosexist history of marriage as a regulatory system. Ultimately, this chapter questions whether same-sex marriage should be expected to produce gender-subversive effects and reviews the discursive anxieties evident on both sides of the debate.

Conjugal Rites concludes by suggesting that the traditional characterization of marriage as a social institution is no longer analytically useful. A different and more accurate theorization of conjugality—one better suited to the range of regulated intimate relationships available in the twenty-first century—is offered. As a whole, *Conjugal Rites* does not point to a neatly prescriptive conclusion. I offer no advice as to how people should organize their sexual-affective relationships. Instead, the book draws a map charting a social journey of matrimonial regulation, tracing the conjugal body politic from a single model replete with coverture to several overlapping constructions of conjugality. This book theorizes marriage and marriage-like relationships, paying attention to sex, sexualities, and "race." In that my account of conjugality includes cohabitation, certified marriage, civil unions, and other forms of marriage, it takes a broad and international sweep, but it is by no means an exhaustive account.

Neither ecclesiastical law nor non-Christian forms of certified marriage are discussed here. Only contemporary (post–World War II) civil marriage is considered. This is not because the various marriage traditions of Islam, Hinduism, and other religions are not interesting or relevant, but because to consider them would be unmanageable in a book of this length. This, along with the complex and fascinating history of marriage in the Christian tradition, I leave to others with expertise better suited to the task. For similar reasons, the global dynamics of migratory marriage are also excluded: this is not a book concerned with conflict of laws, or how situations of legal difference are negotiated across national boundaries. Again, these issues are especially complex and better left to those more adequately equipped to undertake their analysis.[2]

Instead, I aim to present a "history of the present"—*my* present—by analyzing legal discourses of conjugality. Such discourses include cases drawn from contemporary records of law, but also touch on governmental and bureaucratic decisions, as well as scholarship produced in a range of disciplines—from law, cultural studies, philosophy, and politics, to history and sociology. Apposite, here, is Elizabeth Cady Stanton's prescient observation that "[w]e are all what law, custom, and public sentiment have made us, alike fragmentary" (1891, 3). In so much as it is privileged in my account, I do not mean to situate law as any kind of social steering apparatus. Rather, I consider legal discourse to be an important but partial influence on the forms of conjugality we experience today. Case law, in particular, is often peopled idiosyncratically: the woman whose "stunted" vagina presented an obstacle to the validity of her marriage (*S.T. v. S.T.* 1963) hardly represents common experience. Such cases do, however, open the borderlands of legitimate marriage, allowing us to see more clearly what is variously excluded or sanctioned.

The idiosyncratic nature of case law, along with the inconsistent operation of rules across (even similar) jurisdictions, does present particular difficulties in an analysis like mine. My preference for post-structuralist feminist methods means that my inclination is always to analyze the local and particular, and to situate that analysis in its specific context. In fact, this is the approach I have adopted, but *Conjugal Rites* speaks nonetheless about conjugality in generalizing ways. To stretch an overused metaphor, one can discuss the color called "forest green" with reference to individual and unique leaves without asking one tree to represent the forest. An accurate account of the motifs and mechanisms regulating conjugality, then, can be drawn from odd or contradictory sources.

By the same token, I would reject any suggestion that law or legal discourse is a repository of truth. Of course people lie in courts of law, perhaps as often as in any other social arena. When a defendant is pronounced "guilty" or "not guilty," a verdict stands, but verdicts do not always or necessarily represent the truth. As Norma Basch rightly observes, this necessitates (rather than compromises) a discursive approach (1999, 6–7). In law, "truth" may be inaccessible, but what remains is a record of what has *counted* as truth, and such records are instructive. Indeed, they may be especially telling where mechanisms of discursive performativity (such as sentencing and vowing) are under examination. In this sense, then, legal discourses on marriage and marriage-like relationships offer us access to (what has counted as) the "truth" of sexed/gendered intimate relationships, and not the (necessarily multiple and various) subjective truths of people's experience of conjugality.

Exploring and criticizing the "proper" or governmentally desirable relationship of women relative to men is, of course, an important (if not defining) task of feminism. As we will see, marriage is often considered an emblematic form of sexed/gendered relations and, as such, conjugality is a locus of considerable social and political anxiety. As Lynne Halem remarks, statistics on marriage and divorce are routinely accepted as indices of the state's relative health or decline (1980, 1). Americans, she says, "regard divorce as a problem of momentous consequence, a pathological event that threatens not only the institution of the family but also social cohesiveness and order" (3). While this seems still to be true, homophobia has fuelled additional fears concerning marriage in the twenty-first century. Not only divorce, but also (same-sex) marriage is now constituted as a threat to the social order.

The part marriage might play in maintaining or disrupting social order is linked to a number of important arenas, including cultures of love and romance; reproduction and child rearing; domestic and other sexual divisions of labor; and economic relations of wealth, welfare and dependence. These are treated cursorily or not at all in *Conjugal Rites*. My endeavor has been to isolate marriage and marriage-like relationships as artifacts of government rather than to consider how the experience of marriage shapes social life more generally. This is not to dismiss the importance of these fields or to downplay the myriad insights afforded by the long and productive history of feminist engagement with these issues. On the contrary, the feminist trajectory of scholarship around marriage linking fields of oppression like domestic labor and romantic love to the ideology, institution and experience of marriage makes a book like mine possible. The tradition speaks, in fact, to the relevance of *Conjugal Rites* beyond its own analytical terms.

Finally, this is a book about marriage *more or less*. It concerns "more" than marriage because it considers cohabitation and other forms of relationship recognition additional to marriage as such. Since forms of intimate relationship outside or beyond marriage are usually given a subordinate or inferior status relative to bona fide marriage, they are considered to be "less" than marriage. In general, I prefer to consider marriage as one of a number of regulatory frameworks—as part of a broader field of conjugality in which rules, norms and practices of intimacy and interdependence might vary without connoting a hierarchy of relationships at whose apex, inevitably, (bona fide) marriage sits. Moreover, what "marriage" is expands and contracts, including more or fewer subjects depending on its particular incarnation. In Canada, gay and lesbian couples can now be included within the purview of marriage as lawfully married spouses, while in Australia and the United States, they cannot. In this sense, "marriage" is *always* "marriage (more or less)"; that which is not-marriage defines and demarcates that which is. Marriage is, in other words, a floating but privileged signifier in the broader field of conjugality.

CHAPTER 2

THEORIZING CONJUGALITY

In developed western societies, people marry in diverse and sometimes novel ways: some couples write their own ceremony, some take traditional vows; some marry in church, some in hot-air balloons. In recent years, not just wedding ceremonies, but marriage itself has become (arguably) more negotiable and less conventional. Certainly in developed western nations like the United States, marriage is nowhere near as "compulsory" as it once was. These days, women are no longer forced to view marriage as an especially feminine "trade" or "career," but instead see marriage as an optional course on life's menu (cf Hamilton 1909; Friedan 1963). Marriage has become, it would seem, many things to many people. In this climate of conjugal diversity, feminism's long and illustrious history of marriage criticism seems to have lost much of its potency. Feminists no longer seem to care so much about marriage, and the passion with which our political foremothers rallied to decry marriage seems as obsolete as hooped skirts.

In this chapter, I want to introduce some interdisciplinary perspectives on marriage and, in particular, consider the long and fruitful engagement of feminist thinkers in debates about marriage. My aim is not only to identify some shortcomings in these accounts, but also to develop some of their strengths. Ultimately, I want to build on ideas not usually mobilized in scholarship on marriage, but which might offer new and useful avenues of exploration. To this end, this chapter is organized into three main sections. In the first of these, two historically productive lines of feminist critique on marriage will be distinguished. My argument here is that most feminist treatments of marriage present it as either (reformably) sexist or (irredeemably) patriarchal. In the second major section, I will offer some explanation as to why these lines of critique seem to have lost so much purchase. My focus here is on intra-feminist tensions concerning critiques of marriage as an institution, but also explores the somewhat fraught imbrication of marriage and sexualities. In the third and final section, I adapt recent feminist theory on government, corporeality and performativity to show how a range of contemporary feminist concerns can be brought to bear on our understandings of what marriage is and does.

MARRIAGE OF MINDS

Marriage has been studied and theorized within a very broad range of academic disciplines. Interest in the topic is neither merely recent, nor necessarily linked to feminist movements. In anthropology, for example, marriage and kinship studies examining the structures, origins, and rituals of marriage across different cultural contexts comprise some of the discipline's most important texts.[1] Philosophers and theologians have long pondered the sacred or profane nature of love, marriage, and monogamy.[2] Historians and legal theorists have produced analyses concerning the origins and development of marriage customs and matrimonial law.[3] Studies dealing with marriage as a key indicator in monitoring populations and as a foundation for household economics have emerged from demography and sociology.[4] In psychiatry and psychology, analyses of the interpersonal dynamics of intimate relationships have spawned a vast literature on marital satisfaction, marriage counseling, and therapy.[5] It is hardly self-evident, then, what shape any new approach to the study of marriage and marriage-like relationships might take.

Marriage has been a subject of feminist investigation for as long as there have been feminists. This is not surprising given that, at a fundamental level, feminism has problematized relations between the sexes, while marriage represents a formal or structural aspect of sex/gender relations. Indeed, the history of feminist engagement with marriage almost amounts to a history of feminist thought more generally. It goes without saying, then, that the range of feminist opinions on marriage is large and critically diverse. Despite the variety and scope of feminist analyses of marriage, two recurring motifs are discernible. The first of these is that most feminists theorize marriage as an institution. The second theme follows from and extends the first: most feminist analyses of marriage tend to favor either its reform or outright rejection. Let us consider each of these in turn.

THE INSTITUTION OF MARRIAGE

A while back, a pop-art style cartoon featuring a man and woman in earnest conversation surfaced on postcards and tee-shirts around town. The woman's speech bubble read, "Marriage is an institution," to which the man replied, "I'm not sure I want to be institutionalized." Reversing the gender order of a quote usually attributed to Mae West, the joke's humor plays on the way that marriage is spoken of as an institution, yet is unlike the bricks-and-mortar institutions of the prison, church, hospital, mental asylum, or school. When marriage is referred to as an "institution," the import usually conveyed is that marriage has been around for a very long time, and that as an element of societal organization, it is widely accepted and practiced. Marriage is "the done thing"—an "institution." Most non-feminist social theorists characterize marriage as (above all) an institution of *kinship*, and situate it as a relatively discrete, ostensibly private realm. One of the most enduring insights arising from feminist scholarship is that marriage has been revealed to be not only a site of institutional kinship, but also a site of gendered power relationships. Feminist analyses of marriage have demonstrated very clearly that the ostensibly private domain of the family is by no means immune from operations of power.

Feminists as dissimilar as Mary Astell (1706), Germaine Greer (1970), and Carole Pateman (1988) refer to marriage as an institution. In doing so, they attempt to isolate marriage as a social structure from marriage as a personal, lived experience. There are (by degrees) many nuanced and expert definitions of social institutions (Lecours 2005, 6–8; Roy and Sideras 2006, 4–5; Turner 1997, 4–6). My focus here is on that everyday understanding of the term as it has been deployed in feminist thought in general, indicating that which is received, authorized, and expected (after Rich 1977, 13 [et passim] for example). Where marriage is described by feminists as an institution, the implication is that marriage is a received, relatively fixed social structure that draws women's participation in maintaining, organizing, and reproducing a sexed/gendered order (see Jeffreys 2004, 327). Sociologist Stevi Jackson describes marriage as "heterosexuality's central institution" (1996, 24). This institution, she says, "entails a hierarchical relation between (social) men and (social) women. It is women's subordination within institutionalized heterosexuality which is the starting point for feminist analysis. It is resistance to this subordination which is the foundation of feminist politics" (26).

As Jackson's example shows, conceptualizing marriage as an institution means that marriage can be criticized without condemning wives—without "blaming the victim," so to speak. (This is evident in the function of Jackson's parenthetic qualifier, "social.") Characterizing marriage as an institution—as a social structure related to yet distinct from women's lived experience of conjugality—also allows us to conceptualize marriage as an emblematically defended site; that is, as a site of sexist or patriarchal power relations.

Marriage as a Sexist Institution

When feminists describe marriage as a *sexist* institution, they criticize the overtly different treatment of men and women (husbands and wives) in identical or similar circumstances (after Grosz 1988). Marriage is sexist, for example, in that wives but not husbands are expected to change their name and title upon marrying (Popovic 1994); women's marital status is a marker of discrimination in employment, banking, and housing, but men's is not; the domestic work women perform as wives is undervalued and often unrecognized while the husband's contribution to marital prosperity is more obviously and more consistently rewarded. In critiques identifying marriage as a sexist institution, the problem demanding redress is that the consequences of marriage are not identical for men and women, and tend to disadvantage women. However, the basis of the problem is not understood to be necessarily inherent in marriage itself, but rather stems from women's limited opportunities and choices both within and outside of marriage.

Most of the earliest feminist criticisms of wifely subordination tend not to question the propriety of marriage as such. Indeed, many take pains to reassure their readers of the ultimately desirable nature of matrimony. The focus of critiques from a spectrum of thinkers (including Mary Astell 1706; Mary Wollstonecraft 1792; John Stuart Mill 1832; and Betty Friedan 1963) was the argument that marriage could be a stronger, better institution if the roles it demands, and our socialization *for* those roles, were different. Fundamental to this critique is the insistence that marriage should be a choice rather than an economic necessity for women. In order to facilitate such choice, it is argued, women must have access to education and worthwhile employment. Many, including J. S. Mill and Betty Friedan, believed that women would nevertheless *choose* to marry. Their contention is that if the foundation of matrimony were an agreement between economic equals, marriage would no longer be tainted with the resentments and bitterness of necessity.

Some feminists have argued, implicitly or otherwise, that the critique of marriage as a sexist institution has *epistemological* purchase. Women, they say, are excluded as producers of knowledge about marriage. Knowledge produced without adequate consideration of women's experience quarantines marriage and the family as "private" and therefore outside the "public" arena of social theory. This is, in effect, an epistemological male bias. Susan Moller Okin's *Justice, Gender and the Family* (1989) is a good example of this sort of critique. Okin examines mainstream theories of justice to identify problems resulting from their failure to consider marriage and the family as an arena of injustice. Her argument is complex, and draws on such mainstream political theorists as Rawls, Nozick, and Walzer, but its crux is the proposition that "until there is justice within the family, women will not be able to gain equality in politics, at work, or in any other sphere" (Okin 1989, 4). Okin's argument is woven around feminist critiques of the public/private divide and the sexual division of labor. Her understanding of marriage is that it is, in the first place, the product of those who come to it, but beyond this it operates *unjustly*. This conception of marriage is a defining feature of scholarship labeling marriage as "sexist". The effects of marriage are unequal and unfair, according to the critique's proponents, because men and women are not treated as equals either before, during, or at the end of marriage.

Other feminists have identified, in marriage, a sexist structure with empirically sexist effects. Cicely Hamilton's (often overlooked) work from the turn of the century falls within this category, as does Jessie Bernard's celebrated book *The Future of Marriage* (1972).[6] Bernard argues that, while married men experience longer, healthier lives as compared to their bachelor brothers, the reverse is true for women. Bernard's work has spawned many more studies, most being similar sorts of empirical analysis exploring different areas. Among others, the following examples illustrate the usefulness of this approach: Lenore Weitzman's (1985) investigation into the unequal results of property settlements at divorce, Australian women's campaigns to remove the Public Service "marriage bar" and similar discrimination by marital status (Sawer 1996), and studies examining men and women's domestic labor (Bittman and Pixley 1997; Maushart 2001). Indeed, the empirical basis of such work has been crucial in establishing the validity of various feminist claims.

Feminists working on the legal consequences of marriage have been instrumental in its modern-day reform. Feminist legal scholars like Regina Graycar (1990), Jenny Morgan (Graycar and Morgan 1990), Jocelynne Scutt (1990, 1995, Scutt and Graham 1984), Herma Hill Kay (1991), Ruthann Robson (1992), Susan Boyd (2003), and Katherine O'Donovan (Diduck and O'Donovan 2006) have identified and criticized the different legal consequences of marriage for men and women. One of the best-known works of this type is Carol Smart's *The Ties That Bind* (1984). Smart analyzes British matrimonial law to argue that it "both creates marriage as a legal status with certain privileges and sustains women's economic dependence within marriage and the family" (1984, xi). Smart traces British law from the 1950s through to the 70s to show how family law continues to place women in socially and economically disadvantaged positions. She focuses on divorce, in particular, suggesting that this is the "moment" at which the private family becomes public (and, implicitly, thus ripe for reform). She does not suggest that marriage be abolished; such calls, she says, would prove both unpopular and unrealistic (1984, 225). Rather, Smart's chief strategy for reform advocates the removal of those privileges currently attached to marriage, and promotes the continuing intervention of feminist approaches to household and welfare policies.

While the arguments aired by Smart and antecedent thinkers maintain their analytical purchase, this kind of marriage critique is heard less frequently these days. Although feminism continues to question the relative equality of women and men, and although powerful arguments persist concerning the economic dependence of wives, the theoretical fulcrum seems to have shifted from marriage to parenthood and the economic burden of childcare. As Jo VanEvery notes, "Feminists have theorized extensively about . . . marriage and the family, and continue to do so. However, these theories do not always problematise heterosexuality and often look to motherhood for the explanation of continuing inequalities" (1996b, 52).

The trajectory of the critique of marriage as sexist seems to have ended in the mid-1990s in an almost celebratory burst. Dale Spender presents her anthology of contemporary women's writings on marriage as expressing the collective opinion that women now choose to have weddings without adopting the identity or role of "wife." "[W]omen have come of age," she says, "and no longer seek to be subordinate wives" (1994, xxiii). The subordination of women in marriage is, by Spender's account, little more than "ancient history." Nowadays, according to Spender, marriage is merely another "consumer choice" in which one's spouse is exchangeable and, ultimately, expendable: "For so many women now, marriage vows are conditional. When earlier generations of women were married, the contract was for life. . . . Today's young women, who are more conscious of their own worth, rarely put themselves in this invidious position . . . These days a girl can have as many weddings as she wants. She can be a bride as often as she likes" (1994, 16, 18).

Spender's approach is playful, but her light-heartedness hides the fact that some serious issues remain at stake. Marriage is rarely a whimsical choice. For all but the most well-off women, marriage heralds the expectation of, at the very least, some instances of economic dependence on the husband. Moreover, the specter of financial dependence is, for some wives, accompanied by physical and emotional menace.

Marriage as a Patriarchal Institution

The term "patriarchy" has been employed in a variety of complex ways in feminist thought (see Walby 1990). The term has fallen out of fashion in recent years, but remains nonetheless useful.[7] When feminists criticize marriage as an institution of *patriarchy*, the argument is that marriage is structurally and necessarily oppressive toward women. Feminists adopting this position assert that marriage is an institution devised by men to serve men's interests. In many such critiques, marriage is linked to the exploitation of women's domestic labor, men's (hetero)sex rights, sexual-domestic violence, and the household economics of dependency. While critiques labeling marriage "sexist" usually see matrimony as an essentially benign institution whose unequal consequences can be reformed, feminists criticizing marriage as a patriarchal institution see such reforms as treating the symptoms rather than the root of the problem. For example, in most jurisdictions, wife-beating is no longer protected as a husband's right, but has been outlawed as (ostensibly gender-neutral) domestic violence. However, the majority of female homicide victims are murdered by "sexual intimates"—usually their husbands (Carcach and James 1998; Easteal 1993). Feminist adherents of the marriage-as-patriarchy critique might argue, then, that removing the overt sexism of those matrimonial laws that rendered wife-beaters immune from prosecution has not remedied the structural inequality of the husband-wife relationship that leaves wives vulnerable to their violent partners in the first place.

One of the most important and influential books about marriage and feminism explores the politically patriarchal origins of marriage. Carole Pateman's *The Sexual Contract* (1988) investigates marriage, but also considers employment, prostitution, and surrogacy arrangements—all under the conceptual umbrella of contract. Pateman argues that an origin-myth of marriage as endogamous and monogamous operates alongside (and carries similar explanatory weight to) the political myth forming the basis of social contract theory. According to Pateman, the "sexual contract"—that is, the sum of these myths—disguises coercion and subordination as "contract," incorporating women into the body of citizenship as it simultaneously enslaves them. Through and within marriage, argues Pateman, women are subjected to a "fraternal" form of systematized masculine authority and privilege. *The Sexual Contract* is critique rather than construct: Pateman does not offer any clear solutions. She does, however, gesture tentatively toward a model of marriage based on friendship rather than contract.

Pateman's approach represents a significant departure from her predecessors and contemporaries in that she examines marriage as a kind of institutionally *political* patriarchy. Locating the problem of women's subordination in operations of contract and consent, Pateman argues that women are smuggled into the political fiction of social contract theory through marriage. In that marriage is understood as contractual, its real patriarchal purpose—to establish or legitimize a relation of sexual domination and subordination—is concealed. Pateman's argument is, at times, seductive; its greatest strength, I think, is its insistence that gender relations are an integral but often ignored part of "mainstream" political theory. In arguing that men's public, "political" contracts depend on the exclusion of women, Pateman warns against traditional and contemporary political philosophy's tendency to conceptualize the situation of women as institutionally peripheral. Pateman's analysis of marriage has been both highly influential and hotly contested, and I will engage her arguments at a number of points throughout the present volume.

A more recent analysis of marriage as an institution of patriarchy—and one very different from Pateman's—is Christine Delphy and Diana Leonard's *Familiar Exploitation* (1992). As its title suggests, Delphy and Leonard present a materialist account of marriage as, above all, an institution in which men exploit women's labor. Building on those analyses linking the institutional oppression of marriage and labor, they use empirical studies of families in rural France and industrial England to argue that, "[w]ithin the family in our society, women are dominated in order that their work may be exploited and because their work is exploited" (1992, 18).

By their account, marriage is an institution whose structure and consequences are inescapably patriarchal: "[M]arriage . . . is not a personal relationship in the sense of being independently decided upon by each particular couple. Individuals can make choices about which partner to marry, and they choose as a couple how to organize their lives within marriage [to an extent] . . . But they do not choose the nature of marriage . . . Th[is], like the language of their country, they are born into and have to 'speak'" (Delphy and Leonard 1992, 265).

Delphy and Leonard's conclusion is not optimistic. They see marriage as a key problem in feminist theory, but warn against blaming wives for their own situation because to do so would risk alienating women who love men from the women's movement. De facto relationships are not advocated as an alternative to marriage; rather, cohabitation is treated (along with a range of other familial relationships) *as* marriage. The inescapability of marriage and its exploitative despair is, perhaps, the biggest problem pertaining to theorizations of marriage as a patriarchal institution in general. Where women marry because they must, and where marriage oppresses women, there is little room for theorizing or realizing a better situation.

Although it would be a gross oversimplification to suggest that every feminist critique of marriage is either wholly counter-sexist or counter-patriarchal, most do at least incline toward one or the other characterization, perceiving women's marital inequality as either an *effect of* or a major *facilitator of* men's power and privilege. Each tends to suggest either reforming or rejecting marriage (respectively). Both strategies have been enormously productive.[8] As Rosemary Pringle and Sophie Watson remark, "While no one would deny the continued existence of domestic tyranny, the achievement of legal equality has seriously weakened men's authority as husbands and fathers" (1990, 231). Critiques of marriage's sexism have prompted numerous reforms to matrimonial law and other regulations. These range from the nineteenth century enactment of the English *Married Women's Property Act* (which toppled the notion that a wife and all her property belong to her husband), to a more recent Australian ruling on the splitting of superannuation benefits at divorce (Henn and Boujos 2003). Critiques of marriage as a patriarchal institution have contributed to and even spearheaded (some) political and cultural tolerance of "alternative" family and household arrangements, and certainly cleared the way for women to pursue life options apart from (and as well as) marriage. The impact of both critiques amounts to a significant change in our understanding and experience of the nature and consequences of marriage.

The Trouble with Counter-sexist Critiques of Marriage

However, as Pringle and Watson's proviso attests, few feminists would suggest that marriage is now a gender-neutral field into which husbands and wives enter as equals to form the basis of fundamentally egalitarian families.[9] It seems that no matter how the balances are adjusted, the matrimonial scales continue to tip in men's favor: the project of eradicating marriage's sexist consequences seems endless. Indeed, some might argue that the project is futile—where only a man can be a husband and only a woman can be a wife, marriage must surely be fundamentally and structurally gender-skewed. Advocates of the marriage-as-patriarchy critique might also point out the limits of reform as a political strategy. They might argue that it is impossible, for example, to employ strategies of law reform to change the ways people experience sexual-affective relationships. Perhaps, as Martha Fineman suggests, law is "more reflective than constitutive of social realities" (Fineman 1994, xvi). Further, if heterosexuality eroticizes sexist power relations, then no amount of matrimonial law reform will alleviate women's subordination in marriage. Despite the fact that in many nations men and women *are* now formal equals (that is, they are purportedly equal in the eyes of the law), marriage remains the site most likely to harbor the perpetration of a range of atrocities against women. Rape and other sexual assaults, bodily harm, homicide, terror, and exploitation are all more likely to occur within a woman's matrimonial home than outside it, and are much more likely to be committed by the victim's husband than by a stranger (Carcach and James 1998, *inter alia*). However, if counter-sexist remedies for marriage's ills seem endlessly futile, counter-patriarchal remedies are not much better.

The Trouble with Counter-patriarchal Critiques of Marriage

Although trends against formal or certified marriage have been identified in most developed, western countries,[10] few suggest that it is being abandoned in any wholesale fashion. Despite its apparent dangers—despite its oppressive history and legacies—marriage seems unlikely to wither away due to any lack of interest.[11] Feminists criticizing the counter-patriarchal imperative to resist marriage might warn, moreover, that calls for women to abandon or abolish marriage risk seriously alienating a vast feminist constituency—namely, wives. As Michele Barrett and Mary McIntosh explain (in their feminist classic, *The Anti-Social Family*), "In seeing the family as the site of male attempts to control and exploit women, in arguing that heterosexuality and marriage are instruments of male power, feminists have encountered considerable hostility and resistance from women in general" (1982, 132).

Indeed, if marriage is utterly and unavoidably patriarchal, married feminists—whose home lives might not be significantly different from their sisters living in de facto or even lesbian relationships—must count themselves as dupes. This highlights the biggest problem for advocates of the counter-patriarchal critique of marriage. If marriage is to be rejected or abolished, how should such relationships be organized? What is to replace marriage? With the increasing acceptability of de facto relationships, it has become evident that women in merely marriage-*like* relationships face almost exactly the same problems as bona fide wives, and in some respects may be even worse off. Should de facto relationships be understood as marriage *resistance*, then, or are they dangerous simulacra of marriage?

Feminist attempts to reform marriage's sexism and to resist its patriarchal imperatives have met with substantial success, but are neither complete nor sufficient. Here, I have sketched some of the difficulties confounding existing feminist critiques of marriage. In the next section, I want to extricate and expand on those problems by identifying three distinct but inter-related concerns: first, intra-feminist tensions in the feminist marriage debates; second, marriage's status as an institution; and third, the historically interdependent nature of marriage and heterosexuality.

MARRIAGE TROUBLE—INTRA-FEMINIST TENSIONS

Following a pattern that has attached to many sites of feminist scholarship, the two dominant feminist critiques of marriage (counter-sexist and counter-patriarchal, as identified previously) pull in different directions. While some feminists are convinced that marriage is an utterly, irredeemably patriarchal institution, others argue that there is nothing wrong with marriage that can't be fixed. The debate seems to exert a polarizing force of its own, pushing those engaged in it toward declaring themselves either "for" or "against" marriage. Feminist willingness to engage in the debate on these terms has understandably waned. Most feminists, these days, see *families* as neither essentially good nor bad, but as a range of household relationships with the potential to offer love *and* malice, nurture *and* torture. Feminist understandings of marriage seem to be heading in a similar direction, but are not yet as flexible.

While feminist concerns are now less frequently expressed as a problem with marriage as such, a great deal of feminist work continues to pivot on matrimonial hinges. Domestic violence, rape in marriage, women's welfare entitlements or dependence, the economics of divorce, the sexual division of labor in the paid workforce and in household economies, and even surrogacy and prostitution have all been theorized as related to an institutionalized model of marriage. With the advent of post-structuralist approaches which warn against totalizing theory, most feminists are no longer confident to suggest that these problems are *caused* by marriage,[12] and it is not my intention to challenge this. However, the historically productive trajectory of problematizing marriage as such has perhaps stalled, leaving obsolete models of marriage to haunt the subtexts of a range of scholarship. It is important, then, that we not shy away from the task of negotiating a way past this stalemate, but look for new ways to approach the theorization of conjugality which might feed into understanding the variety of issues with which marriage is imbricated.

As we have seen, the tensions that have until recently demanded feminist attention in scholarship on marriage ask whether the institution of marriage is essentially sexist or patriarchal, reformable or irredeemable. I want to take a step back from those intra-feminist tensions and suggest that there is a problem more fundamental than defining marriage's institutional character. The theoretical ghoul disturbing feminist scholarship on and around marriage is the notion that marriage is, in the first place, an *institution*. In debating an institutional model of marriage whose consequences (but not whose structure) might vary, the impetus to polarize arguments toward either reform or abolition is reinforced. As previously noted, conceptualizing marriage as an institution has had some useful outcomes—the most important being that it has allowed feminists to decry marriage without condemning wives. But theorizing marriage as an institution also carries with it some serious limitations—limitations that, to my mind, outweigh its strengths.

INSTITUTIONAL ANXIETIES

In his 1983 essay "The Subject and Power," Michel Foucault identified several problems associated with the analysis of institutions. It should be noted that Foucault, along with many more mainstream institutional analysts, would probably not have expected marriage to be included under the auspices of "institutional analysis." It is something of an irony that while feminist critiques of marriage characterize it as an institution over and over again, marriage tends not to appear in its own right as a topic of mainstream institutional analysis (see Roy and Sideras 2006; Lecours 2005).[13] We should therefore take Foucault's typically androcentric advice with a grain of feminist salt rather than as any kind of "master" blueprint on the subject. Apposite, here, is Nancy Fraser's appropriately conjugal assessment of Foucault's uses for feminism: "Foucault," she writes, "isn't much good as a husband; one wouldn't want, politically speaking, to cohabit with him indefinitely" (1983, 70). For present purposes, then, Foucault's suggestions serve as a springboard for thinking about the consequences of characterizing marriage as an institution.

Foucault warns that in the study of institutions, we are apt to confuse mechanisms designed to secure the preservation of the institution itself with its broader political or disciplinary agenda (Foucault 1983).[14] He goes on to suggest that, "In analyzing power relations from the standpoint of institutions one lays oneself open to seeking the explanation and the origin of the former (power relations) in the latter (institutions), that is to say finally, to explain power to power" (222). There are several ways in which analyses of the institution of marriage illustrate these concerns. Most obviously, counter-sexist critiques, which argue that boys and girls are "socialized" for different marital roles, assert, essentially, that marriage reproduces women as wives—or that marriage begets itself. Other kinds of feminist marriage criticisms exhibit a more nuanced version of this problem. In discussions about the relation between marriage and women's labor, for example, the institution of housewifery and its fundamentally reproductive labor is problematized as constraining women's broader labor market participation. The question becomes like the riddle of the chicken and the egg—each seems to reproduce the other.

This problem of circularity is rife in feminist theorizations of marriage. Even some of the most influential critiques of marriage conclude, in essence, that marriage oppresses women, and that women marry *because* they are oppressed. Consider Delphy and Leonard's influential *Familiar Exploitation* (1994). They argue that marriage is a coercive relation of sexed and sexual labor in which women's work (whether paid or unpaid) is undervalued *because* it is work performed by women. Critiques of marriage exploring its relation to violence often betray a similar problem: to say that power relations exercised to women's detriment in the home originate in marriage is somewhat tautological. After all, what does it mean to say that the effects of marriage are produced by marriage? The arguments get a little more complicated (as we will see) when we explore the proposition that *heterosexual* power relations originate in or are produced through marriage, but what *is* marriage if not the institutionalized organization of heterosexual relations? We seem to arrive, over and over, at an empty, circular destination where women are oppressed in marriage "because" marriage oppresses women.

Most characterizations of marriage as an institution unwittingly reinforce a particular, historically specific model of marriage as *the* institution. That is, even as feminists challenge its justness, we reiterate and reinstitutionalize a single, historically fixed, theoretically rigid model of marriage. In other words, that "distancing" mechanism of institutionalization, which operates as a strength in some circumstances (allowing us to criticize marriage without attacking wives), can be seen, simultaneously, as a weakness. If the institution does not accurately represent the reality or experience of marriage, then its usefulness as a model is obviously compromised.

Foucault makes a final point in relation to the analysis of institutions. He says, "Insofar as institutions act essentially by bringing into play two elements, explicit or tacit regulations and an apparatus, one risks giving to one or the other an exaggerated privilege in the relations of power and hence to see in the latter (institutional apparatus) only modulations of the law and of coercion" (Foucault 1983, 222). This problem raises some very difficult questions in relation to feminist theorizations of marriage as an institution. Clearly, marriage brings both explicit and tacit regulations into play; its explicit regulations include matrimonial law and policies relating to marriage, while its tacit regulations include all manner of social-cultural material (including the myriad representations of romantic love in television, films, books, and magazines). But if marriage is an institution with a regulatory program, what is its apparatus? What or who implements matrimonial programs? The family? Labor? Sex? Violence? Gender? All of the above? Feminists have certainly identified each of these areas as intrinsically linked to marriage. One suggestion for conceptualizing marriage's institutional apparatus will be posited later, but for now, the question will be put to one side. Having looked at what Foucault has sketched as perils accompanying the study of institutionalized power relations, we need to examine his suggestions for avoiding these problems.

Foucault asserts, in "The Subject and Power," that the "anchorage" of institutionalized power relations is to be found *outside* the institution; that we might understand sanity by investigating insanity, legality through crime, power through resistance, and so on (Foucault 1983, 211, 222). But with an institution like marriage, whose regulations seem so pervasive, it is difficult to pinpoint any specific nexus of resistance. If, as some have argued, marriage is, above all, a (power) relation constituting sexual divisions of labor, for example, perhaps hiring a male housekeeper or marrying a house-husband is its ultimate expression of resistance. However, some avenues strike me as more promising than others. Divorce, for example, seems an obvious pair for marriage in the binary sets previously noted, but single life, homosexuality, and "not-marriage" might also fit the gap. In those discourses of marriage linking race and the repro-duction of nationality, inter-racial pairings struck in defiance of anti-miscegenation laws might amount to marriage-resistance. Exploring these paths constitutes, in sum, the trajectory of this book, and will be more completely elucidated in later chapters.

SEX AND MARRIAGE

That marriage may not be living up (or down) to its institutional reputation is nowhere more obvious than in recent (and it seems snowballing) efforts to include lesbian and gay relationships in the regulatory field of marriage and de facto relationships laws and poli-cies.[15] The injustices and indignities suffered by lesbians and gay men through the legal and social non-recognition of their partner-ships is grave. However, it is not my intention to list those com-plaints or debate the relative merits of strategies being mooted to redress them here.[16] I want to focus instead on the impact of the "same-sex marriage" debates[17] on the feminist problematization of marriage.

The dilemma is obvious, yet disarmingly complex. If the patriar-chal and (hetero)sexist imperatives of marriage (presumed to both construct and police an unequal power relationship between hus-bands and wives, or men and women) are removed, feminist cri-tiques of marriage peel away from the social-institutional structures of marriage like so much old wallpaper. If marriage no longer neces-sitates the (de jure or de facto) union of one man and one woman, it no longer seems to have very much to do with either counter-sexist or counter-patriarchal critiques. If women are dealt a smaller share of matrimonial assets than their husbands upon divorce, for example, the counter-sexist argument that this reflects systemic discrimination against women might be difficult to sustain, especially if property settlements struck between divorcing men likewise disadvantage the less "productive" or economically weaker partner. Similarly, the counter-patriarchal feminist assertion that marriage is implicated in, for example, sexual domestic violence against women must be squared against two complicating factors. First, women who deliberately choose not to marry but live instead in de facto relationships are also subject to such sexual violence. Second, gay and lesbian relationships are by no means immune from similar problems. In both cases, neither marriage nor heterosexuality can be cleanly singled out as the culprit.

So what would the inclusion of gay and lesbian relationships mean for feminist critiques of marriage and marriage-like relationships? So far, most feminist commentary on same-sex marriage divides along lines broadly corresponding to the counter-sexist versus counter-patriarchal positions outlined earlier (although their theoretical affiliation is generally implied rather than explicit). Those inclined to see marriage as recuperable—those who see nothing necessarily or inherently oppressive in marriage—argue that if same-sex couples could marry lawfully, the historically heterosexist and patriarchal imperatives of marriage would be thwarted. They suggest that if all couples had access to the same range of relationships regulation regardless of sexual orientation, marriage would truly speak to individuals and their relationship choices. Marriage would continue to regulate relationships, but would no longer be emblematic of relations between (social) men and (social) women (after Jackson 1996). The heterosexist history of marriage would no doubt exert some residual influence in the experience of conjugality, but its systemic equation of women as wives serving men as husbands would begin to be undone. E. J. Graff, for example, describes same-sex marriage as "a breathtakingly subversive idea" (1997, 135). She goes on to argue that, "[s]ince same-sex couples will enter the existing institution, not some back-of-the-bus version called 'domestic partnership' . . . marriage law will have to become gender blind. Once we can marry, jurists will have to decide every marriage, divorce and custody question (theoretically at least) for equal partners, neither having more historical authority. Our entrance might thus rock marriage toward its egalitarian shore" (1997, 137). Some suggest, then, that the legalization of same-sex marriage would herald a victory of revolutionary proportions not just for gay and lesbian couples but against gender oppression generally.

Others argue that this rather optimistic anticipation of same-sex marriage's potential for social transformation is naïve and possibly foolish. They suggest, conversely, that the legalization of same-sex

marriage would simply reinforce and proliferate hopelessly heterosexist roles and ideologies. Lesbian and gay couples whose living
arrangements contest and destabilize the heterosexual norm would
be shifted into architectures drafted at exclusively heterosexual
desks. The gay and lesbian community would be divided, they say,
into "good" homosexuals (who accept the heterosexist and patriarchal norms of marriage) versus "bad" queers who disdain and
oppose those norms. Catherine Saalfield suggests that the history of
marriage is so misogynistic that it is beyond repair as a familial linch-
pin for lesbians. Marriage, she says, "should already be a relic of heterosexuality" (1993, 191). Paula Ettelbrick sounds a similar
warning: "Since when," she asks, "has marriage been a path to liberation?" (1997; see also Ettelbrick 2001). If there are material privileges attached to marriage, she says (echoing a key element of Carol
Smart's earlier analysis), then the task at hand should be to unshackle
those benefits from marriage rather than to clamor for them on historically heterosexist terms.

These two main strands of feminist debate on same-sex marriage
resound with the institutional echoes of existing critiques of marriage. The approach represented by E. J. Graff conceptualizes marriage as inherently benign in much the same way that feminist
critiques of the sexist effects of marriage have stressed its reformabil-
ity. In Graff's account, marriage is a bastion of privilege ripe for
queer infiltration. The implication is that once lesbian and gay couples are ensconced within marriage's institutional walls, the project
of its queer refurbishment might begin. The stance represented by
Saalfield, Ettelbrick, and Polikoff (1993) is more reminiscent of
counter-patriarchal critiques of marriage. The institutional model of
marriage they evoke is an edifice of patriarchal privilege; the opera-
tive motif in their critique is not infiltration but assimilation. Here,
the institution of marriage is believed to exert a homogenizing influence. Critiques like Polikoff's warn that no matter how much time
and money is spent on queer décor, the institutional structure of
marriage will remain steadfastly straight.

It would seem, then, that debates concerning the legal recognition of same-sex relationships destabilize and even disarm existing
feminist critiques of marriage while simultaneously replicating their
limitations. Though the critical target shifts (from sexism or patriarchy to heterosexism), the nature of the problem with marriage
seems to remain always just out of reach. How, then, can we move

into this theoretical "beyond"? I have suggested that the difficulties we are currently experiencing in negotiating conjugality and its effects stem from its continuing theorization as an institution. It is a matter of some urgency, then, that we explore new ways to conceptualize marriage which do not perpetuate its theoretical rigidity.

MOVING OUT AND MOVING IN—RETHINKING INSTITUTIONS

In some respects this may be easier than it sounds. Susan Hekman has argued that to develop theoretical frameworks that accommodate plurality, we should attend to "what we (already) do rather than what the philosophers say we should do" (1999, 105). She suggests that "if we look at what we actually do—in epistemology, morality, and the law—we can learn a valuable lesson. . . . [I]n practice, multiple paths to truth exist in each of these areas. . . . We already engage in these activities; we recognize their legitimacy in practice if not in theory" (104).

Hekman's argument is in essence epistemological, but it is not difficult to see how her approach might be applied more broadly. For example, in Australia (and similar societies) there are several senses in which one might be "married." Most obviously, if a wedding occurs according to the rules set out in the (Australian) *Marriage Act* 1961 (or its counterparts elsewhere), a couple is unequivocally married. But there are also presumptive policies and laws operating to determine whether or not a person is in a "de facto" marriage, or a marriage-like relationship. Such regulations give rise to what legal scholar John Wade calls the "limping" marriage, in which the same couple may be deemed married or not for various purposes (Wade 1990).[18] Moreover, one can be understood to be "married" under such legislation by accident or by design.

While some jurisdictions have opened access to bona fide marriage to gay and lesbian couples, others have begun to recognize same-sex partnerships as marriage-like. Not just state authorities but also employers, businesses, and service providers recognize a range of different kinds of relationship for various purposes—insurance as a "couple," for example, or season tickets as a "family." Although not necessarily recognized by the state, some churches perform wedding or "commitment" ceremonies for gay and lesbian couples. In some jurisdictions, "opt-in" regulations allow unmarried couples to register their relationships for certain purposes. In any case, many not-lawfully-married couples are addressed (by the state, family, and friends, or others) as "married."

It is clear, then, that although marriage organizes social relationships in various fundamental ways, it is neither regulated nor experienced in any necessarily uniform fashion. This suggests that we need to reexamine what "marriage" is and does. The task, here, is to find ways of theorizing marriage that build on the strengths of existing feminist critiques without replicating or exacerbating their shortcomings. We need an analysis that takes account of the long and valuable history of feminist marriage critique but also accommodates the diverse and plural nature of contemporary marriage. To promote such an analysis, it is necessary to stop conceptualizing marriage as an institution and instead theorize it as a site of more or less "permanent provocation" (Foucault 1983, 222). Marriage might then be understood as a site of various and dynamic relations, in which new conceptual tools in political and social theory might be put to work. There are three such conceptual tools that, I believe, are especially suited to the task: relations of government, corporeality, and performativity.

GOVERNMENT

Marriage, in its various degrees and guises, should be understood as a relation of government. Foucault's concept of government does not pertain only to political bodies (parliaments, bureaucracies, dictators, and so on) and their edicts, but refers, much more broadly, to "the conduct of conduct" (Dean 1999, 2). "Governing conduct" can include less overt directives internalized by the populace and does not quarantine "the private" or familial relations from the scope of government. This is not to suggest that marriage is, *above all*, a governmental relation. My claim is more modest and simply suggests that analyzing marriage as a relation of government may be a fruitful line of inquiry. There are several benefits attaching to such an approach.

Investigating marriage as a relation of government stresses the *overtly* political nature of conjugality (Cott 2000). Marriage is, in this sense, something regulated and governed through acts, statutes, and policies. As Nan Hunter observes, marriage is an artifact of government. She contends that "[western m]arriage is, after all, a complete creation of the law, secular or ecclesiastical. Like the derivative concept of illegitimacy, for example, and unlike parenthood, it did not and does not exist without the power of the state (or some comparable social authority) to establish, define, regulate and restrict it. Beyond such social constructs, individuals may couple, but they do not 'marry'" (Hunter 1995, 110).

In their exclusion and differentiation from bona fide marriage, gay and lesbian relationships are also governed, as is cohabitation—sometimes through separate legislation, sometimes constituting "bona fide" marriage's shadowy other. In any case, marriage is frequently debated, defended, and amended in various political and legal discourses of government. Feminist investigations into contemporary marriage must inquire into the nature of governmental investments in marriage. Why, in liberal democratic societies that continually iterate the realm of "private life" as immune from government interference, is marriage so passionately "defended," circumscribed, and regulated? What are the political subjectivities of conjugality, and what do they entail? How have the political subjectivities of marriage shifted, expanded, or contracted?

Although she does not adopt a specifically governmental approach, these are the kinds of questions addressed by American historian Nancy Cott in her book on marriage in the United States, *Public Vows* (2000). Cott maintains that marriage defines who "belongs" to the nation, and in this way marriage and citizenship are thoroughly connected. The great strength of Cott's analysis is that she demonstrates how many historically crucial and clearly political issues have been worked through marriage. In relation to labor economics in the early twentieth century, for example, she shows how marriage became a way "to stabilize the essential activities of sex and labor and their consequence, children and property" (Cott 2000, 6). Assessing marriage as it is continually renovated and rebuilt allows her to evaluate its meanings and consequences in different times and places without resorting to an irredeemably oppressive *or* intrinsically benign model. Most importantly of all, analyzing marriage as a relation of government attacks the myth that marriage belongs to the private realm and is therefore "beyond" politics (see Caldwell 1998, Cott 2000). In this way, feminism's most enduring legacy of marriage critique—that "the personal is political," and that marriage is a site of gendered power relations—is not dismissed but acknowledged, reiterated, and reworked.

In suggesting that marriage is a governmental relation, it should not be inferred that married subjects are merely passively inscribed with governmental regulations. Marriage might well have a disciplinary role; it might operate to police or produce "docile" wives (and husbands, too)—feminist work on compulsory heterosexuality and women's economic dependency has suggested as much. But the government of conjugality does not exist outside of or above its subjects. Rather, marriage is produced, reiterated, and contested by the same conjugal subjects it governs. Thus, while marriage may be like the language of a country into which we are born and must speak (Delphy and Leonard 1992, 265), the potential to contest its terms and debate their meanings is always inherent.

The adoption of an approach emphasizing marriage as a relation of government accommodates the best of both counter-sexist and counter-patriarchal feminist traditions. It allows the consequences and especially the rationales for matrimonial law reform to be assessed, but acknowledges that such changes are enacted in male-dominated political contexts. This is not simply to invoke the "man-as-author" critique of law, in which masculine privilege is understood to be produced by male-dominated executives. Rather, it acknowledges and accepts the kinds of critiques espoused by Pateman (1988) and Gatens (1996) that demonstrate the body politic's reliance on the exclusion and relegation of women. Theorizing marriage as a governmental relation also draws the regulation of women's *bodies* into the political spotlight.

CORPOREALITY

In feminist thought, "corporeality" is revealed as a concept whose immediate simplicity—the acknowledgment that embodiment is the arena of human exitence—presents a disarmingly complex array of theoretical consequences. Throughout the dominant traditions of political philosophy, Cartesian models of humanness have occupied theoretical pride of place. Such models establish a binary framework in which "woman" is identified with nature and body, subject to the authority of male-identified mind, reason, and culture. These philosophical and political traditions universalize "man" as *the* citizen-subject: in his mythically parthenogenetic establishment of civil society, man exercises his ability to *transcend* embodiment.[19]

Feminists argue that this transcendent, "disembodied" liberal individual assumes a corporeality resonant with men's—but not
women's—social experience. Women's lives and bodies are not so
easily separated from the bodies and lives of others, especially in
reproductive matters (lactation and pregnancy, for example).
Moreover, the activities held to constitute transcendence—creative
public enterprise, for example—have tended to be fields barred to
women. Women's historical exclusion from transcendent projects,
then, has been deemed to reflect a natural incapacity or unfitness for
public life, and has seen the entrenchment of divisions associating
women, or the feminine, with domesticity and the private. Men and
masculinity, on the other hand, are understood to be the proper
inhabitants of the public sphere. As Moira Gatens notes, "This division between nature and culture, between the reproduction of mere
biological life as against the production and regulation of social life,
is reflected in the distinction between the private and the public
spheres, the family and the state." (1996, 51). The liberal tradition's
refusal to countenance the significance of different embodiment has
reinforced divisions between public and private spheres, constructing "the masculine" and "the feminine" always in opposition to each
other, privileging the political capacities of men. Thus, "[i]t is the
male body, and its historically and culturally determined powers and
capacities, that is taken as the norm or the standard of the liberal
'individual'" (64).[20]

Ironically, feminist attention to corporeality has often been highly
abstract. Gatens, for example, discusses the isomorphism between
representations of the body politic and masculine political subjects.
She argues that "[w]hat is required is a theoretical space that is not
dominated by the isomorphism between male bodies and political
bodies" (55). In the government of marriage, however, the body is
neither disavowed, relegated, nor universalized, but is the subject of
specifically regulatory and heavily sexed inscriptions. Sexed human
bodies are the subjects of marriage legislation; marriage is the scene
of lawful, "productive," and "proper" sexual relations. In this sense,
then, the government of marriage might well offer some theoretical
space for understanding and criticizing not the *disavowal* of
women's bodies, but their production as political subjects.

This theoretical space is discursive, but neither abstract nor
abstruse. Early in our feminist education we learn that until 1870,
under English law, women became the property of their husband

upon marriage. A wife's very being was incorporated into her husband's. As Blackstone's famous commentary goes: in marriage, two become one, and that one is the husband. But of course women did not actually vanish into the bodies of their husbands upon marriage. Rather, under coverture, a husband could direct and control his wife's body *as if* it were his own (Wolfram 1990). Today we find this absence of wifely autonomy shocking and archaic—and rightly so. We have undoubtedly come a long way since the enactment of the *Married Women's Property Act*. However, marriage and marriage-like relationships have continued to govern at least some aspects of bodily conduct. For example, in many liberal-democratic jurisdictions, adultery is a ground for divorce. In governmental terms, what constitutes adultery? Not the transference of emotional attachment or love from a spouse to another, but a physical and corporeal act of sex. Adultery is "the voluntary act of sexual intercourse committed by a husband or wife with some person of the opposite sex other than the wife or husband" (Joske 1969, 308). The corporeal nature of the act is spelled out in governmental discourse; the main criteria for determining whether a particular sex act "counts" as adultery are penetration of the vagina by the penis, sexual gratification, and an "element of mutuality" (Joske 1969, 308, see also Chapter 4 of this volume). There is nothing abstract or even representational in such provisions: they are firmly and unmistakably corporeal.

While wives are no longer subsumed and incorporated into their husband's being, the subjects of marriage are not yet the autonomous individuals of liberal political theory. Conjugal subjects are neither entirely individual nor wholly incorporated. Married subjects are governmentally inscribed as a somewhat volatile coalition whose unity is corporeally figured. A cleric's advice to new brides in the early 1960s illustrates this point: "A young woman becoming a wife should think of her new state not as one that is to make her happy but as one in which she is to make her husband happy. . . . The good wife realizes that in becoming a wife she contracts to forget [her]self and put her husband's happiness above her own . . . In the marriage contract she handed over the right to her body for the actions of marriage . . . " (Rev. Father D. F. Miller, as cited by MacKenzie 1962, 86).

The operation of *condonation* as a bar to divorce (discussed in Chapter 4) illustrates the same phenomenon. Moreover, these sorts of corporeal inscriptions are not merely "written onto" passive bodies but can be mobilized by agent-subjects. In this way, marriage is *perfor-mative* in several senses.

PERFORMATIVITY

In her introduction to a collection of essays on feminism and Foucault, Susan Hekman says, "Foucault's treatment of the body and sexuality has stimulated the most extensive feminist interest in his work. Judith Butler's feminist appropriation of Foucault has been at the forefront of these discussions" (1996, 5). This "appro-priation" is complex. Butler's subject matter broadly concerns iden-tity, sexuality, gender, and feminism, and draws on a variety of theoretical traditions—most notably, linguistic philosophy, psycho-analysis, and its feminist offshoots (Butler 1990, 1993, 1997). Much of Butler's work is, in her own words, "dense or difficult to read or theoretically rarefied" (1992, 85). Given the scope and depth of her work, it is not my intention to offer any sort of exeget-ical account of Butler's commonalities with and departures from Foucault. Instead, I want to take up one of her key formulations, "performativity," and direct it back into the field of the govern-mental regulation of marriage.

Butler argues that embodiment is discursively informed; that gen-der is both inscribed upon and performed through the body. In a sense, she seems to figure bodies as utterances. That is, she suggests that bodies are both discursively informed and discursively produc-tive. "We do things with language, produce effects with language, and we do things to language," she says, "but language is also the thing that we do," (1997, 8). She contends that gendered and sexed identities are constituted in the repetitive performance of social norms; norms that police and construct "compulsory heterosexual-ity" (after Rich 1980). Like Gatens, and again, after Foucault, she posits a subject which does not precede its social construction in any essential way. "There is no 'sex' to which a supervening law attends; in attending to sex, in monitoring sex, the law constructs sex, pro-ducing it as that which calls to be monitored and is inherently regu-latable" (Butler 1996, 64). Thus, Butler argues that gender performance proceeds as iterative mimicry without reference to any "original," or prior, standard. In *Gender Trouble*, she uses drag as an example or illustration of her notion of gender performativity (1990,

136–9). While she celebrates the subversive potential of drag, Butler means to expose the material referentlessness of gendered identity: no person ever actually inhabits gender perfectly, for the standards of "correct" gender performance are not fixed, but float in a perpetual reconstruction of symbolic or psychic binaries pitting heterosexuality against non-heterosexuality. She asserts, *"[G]ender is a kind of imitation for which there is no original*; in fact, it is a kind of imitation that produces the very notion of the original as an *effect* and consequence of the imitation itself. In other words, the naturalistic effects of heterosexualized genders are produced through imitative strategies; what they imitate is a phantasmatic ideal of heterosexual identity, one that is produced by the imitation as its effect" (1991, 21, her emphasis).[21]

Butler's theoretical fascination with drag has seen a certain misreading of her notion of performance. In her contention that "gender . . . produces on the skin, through the gesture, the move, the gait (that array of corporeal theatrics understood as gender presentation)" (1990, 28), some have understood Butler to be figuring gender as a kind of vast costume box from which one might whimsically select the significatory accoutrements of one's preferred gender of the day (1992, 83). But gender performance is not mere masquerade bedecking some "truer" sexed self or biologically irreducible fact of sex. For Butler, "[G]ender is not a performance that a prior subject elects to do, but gender is performative in the sense that it constitutes as an effect the very subject it appears to express. It is a *compulsory* performance in the sense that acting out of line with heterosexual norms brings with it ostracism, punishment, and violence, not to mention the transgressive pleasures produced by those very prohibitions" (1991, 24).

The consequences of the performative utterances of marriage are obviously related to projects of subjectivity, gender, and identity. The social conventions attaching to marriage in the 1950s included such fundamental identificatory mechanisms as name-change. If Sam Stuart were to marry Wendy Wong, for example, Wendy would ordinarily become known as "Mrs. Sam Stuart." Sam, meanwhile, would see a name he formerly occupied as his alone used to refer to Wendy. Moreover, upon marriage, Sam and Wendy's relationship would be codified and inscribed in a number of socially meaningful ways.

However, these days one does not need to have uttered the performative speech acts of a wedding ceremony in order to be constructed (or to construct oneself) as "married." Performative *utterance* is no longer the only route to the social conventions of marriage. Comparing the governmental regulation of marriage and de facto relationships shows that the defining performance of conjugality occurs as it is corporeally inscribed—that is, through specifically *sexual* performatives. In so far as Butler ties gender performance to normative projects of compulsory heterosexuality, recent calls from gay and lesbian lobby groups for the legal recognition of same-sex marriage might carry profound implications for the iterative integrity of marriage's largely heterosexual history. To restate Foucault's question: if the corporeal imperatives or defining sexual performatives of marriage were no longer exclusively heterosexual, what kind of (sexual) bodies would society be demanding?

THEORIZING CONJUGALITY

I suggested at the beginning of this chapter that feminist critiques of marriage can be seen in sum as a polarized debate in which competing campaigns to reform or abolish marriage are promoted. Where the option to reform matrimony is pursued, marriage takes on the character of a whole menu of unpalatable dishes which warrant striking off, one by one, until we end up with something more appetizing. But like so many feminist issues, the problems seem impossible to pin down—the bad taste is mercurial, and seems to slip and shift between the prongs of our every attempt to remove it from our plates. So how do we reconcile those feminist critiques of marriage that are deeply pessimistic about the prospects for rehabilitating conjugality with the actual (albeit limited) transformations and improvements to marriage and matrimonial law that feminists have struggled to achieve, and for which we continue fighting to protect and extend?

A second issue concerns what we might understand as *alternatives* to marriage. Is cohabitation in any (feminist) way *better* than certified marriage, or does it merely mimic or simulate marriage? If de facto relationships are essentially identical to bona fide marriage, should we challenge and investigate them along with marriage, or is some other issue at the heart of women's subordination? What of those differences that do exist between the two? What should we make of calls to legalize or recognize same-sex marriage? If men can marry men, and if women can marry women, will the hegemonically heterosexist institution of marriage be blown down like a discursive house of cards, or will historically heterosexist norms be mortared into gay and lesbian relationships? Would "normalizing" queer conjugality see marriage's institutional patina applied to relationships whose very attractiveness might adhere in their subversively portable and flexible foundations?

The apparently intractable nature of these questions does not warrant the evacuation of marriage as a site of feminist investigation. While analyzing regulations concerning marriage and marriage-like relationships might demonstrate the usefulness of adopting a particular, local focus (underlining the flexible and contestable nature of such regulations), this does not mean that any generalizations drawn from such an analysis are necessarily invalid. On the contrary, marriage can be understood as both an effect and a mechanism of political subjectivities. Conjugality can certainly be understood to be, in some respects, emblematic of the broader relationships held and constructed in relations of sex, sexuality, identity, and politics.

The benefits of theorizing marriage as a governmental, corporeal and performative relation are several. First and foremost, focusing on the overtly regulatory government of marriage ensures that the personal remains steadfastly political (without redrawing or reinforcing that division). Secondly, theorizing the subjects of marriage as necessarily embodied means that we might avoid some of the inadequacies of the "autonomous individual" model assumed by most legal-political theory. As an added bonus, where such an approach is adopted, men as well as women might—indeed, *must*—be understood as embodied conjugal subjects. Furthermore, by theorizing the subjects of marriage as agents producing various sorts of performatives, we avoid casting wives as social dupes and might instead show how conjugal subjects negotiate a web of very sticky regulations and norms. In this way, we might begin to analyze and assess *degrees* of conjugality and their consequences, continuing the feminist tradition of marriage analysis even as forms of marriage potentially divested of any heterosexist import loom into view. Re-theorizing marriage in this way allows us to avoid semantic entrapment over whether marriage can or cannot be queered, and instead opens up the task of working out how various governmental bodies attach and measure the performative import of different kinds of sex.

CHAPTER 3

MAKING MARRIAGE:
VALIDITY AND NULLITY

What is "marriage," anyway? As with art and pornography, most of us might claim to know it when we see it, but very few people are ever called on to define or determine whether a particular marriage exists or not. The people to whom we assign such tasks are legal (and sometimes religious) systems and practitioners. Religious annulment is a complex matter in itself and will be left for theologians to debate.[1] This chapter explores civil decisions, variously referred to as "annulment" (in the United States) and "nullity" (in the United Kingdom).[2] Divorce and annulment both dissolve marriage, but in different ways. Divorce declares that a valid marriage has ended; annulment declares that a purported marriage never really existed, or was invalid. Until the middle of the nineteenth century, annulment was the only way to terminate a marriage between living spouses, and in this sense, it is reasonable to suggest that suits for nullity have largely been superseded by the ready availability of divorce (Grossman and Guthrie 1996, 308). However, in most jurisdictions, annulment remains available as a means to dissolve a marriage. As Grossman and Guthrie note, "the endurance of annulment . . . defies easy explanation" (1996, 308).

My view is that the continuing availability of annulment constructs marriage as the subject of state regulation, reiteratively positioning it as a matter of public interest. When we examine rules and cases concerning the validity of marriage, we can identify what has been excluded or what remains outside, and the boundaries of something that appears solid and straightforward are revealed to be much less certain and more permeable. Examination of the nuts and bolts of social and legal judgments on the validity of marriage exposes the institutional architecture of matrimony. What emerges is a blueprint for the naturalization of gender dimorphism: marriage naturalizes, produces, and protects the "logic" of the man–woman binary and its social corollaries. The chief aim of this chapter, then, is to examine how marriage is *made* in places like the United Kingdom, the United States, and Australia. Two main elements of marriage-making correspond to the two major sections of this chapter: weddings and consummation.

WEDDINGS

Even very small children know that to make a marriage, there has to be a wedding. In fact, even this truism masks a more complex reality, as we will see in Chapter 6. Nonetheless, weddings are typically crucial: a wedding is the main mechanism by which the marriage of two people is brought into being. Today, weddings are celebrated in diverse ways. Couples marry in hot-air balloons, on bungee ropes and beaches as well as in registry offices, chapels, and churches. Weddings are an occasion for conspicuous or understated celebration according to myriad tastes and budgets. If we clear away the costumes and cakes, the bare bones of any wedding ceremony are remarkably simple: in most jurisdictions, the bride and groom must declare their consent to marry each other before some authorized person, who records the marriage for county, state, or national registers. Saying "I do" (or "I will") is a key moment in any wedding. It is also a prime—arguably archetypal—example of performative utterance (Parker and Sedgwick 1995, 9).

Saying "I Do"

A performative utterance is a speech act or linguistic event in which to say something is simultaneously to do something. The most influential theorist of performative utterance is J. L. Austin. Austin was a linguistic philosopher whose collection of lectures, entitled *How To Do Things With Words*, endures as a classic text in its field. Austin describes performative utterance as speech, which, by social convention, entails consequences that are understood to arise out of that speech (1962). Examples of performative utterance include sentencing, betting, promising, naming, and so on. Judges pass sentence as the sentence is uttered; a bet is placed as the gambler presents the wager; a promise is made as it is spoken. As John Searle explains, "I can't fix the roof by saying, 'I fix the roof' and I can't fry an egg by saying, 'I fry an egg,' but I can promise to come and see you just by saying, 'I promise to come and see you'" (Searle 1989, 535).

Perhaps the most telling illustration of performative utterance is the magician's "Abracadabra!" Suspending disbelief, the rabbit appears from a hat, the watch vanishes, the bisected assistant is rendered whole again—all seemingly on the strength of a word. Saying a single word, in this instance, is understood to accomplish something consequential to its utterance. We know, however, that the magician's "Abracadabra," in fact, produces its transformations by other, more pedestrian means.

So it is with other performative utterances. Unlike descriptive speech, which often offers an occasion for contests of truth (for example, the statement "It is hot today" may be true or false, literally by degrees), performative utterances cannot be judged true or false. Rather, like magic tricks, performatives either succeed or fail (again, sometimes by degrees). Austin's preference is to describe performative utterances as "happy" or "unhappy." In doing so, he highlights the dependence of any performative utterance on its context: performative utterances require conventions to sustain them. The performative utterance "I christen this ship the Titanic" may be "happy" when it is uttered by a dignitary at a formal dockyard launch, for example, but less happy when uttered by a child playing with toy boats in a bathtub. Conventions governing the success or failure of performative utterances are like the magician's mirror or trick sleeve—they are the means allowing the utterance to effect its accomplishment.

The key performative utterances in a wedding are the bride and groom's vows; their "I dos." But what sorts of conditions govern the success or failure of bridal speech acts? For the most part, regulations outlining the "happy" circumstances, which must exist for a wedding ceremony to produce a valid marriage, are detailed in legislation current at the time and place the marriage was celebrated. Such legislation includes the various marriage codes of American states, the United Kingdom's *Marriage Act* 1949 or the *Matrimonial Causes Act* 1973, the Australian *Marriage Act* 1961, and so on, each with their many amendments and variations. Such legislation is used to determine the validity or nullity of a marriage. Thus, the array of conditions that can invalidate a marriage varies significantly, not only across but also *within* jurisdictions: a couple married in 1950 might have grounds for annulment today which would not be available to a couple married in 1980.[3] Typically, however, a distinction is drawn between "void" and "voidable" unions (Cretney and Masson 1997, 40).

A void marriage occurs when a wedding's conditions are so thoroughly compromised that the invalidity of the ceremony is barely questionable (Passingham and Harmer 1985, 46). To use an extreme example, when two actors utter marriage's performative speech in a drama, their "marriage" is clearly void. A void marriage is one that never really existed, and does not require any legal declaration to substantiate its invalidity. (Actors who have been "married" on stage do not need any decree concerning the invalidity of their stage "marriage" in order to marry other partners in real life.) A wedding in which both bride and groom were aware that the celebrant performing the ceremony was not authorized to do so, and who merely pretend its performatives, could not maintain that they had, in fact, married. Hence, the "marriage" is null and void *ab initio* (from the beginning).

A voidable marriage, however, exists until the point of its being declared null. Thus, if an improperly solemnized wedding is never called into question by either party, the marriage is assumed to be valid. For present purposes, the distinction between void and voidable marriage is largely technical and is not especially germane (see Goda 1967; Cretney and Masson 1997, 39–40). Nor are the historical and geographical specifics of nullity especially pertinent. More important is the effect such exclusions have on defining and limiting what counts as a valid marriage.

WHEN GOOD WEDDINGS GO BAD

Civil courts rarely hear cases concerning nullity or annulment of marriage. This does not mean, however, that this aspect of matrimonial law is irrelevant. It suggests, rather, that laws governing the establishment of marriage are so readily assumed that they routinely evade critical attention. However, at present, rules governing the validity of marriage vows are being scrutinized in many jurisdictions in the interests of securing or denying transsexual individuals and gay and lesbian couples access to marriage. A more precise understanding of what marriage is and does illuminates these debates in interesting ways. If, for example, marriage does not reflect gender dimorphism, but rather creates it in the service of heterosexism, the moment at which gay and lesbian marriages are legitimated might well turn out to be the moment at which marriage outlives its hegemonic use. Whether one celebrates or mourns its passing would, of course, remain subject to any number of personal and political convictions. The significance of challenges to marriage's heterosexist and gender-dimorphous history will be discussed in more detail later.

For now, the kinds of "unhappy" circumstances that have historically compromised the performative utterances of wedding vows can be grouped into two (related) categories: mistake and other problems relating to consent, and ineligibility to marry. Where ineligibility is at issue, the problem has sometimes turned on the ability of spouses to consummate their marriage or the related requirement that spouses be of different sex. Sex/gender conundrums in marriage and especially consummation will be considered in the final part of this chapter. First, let us consider the categories of "mistake" and "spousal ineligibility," and their imbrication with issues of consent.

Married by Mistake

"By The Power Invested in Me . . . "

Mistakes in the solemnization of weddings are rarely severe enough to render the purported marriage invalid. From time to time, however, doubts arise as to a celebrant's authority to solemnize marriage, or the nature of the ceremony performed is questioned. When news services in the United States reported the arrest of a man alleged to have successfully posed as a Catholic priest, county officials rushed to reassure people married by "Father O'Brian" that their weddings were valid (Arlington County Public Affairs Division 2006). As in most jurisdictions, the actual qualification of the person solemnizing a wedding is less important than the bride and groom's belief that they are marrying lawfully. Problems of nullity might arise, however, where both parties were aware *at the time* that they were being married by a person not authorized to do so. Mistakes concerning the nature of the ceremony being performed turn on a similar logic: if people believe they are party to a wedding ceremony, they will usually be deemed to have been validly married—even if the ceremony was not, in fact, a wedding but some other ritual. However, the usual requirement is that wedding ceremonies must be performed according to the rules of the country in which they were solemnized. Thus, when it turned out that celebrity couple Mick Jagger and Jerry Hall's 1990 Balinese wedding did not comply with Indonesian formalities, the couple had grounds for their putative marriage to be annulled (Oldham 2000; Roe 2007). This meant that neither spouse could make any claim on the estate of the other (beyond child support).[4] If, on the other hand, a person goes through a wedding ceremony in the mistaken belief that it is some other celebration—such as a ceremony of religious conversion or a betrothal ritual—the marriage may indeed be null (*Mehta v. Mehta* 1945; *Parojcic v. Parojcic* 1959).

The "Marriage of Convenience"

Ignorance of the consequences of being married does not invalidate the union. Nor is a "marriage of convenience"—in which parties marry according to a secret agreement that the union will be in name only, to achieve certain purposes—invalid. Where bride and groom consent to undergo what they both know to be a wedding ceremony, they cannot figuratively cross their fingers behind their backs. A couple cannot marry for the privileges it endows in relation to immigration and later seek to annul that marriage on the grounds of some "mistake" as to the nature or intention of their commitment (*Silver v. Silver* 1955). As June Sinclair notes, "Parties who have declared their consent to marry each other in a public ceremony before a marriage officer and witnesses should not subsequently be heard to say that they did not mean what they said" (1996, 364). In other words, "If the parties intend to contract a marriage—even though the marriage is only to be for a limited purpose—it will in the absence of fear or duress be unimpeachable in English law" (Cretney and Masson 1997, 67).

In the United States, marriages of convenience—particularly those entered into for immigration purposes—have been treated a little differently, and have been subject to a number of rules and interpretations pertaining to fraud (Gordon 1986; Tucker 1991). In the United States and elsewhere, matters that depend on the establishment of a valid marriage (such as immigration and taxation) are complex and ever changing. For now, it is sufficient to note that "marriages of convenience" present some interesting questions. When parties are suspected of simulating marriage in order to obtain some benefit, the question of the genuineness of the bride and groom's feelings for each other—ostensibly, the "problem"— slides into their prepared-ness to act out the corporeal relationship. In such cases, the question as to whether the marriage has been consummated or not has some-times been pivotal and will be considered in more detail later. In general, however, various kinds of mistakes come into play only where they have significant bearing on the parties' consent to be married—a crucial condition, to which we will return in a moment.

Not the Man I Married

At first glance, regulations concerning the validity of marriage when a bride or groom's identity is in question seem to reflect this consis-tent interest in valid consent. If, for example, a groom believes he is marrying Selma, but in fact weds her twin sister Patti, the groom's consent to the union is obviously compromised. Mistakes of this kind are very rare indeed. Mistakes concerning the true personality, feelings, habits, or fortunes of one's spouse are undoubtedly much more common (if not the norm) but do not, in general, offer grounds for annulment. Rather, the expectation is that where a per-son is a willing party to a wedding ceremony, the onus is on each party to ascertain the true character, history, and fortunes of their prospective spouse (Finlay 1980). "Identity," here, means the per-son as known to the other party. Henry Finlay explains that as a gen-eral rule, if a person means to marry Chris Brown, and the person they marry is the person known to them as Chris Brown, there can be no mistake of identity. Identity, then, is firmly *corporeal*. A notable Australian case confirms this, albeit in a strange way.

The petitioner in *Re the Marriage of C and D* was a woman who had been purportedly married for over ten years. In 1979, she sought a declaration of nullity on the grounds of mistaken identity (Finlay 1980; Otlowski 1990; Bailey 1979). Though the person with whom she exchanged wedding vows was indeed the person she had intended to marry, she alleged that the groom was not, in fact, *a man*. This, she said, constituted a mistake of identity: she thought she was marrying *a man*, but she was not. Evidence presented to the court showed that the husband was what medical experts of the day termed a "true hermaphrodite." Though recorded at birth as being a boy, the respondent had characteristics of both sexes: one teste, one ovary, a penis, and breasts. The husband had undergone several operations prior to marrying in order to bring his body into greater conformity to his identity as a man. The wife knew nothing of this. The judge ruled that the marriage was null and void on two grounds. One of these concerned the requirement that marriage be the union of a man and a woman—an issue to which we will return in due course. But in the first instance, Justice Bell confirmed that this was a case of mistaken identity. The wife's belief that she had married a man was, in fact (according to Bell J, at least), mistaken. Finlay argues that this case should not have been decided as a matter of mistaken identity. His logic is entirely sound: the wife married the person she meant to, so there really was no mistake of *identity*. However, one might argue that this "mistake" did not pertain to the husband's fortune, history, or character. The mistake, if we can call it that, was *corporeal*. Regardless, if the principal ground had been the more appropriate question as to whether the husband was a man, the result is sure to have been the same.

In most instances where mistake constitutes a legal impediment to marriage, the nature of the mistake speaks in one way or another to the issue of consent. A number of other grounds for annulment speak even more directly to the significance of consent, including cases where one party's consent to marry was compromised by means of duress or fraud.

Shotguns and Shysters

In the absence of that very narrowly defined mistake as to identity previously discussed, in the English tradition fraud rarely invalidates marriage. According to Cretney and Masson, "[f]raud is only a vitiating factor if it procures the appearance without the reality of consent" (1997, 66). If a person were to convince a prospective spouse, for example, that what was in fact a ceremony of marriage was merely a charade, the unwitting spouse might petition for an annulment on the grounds that his or her consent was fraudulently engineered. In the United States, fraud is a little more complex: if a groom unwittingly marries a bride who is pregnant to another; if a sexually transmitted disease is concealed from one party; or if a party misrepresents their intent in marrying, a marriage might be annulled on the grounds of fraud.[5] All these situations will be discussed later.

A marriage is voidable where either party's consent is vitiated by duress. "Duress," however, is narrowly defined: the exertion of pressure and the threat of punishment (that might often occur in "arranged" marriages, for example) do not ordinarily amount to duress. Rather, a more immediate and severe physical threat is required (Webb 1959). A British man arrested on a trumped-up charge and presented with the choice either to marry or to serve several years in prison for a crime he did not commit was held to have married under duress, and was granted an annulment of his Maltese wedding (*Buckland v. Buckland* 1965). Likewise, in a case whose details resemble a Hollywood script more than English law, a woman whose purported marriage was merely a daring means to secure her release from a Polish prison was granted a suit of nullity (*Szechter v. Szechter* 1971). The threat to the person claiming compromised consent must be external; the fears of the party alleging to have acted under duress cannot be a consequence of some situation of their own making. This means that what is colloquially called a "shotgun wedding"—in which the father of a pregnant bride marches her boyfriend into church with a metaphorical rifle behind the boy's back—is not deemed to invalidate the groom's consent.[6] The "duress" is, in this case, said to have been of the groom's own making and therefore negligible.

Not the "Marrying Kind"?

Some people are ineligible marriage partners. People whose capacity to consent is *ordinarily* understood to be compromised risk being party to a voidable marriage. Children, for example, are prohibited from marrying. This is a relatively recent innovation. Until 1929, in England, the marriageable age for girls was twelve years, and for boys fourteen. This was in itself an advance on the old ecclesiastical law, which held that "children could marry upon attaining the age of reason, for they were then capable of giving consent. This age was fixed at seven years" (Dickey 2002, 143–144). People with intellectual disabilities rendering them unable to understand the nature and effect of a wedding ceremony are also ineligible to marry, along with people who, at the time of their purported marriage, are inebriated or otherwise of "unsound" mind (Cretney and Masson 1997, 60–62; McGregor 1957, 31). The best-known prohibition relating to a person's eligibility to marry is the rule prohibiting bigamy.

Eligible Bachelors

Anyone currently married is prohibited from entering into a subsequent marriage. Bigamous marriages are void; that is, the rule is that a person is permitted to contract only one valid marriage at a time. (In a sense, this means that where bigamy is outlawed, it is technically impossible to be married to more than one person at a time, since a bigamous marriage is void ab initio.) Bigamy voids a marriage, but it is also punishable as a statutory offense whose maximum penalty extends to imprisonment (for up to two years in England; five in Australia and the United States). In this respect, bigamy is curious—it is not readily apparent why bigamy should attract a felony conviction, whereas forcing marriage by duress or contriving one fraudulently should not.[7] To make matters even more perplexing, there is, of course, no prohibition against a person entering into additional cohabitative relationships that, if they were bona fide marriages, would be bigamous.

Perhaps the most convincing reason behind the outlawing of bigamy concerns the "equitable" distribution of marriage partners. In *The Sexual Contract* (1988), Carole Pateman argues that the regulation of marriage has, at its mythical genesis, a fraternal contract. Together, the brothers plot to kill the father and share his many wives. To ensure that the brothers are not in turn murdered by their own sons, monogamous marriage regulations are established. Pateman uses this story alongside social contract theory to argue that the "overthrow" of patriarchal politics for egalitarian democracy is a reconfiguration of masculine privilege. The "free and equal" subjects of social contract democracy are men whose fraternal power is established in the "private" realm of the familial.

Without wanting to debate the many points of tension Pateman's work has aroused among feminists, her fusing of social contract democracy and marriage as a politics of women's exclusion should be taken seriously. One man, one vote; one man, one wife. Especially when discussed in relation to traditions of non-monogamous marriage, law-makers repeatedly characterize their own kind of marriage as a mark of civilization and a foundation of national prosperity. In an Australian debate on marriage legislation, one member of parliament drew the House's attention to the fact that "[t]he Attorney-General has stressed time and time again that the family is the basis of *our democratic way of life* and that the happy family is the bulwark of any nation" (Australia, House of Representatives 1959, 2740;

emphasis added). Chris Grover and Keith Soothill allude to a similar sentiment in their analysis of contemporary press reports of bigamy. They argue that bigamy is typically represented in British newspapers as "a threat to the nation" (1999). In the absence of an account like Pateman's, this evocation of "proper," monogamous marriage as a sign of political maturity and public good—one whose enemy is bigamy—is puzzling. Unless we understand marriage as intimately connected to the social contract and, thus, (by definition) a matter of public interest, it is hard to see why bigamy should be outlawed. If Pateman is right, the requirement that one marriage must be dissolved before another can be entered into could construct or reflect a form of family life that might be described as characteristically liberal-democratic.

Incest and Affinity

We have seen that some situations compromise or negate an individual's consent to marry. Beyond issues that render individuals ineligible to be marriage partners, some pairings are forbidden. Universally, marriage is void if its parties are related in prohibited ways, but the barred degree of relatedness varies across time and space. Prohibited relationships sometimes include affinal (that is, in-law) relationships, and aunt–nephew, niece–uncle marriages. The least restrictive regulations prohibit only "direct" relatedness by "whole or half blood." That is, a woman will not be granted permission to marry her brother or half-brother, father or grandfather, son or grandson. In each case, the marriage of such relatives is banned whether the relatedness is by "blood" or by adoption. This is, of course, a legal articulation of the incest taboo.[8]

It is interesting to note that, historically, the act of having sex *established* a degree of relatedness. Henry Finlay, describing King Henry VIII's colorful matrimonial career, explains how the English King was granted a decree of nullity in his marriage to Anne Boleyn. He writes, "[King Henry] 'remembered' that, among other transgressions before his marriage to Anne Boleyn, he had slept with Anne's sister Mary. This constituted a close relationship between himself and Anne, rendering their marriage incestuous" (1997, 45).[9] In other words, in the court of King Henry VIII, sex between two otherwise unrelated individuals established a degree of relatedness between those individuals. In this (highly idiosyncratic) instance, sex produced dramatically performative effects. More generally, when accusations of incestuous marriage arise, consent and knowledge are immaterial. A man who unwittingly marries his sister enters an incestuous relationship as much as a man who knowingly does so. However, in most other cases, when the validity of a particular matrimonial pairing is brought into question, knowledge and consent are crucial factors.

Pregnant by Another

It has sometimes been held that if a man marries a woman who is pregnant to another man, and if the groom is unaware of the bride's condition, his consent to marry is compromised (McGregor 1957, 31). This provision, clearly, is a strategy to police (and construct) paternity. A marriage would not be similarly voidable if the groom had impregnated a woman other than the bride. This is one example of the diverse operations of a sexual double-standard with regard to parenthood and marriage. The means by which children are made "legitimate" are entirely tied up with the marital status of their mother. Not so long ago, a child born to an unmarried woman was filius nullius, or *nobody's* child.[10] Discussing an English case of 1959 in which a mother tried (unsuccessfully) to adopt her own illegitimate daughter, Jenny Teichman notes that there existed "a very widespread social rule, namely, the rule that *only a man can legitimate a child*" (1982, 74, her emphasis). Further, a man "legitimizes the child not by adopting it but by marrying its mother or by being already married to her" (75). Thankfully, the legal category of "illegitimacy" has now lost most of its historical status and effects.

Syphilis and Similar Problems

In some jurisdictions, a purported marriage could be annulled if at the time of the marriage, one of the parties has a sexually transmitted disease of which the other party is unaware.[11] Similarly, a person who, unbeknownst to their bride or groom, suffers "incurable" mental illness risks contracting a void marriage.[12] These kinds of provisions construct "lawful" sexual relations as necessarily wholesome—in the modest, medical sense, at least. Given that a prospective marriage partner could hide a serious illness such as hemophilia, cancer, or diabetes without risking a future annulment, and given that weddings vows traditionally include a promise to maintain one's partner "in sickness and in health," the focus on sexually transmitted disease and mental illness can only underline the fundamentally sexual nature of marriage. The science of perversion—with its myriad connections between health and sexual desire—is the garden in which these particular grounds for annulment flourish.

Each of these categories of problem that might justify a declaration of nullity of marriage speaks to what conjugality is and does. Where and when such rules have prevailed matters less than their role in shaping the "normal" bounds of marriage as (above all) a consensual and heterosexual relationship. Nowhere is this clearer than in a final category of rules, which are now being challenged, sometimes successfully. This is the requirement that parties to a marriage must be able to consummate their marriage and be of different sexes.

CONSUMMATION

Consummation is the first instance of marital sex. It has served, historically, to finalize a wedding. In some jurisdictions, its operation is ostensibly obsolete, but its normative basis continues to shape and inform what marriage is and does. Consummation is very much like the handshake that seals a business agreement—it is a kind of corporeal communication. Tony Honoré defines consummation as follows: "To consummate the marriage means to have sexual intercourse at least once. The requirements for this are stricter than are needed to establish a case of rape. The husband's penis must penetrate the wife's vagina if not to its full extent at least to a certain depth, and he must be able to keep up the penetration for a reasonable length of time" (1978, 17).

Doing "I Do"; Consummation as a Sexual Performative

Consummation might be like a handshake, but no legal system defines the firmness of grip or duration required for a handshake to stand as evidence of agreement. Consummation, on the other hand, has been the subject of considerable definitional anxiety. In the previous quotation, Honoré refers to an English case of 1967 in which consummation was relentlessly and explicitly defined. In *W. v. W.* (1967), Justice Brandon said, "[P]enetration maintained for . . . [only a short time], resulting in no emission either inside the wife or outside her, cannot . . . be described as ordinary and complete intercourse. I

do not think that there is any authority which binds me to hold that
any penetration, however transient, amounts to consummation of a
marriage" (*W. v. W.* 1967, 178).

While sex in general can be understood as a range of actions and
behaviors, consummation refers to a particular type of sex invested
with legal meaning such that it, rather than other sexual acts, comes
to stand as "sex" as such, or as *all* sex. It is defined in case law as *vera
copula*, or "the true conjunction of bodies" (Hambly and Turner
1971, 96, 98). The notion of consummation, then, is a corporeal
yoke linking law and marriage. The kind of sex act required to consummate a marriage stands as the historically unmarked, universal
standard of "sex" and as an archetype for *conjugal* sex. Where the
sexual performative of consummation "fails," this speaks to the otherwise not-so-explicit conditions required for the sexual performatives of consummation to succeed.

A party's consent to have marital sex with their purported spouse
has sometimes been taken as implicit proof of their having consented
to marry. In many historical decisions concerning the validity of marriage, the question of whether the marriage was consummated or
not—that is, whether the bride and groom had performed a certain
type of sexual intercourse—was pivotal. Being *unable* to consummate marriage is different from being *unwilling* to do so, although
both have offered grounds for dissolving a marriage. Refusal to consummate will be considered in more detail in Chapter 4. For the
time being, the main focus will be on the requirement that parties to
a marriage must have the *ability* to consummate it.

In a 1952 case in the Australian state of Victoria, a woman petitioned for her marriage to be declared null and void on the ground
that the marriage had not been consummated. She described the
marriage as "unconsummated" because, though her husband had
"achieve[d] an erection and effected penetration of her sexual organs,
on no occasion did he succeed in completing the act of coition
because he was incapable of having a seminal emission" (Hambly and
Turner 1971, 94–95). The case required legal definitions of "consummation" and "sexual intercourse" to be articulated. The judge,
in his deliberations, cited medical authorities Winton and Bayliss
(1949, 276): the "essential parts of the act [of coitus] are erection,
which enables the penis to be inserted into the vagina, and ejaculation" (cited in Hambly and Turner 1971, 96). In this case, it was
decided that because erection and penetration did not in themselves

constitute "sexual intercourse," the marriage had *not* been consummated. The marriage was therefore annulled. This case invites the inference that "proper" consummation must be procreative, but this is not so.

In an earlier English case, a husband sought a decree of nullity on the ground of his wife's refusal to consummate the marriage (*Baxter v. Baxter* 1948). The wife, in this case, would not have intercourse with her husband unless he wore a condom. This he did, under protest, in order for any intercourse to occur at all. This case was dismissed. After all, the defining features of *vera copula* (erection, penetration, and ejaculation) were present and correct. Thus, there is no need for "consummative" sex to be procreative. Indeed, despite the wealth of detail articulated in the law as it concerns marital sex, nowhere is it demanded that the conjugal body produce offspring.[13] In one notable English case, we see that even where a marriage has produced legitimate offspring—a (biological) child of both the wife and the husband—the marriage might nonetheless never have been consummated (*L. v. L.* 1949).[14] Nor is there any reference to mutual gratification. The important player in the drama of consummation—the "speaking" part, if you like—is the penis. This is not to suggest that the only important role is the husband's: consummation is always a double act.

A case focusing on the wife's part in consummation was raised in England in 1963 (*S.Y. v. S.Y.*). A husband sought to have his marriage annulled on the grounds that the marriage had not been consummated. The problem, it was argued, pertained to the wife's "abnormal" vagina, which was described as "no more than an incipient vagina in the form of a cul-de-sac; [the wife] had never menstruated, had no uterus and was incapable of conceiving children, although she had perfectly normal external sex characteristics" (*S.Y. v. S.Y.* 1963, 3–4). It was held that if the wife were willing to have an operation to extend her vagina, she would be capable of consummating the marriage. The wife was willing to undergo such surgery, so the question rested on whether sex with an "artificially extended" vagina would "amount to *vera copula*." Counsel for the husband argued that "[i]ntercourse which is not within a natural vagina is not natural intercourse; it is a perversion. Penetration of the cavity in this case would be nothing but masturbation inside the wife's body" (*S.Y. v. S.Y.* 1963, 48). In his decision, Lord Justice Willmer disagreed, and denied the husband an annulment. He noted that if the wife couldn't be said to be capable of consummating her marriage (with her surgically "corrected" vagina), it must also be held that she could not be raped or, "even more startling," commit adultery (*S.T. v. S.T.* 1963, 61).

In each of these cases there was never any doubt over the sex/gender identity of the bride and groom: the husband is a man, the wife is a woman. The "problem," if it can be pinpointed as such, is with malfunctioning or dubiously effective genital equipment. Indeed, the idea that marriage is the union of one *man* and one *woman* has functioned axiomatically—so much so that it has not generally needed to be defined, defended, or even clearly stated (Dickey 2002, 145; Sharpe 2002, 91). The presupposition this "truth" rests upon is that legitimate unions endorse a "natural" order of sexuality, and this assumption has shaped marriage law in profound ways. This "natural" order, however, is anything but.

Sex Changes (Everything)

We know that "sex" and "gender" are not always coterminous: a person might have "male" biological and anatomical attributes but exhibit or practice traits and behavior considered "feminine" (that is, associated with what is thought to be appropriate to or for women). This, in itself, is not a problem for marriage; as a regulatory system, marriage polices sex, not gender. An "effeminate" man might marry a "masculine" woman—indeed, the wife who "wears the pants" and the henpecked husband are enduring matrimonial stereotypes. Marriage is not primarily concerned with "appropriately" gendered costumes: a tuxedoed woman might marry a man wearing full bridal regalia. A wedding can be celebrated in gender-novel ways (with a "best woman" rather than a best man, "bridesmates" rather than bridesmaids, and so on) without invalidating the marriage. In laws pertaining to the validity of marriage, few connections are drawn between sex and gender. There is no demand for women to be "feminine" or for men to be "masculine." Rather, the requirement that marriage be the union of one man and one woman emphasizes, again, its *corporeal* grasp.

As we have already seen, a spouse with "deficient" or "defective" genital equipment risks being party to an invalid marriage. If an "insufficiently" deep vagina or a non-ejaculating penis can constitute grounds for annulment, it is easy to see how transsexual[15] spouses might pose a legal drama of epic proportions. In the legal arena of matrimony, rules and decisions affecting transsexual people reflect governmental concerns about corporeal sex/gender identities and their status. The question at the center of things is not whether a man might marry another man, but how admission to the ostensibly exhaustive categories "men" and "women" is to be determined.[16] That such determinations turn on a party's capacity for *vera copula* (hetero-) sex is very clear, and points to the interconnectedness of legal anxieties directed at bodies whose sex is ambiguous or changed, and those related to sexualities.

The complex legal debate regarding transsexual people and marriage can be very simply summarized. Until recently, a person's sex for the purposes of marriage was held to be determined *at birth*. That is, matrimonial law denied the fact that a person's corporeal status might change from "man" to "woman" (or from "woman" to "man") between their birth and the time that they sought to marry. This is not an isolated or novel hurdle for transsexual people, who have generally had to struggle for recognition as coherently sexed people in virtually every aspect of their lives. However, marriage law seems to be especially sensitive and resistant to the possibility that its "traditional" sexual and corporeal categories might be flawed.

We will see in Chapter 6 how cohabitation has disturbed the institutional foundations of marriage. Treating cohabitation as part of a spectrum of conjugal relationships does away with marriage's performative magic and brings into being a different order of conjugal body politic. I will suggest later in the book that cohabitation can be theorized as a kind of simulacra of marriage—a simulation in which the norms of marriage are not merely pretended but are in fact produced. Transsexuality offers a theoretical arena that, at first, sight seems to require similar sorts of analytical tools. It could be argued (after Baudrillard as much as Butler) that transsexuality produces the *simulation* of fixed sex/gender boundaries; a simulation that generates the very "truths" it apparently reflects. Baudrillard suggests that simulacra are generally taken to be real. He surmises that when doubt or ambiguity arises, "order always opts for the real" (1988, 178). Where transsexuals enter into the legal arena of marriage, however, the social order has seemed historically *not* to opt for the real—that is, the simulacra of sex (and its transsexual hyperreality)— has *not* been taken as the reality of sex. Rather, the social-legal order continually underscores transsexuality as something *other* than real. The truth of transsexual identity—that a female-to-male transsexual

is *really* a man and that a male-to-female transsexual *really is* a
woman—is denied, and represented instead as something pretended
and imperfect; something at a temporal or corporeal distance from
the "truth."[17] It is necessary, then, to inquire after the state's dogged
reluctance to "opt for the real" in relation to marriage.

The author of a recent book investigating the situation of transsexual people as legal subjects argues that anxieties over transsexual
people in relation to marriage mobilize law's homophobia (Sharpe
2002). Andrew Sharpe positions marriage as one of a number of
grounds in which the "truth" about transsexuality is contested,
offering a wealth of persuasive detail and an intriguing argument. I
would suggest, however, that Sharpe tells only part of the story.

Trans Trouble

Transsexual individuals who marry in their ("new," true) sex run
aground on two connected matrimonial reefs. Where incapacity to
consummate is a ground for a declaration of nullity, transsexual
spouses have risked contracting invalid marriages on account of their
sexual "inability" or inadequacy. More consistently, marriages in
which one spouse is transsexual have been deemed to be invalid on
the ground that the parties to it are not of different sex—that is, they
are said to be not "male" and "female"; not "man" and "woman."
In either case, the crux of the matter is virtually identical: marriage
demands a specifically heterosexual relation that is desperately and
repetitively naturalized. One mechanism for naturalizing *vera copula*
has been to challenge any transsexual performance of consummation
as "unhappy" or unsuccessful.

A number of cases illustrate this. The most notorious and influential of these is *Corbett v. Corbett*, in which the husband, Arthur
Corbett, sought an annulment of his 1963 marriage to April Ashley,
a model whom he had purportedly married just three months earlier.
Deemed at birth to have been male, Ashley underwent a "sex
change" operation in 1960. The husband, who was fully aware of his
wife's corporeal and personal history, sought to have the marriage
declared invalid on the ground that the parties to it were not of different sexes. The case was heard in 1970 by Justice Ormrod, a man
qualified in medicine as well as law. The gist of his ruling, which was
to dominate similar cases for the next thirty years, was that for the
purposes of marriage, a person's sex is to be determined by their
gonadal, genital, and chromosomal characteristics at birth.

Ormrod's decision in *Corbett* is well known and considered by many to be deeply offensive. Ormrod sees fit to judge how "convincing" Ashley is, "as" a woman, inspecting her gestures and voice for traces of "female impersonation" (*Corbett v. Corbett* 1970, 104). Worse, Ormrod dismisses the difference between penile-vaginal sex and penile-anal sex as, in this case, a "difference . . . to be measured in centimetres" (107). Indeed, Ormrod refuses to acknowledge even that Ashley's vagina is a vagina, preferring to refer to her reconstructed genitals as a "pouch or cavity" (90). This is not to deny that this story is a strange one. Corbett, in particular, appears as a gender-confused popular mechanical, marrying Ashley in obsessed envy more than love. The judicial stage positions their drama as comedy rather than tragedy, marking Corbett and Ashley as subjects of legal ridicule. That a judgment as inhumane as this should hold sway for thirty years is testament to judicial affection for and dependence on what Sharpe calls "'[bio]logical" sexual dimorphism (2002, 9–10).

Ormrod's three-part test of sexual congruity has held sway in England even until very recently. It acknowledges only two "natural" sexes, which are positioned as naturally or normally exhaustive and exclusive. However, recent appeals to the European Court of Human Rights (Singer 2004) suggest that Ormrod's test is being seen as increasingly anachronistic. The case principally responsible for this questioning of *Corbett* concerns an English couple, the Bellingers. Mrs. Bellinger, a male-to-female transsexual, was married to Mr. Bellinger in 1981. They have lived ever since as a happily married couple. Mrs. Bellinger sought a declaration that her marriage was valid and subsisting. The English court denied her application, but noted that its finding was inconsistent with articles in the European Convention of Human Rights, and recommended a legislative remedy (*Bellinger v. Bellinger* 2003). The problem—or at least part of the problem—for the English court was that it was hamstrung by a *Corbett*-inspired amendment to English matrimonial law specifying that parties to a marriage must be "male" and "female." These terms are routinely differentiated from "man" and "woman": the distinction speaks to a dimorphic understanding of sex as biologically ordained and fixed—as "natural." There are many who understand and even embrace the fluidity of "gender" with its emphasis on roles, behaviors, and cultural constructions of masculinity and femininity, who nonetheless struggle to understand sex as anything other than completely and finally determined at birth. The limits of such understandings figure the body as the (fundamentally "blue" or "pink') page on which "gender" is (subsequently, socially) written. The theoretical and empirical difficulties countenanced even by experts in gender studies concerning the potential instability of the body as a ground for gender has been the subject of much debate, both before and after Judith Butler's important text on the subject, *Bodies That Matter* (1993). Insisting that parties to a marriage be "male" and "female" builds in and on a biological foundation to marriage, which is, in fact, thoroughly unstable.

In Australia, the requirement is not that parties to a marriage be "male" and "female" or even "of different sex," but rather that marriage is the union of a man and a woman. In a recent landmark decision, Justice Chisholm ruled that the words "man" and "woman" should, for the purposes of marriage, be understood in their everyday sense (*Re Kevin* 2001). He discarded Ormrod's test, determining that a female-to-male transsexual man, Kevin, was a man at the time of his 1999 marriage to Jennifer. Kevin and Jennifer sought a declaration that their marriage was valid—like the Bellingers in England, the case involved no conflict between the spouses. This decision is likely to have repercussions in many jurisdictions, including the United States. Indeed, in a recent and hotly publicized divorce case concerning Michael Kantaras (a female-to-male transsexual), the Texas court cited Chisholm, finding that Michael Kantaras's marriage was similarly valid (*Kantaras* 1998). The decision has since been reversed on appeal, but may yet be subject to further challenge.

Disclosure

In a number of cases, transsexuality has been subject to judicial anxieties concerning knowledge and consent—which, as we have already seen, play an important part in almost every determination of validity. When a wife "discovered" (improbably enough) that her husband was "female" after seventeen years of marriage, for example, the husband's "deception" was roundly denounced (*S.T. [formerly J v. J]* 1998). Sharpe argues that this and similar cases wrongly require transsexual people to "out" themselves to potential spouses. He says, "a decree of nullity may not be granted where a petitioner was aware of the respondent's 'inability' to consummate a marriage or where the petitioner has subsequently ratified the marriage. Thus, it is the knowledge and consent of the parties rather than the presence/absence of heterosexual intercourse, or its characterization as 'unnatural,' which ultimately determines the question of nullity" (2002, 92). Sharpe argues that any requirement that prospective spouses must know about their partner's transsexual history would be inconsistent with existing practice; that any requirement to disclose would constitute an unreasonable burden on transsexual people.

"Inability to consummate" is, however, related to other issues of knowledge and consent. A bride already pregnant to a man other than the groom, for example, must disclose her corporeal status if she wants to avoid the risk of a nullity suit. Further, as we saw in the case of *C and D* discussed earlier, "identity" is firmly corporeal and subject to mistakes that might vitiate consent. In any case, the desirability (or otherwise) of transsexual disclosure neither accounts for nor drives judicial disquiet concerning transsexual brides and grooms.

Arthur Corbett, for example, was fully aware of April Ashley's corporeal history, as were Mr. Bellinger and Linda Kantaras with respect to their spouses. What is significant about judicial engagement with the issue of transsexual disclosure is that the body is taken to both hide and reveal things more significant to marriage than a spouse's true character, fortune, or history. In this sense we can figure the body as a kind of repository of sexed and sexual communications—a sexually performative body, in fact.

Sharpe asserts that "laws pertaining to consummation and/or premarital 'fraud' have no, or little, relevance to the question of validity of marriages involving transgender people" (2002, 93). I happily agree with the normative claim that such laws ought not to be relevant, but the descriptive case is not made. This departure does not detract from the rest of Sharpe's analysis, which I find deeply persuasive. Rather, it suggests that the operation of consummation cannot be held distinct from the kinds of issues Sharpe raises—particularly those concerning the judicial conflation of transsexuality and homosexuality.

Homosexualization
Sharpe argues that the refusal to allow transsexual people to marry can be understood as an instance of law's homophobia. In *Corbett*, he says, "the overriding concern . . . is to insulate marriage, the institution of 'natural' heterosexual intercourse, from perceived 'homosexual' practice" (Sharpe 2002, 96). Ormrod's narration of both Arthur Corbett and April Ashley's "homosexual" histories, for

example, positions their marriage as a continuation of Ashley's pre-operative sexual career, thus "inscrib[ing] homosexuality onto the body of April Ashley" (2002, 97). Ashley and Corbett are thoroughly (homo-)sexualized: Ashley's surgical transition is represented as an elaborate dress-up, a corporeal costume whose sole purpose is perverse titillation. Similar tactics are equally apparent in Linda Kantaras's evidence against her former husband. While I agree with the sentiment of Sharpe's argument, judicial homophobia does not completely explain the "threat" of transsexuality in marriage.

There are several elements to my objection. First and foremost, as Sharpe notes, transsexuality is *rendered proximate* to homosexuality in *Corbett* and similar cases. Transsexuality is not homosexuality: the two must be (strategically, tactically) likened. Sharpe says that in *Corbett*, "the facts of the case serve to dramatize judicial anxiety over an imagined proximity to the homosexual body" (2002, 100), but in some ways this places the cart before the horse. The facts of the case are rendered proximate to the homosexual body in order to dramatize the case as the "proper" source of legal anxiety. Homophobia is not so much revealed as mobilized: the judgment brings the proximity into being. Legal anxiety over transsexual marriage has less to do with homosexual panic and more to do with the maintenance of "natural" and "obvious" distinctions between men and women, and their supposedly foundational role in a gendered and sexualized social order. "Confusion" between transsexuality and homosexuality is a legal production whose foundation is a "coherently" dimorphous sexed, sexual, and gendered order. Where anxiety over sexual differentiation occurs, the category threat is either assimilated or expunged. In *Corbett* it was expunged, in *Kevin* it was assimilated. Where the response is to expunge, the category threat is (homo)sexualized—bringing transsexuality into proximity with homosexuality *accomplishes* its exclusion.

If insulating marriage from homosexuality were the main or sole concern, a lesbian woman could not validly marry a gay man. Even in jurisdictions where non-consummation of marriage continues to offer grounds for dissolution, the conditions for establishing a valid marriage are easily accomplished. A marriage between a gay man and a lesbian woman presents no real legal difficulty. Moreover, many bisexual and homosexual people are validly married. A person's sexuality is not a determining factor in their capacity to marry so much as their corporeal coherence as a man or a woman. A husband or wife is not required to *enjoy* consummative sex, after all, but merely to be willing and able to go through its corporeal motions. In this sense, marriage has never been insulated from homosexuality, try though it might to mark itself thus. Where law homosexualizes transsexual people in order to exclude them from marriage, it is in the service of something additional to or apart from homophobia; it is in the interests of maintaining some corporeal coherence between sex, sexualities, and gender.

Homophobia is nevertheless clearly a factor or strategy in policing transsexuality in marriage—anxieties are not only reserved for those unions that might be "really" homosexual, but also for any that might merely "seem" to be so. Thus, as Justice Ellis observed in an Aotearoa New Zealand case, "[i]f the law insists that genetic sex is the pre-determinant for entry into a valid marriage, then a male-to-female transsexual can contract a valid marriage with a woman.[18] To all outward appearances, such 'marriages' would be homosexual marriages. The marriage could not be consummated" (*Otahuhu* 1995, 629). Similarly, one might surmise that if a natal man and natal woman marry, and later one of them undergoes sex reassignment surgery, their marriage could remain valid, despite its subsequent semblance as homosexual.

Precisely this scenario arose in the Canadian case of *M. v. M. (A.)* (1984). In this case, a natal man married a natal woman, and their marriage continued for the best part of six years, until the wife instigated transition toward bringing her corporeality into line with her emerging identity as a man. Ruling in favor of annulment, the judge found that the wife had *always* had an incapacity for "natural heterosexual intercourse"—despite the marriage having been consummated. The fatal incapacity was held to be "latent," along with the wife's transsexualism. Sharpe rightly describes this legal reasoning as "strange" (2002a, 112). Its strangeness inheres not in its figuring of Mrs. M's body as "a locus of/for homosexual practice" as Sharpe suggests (112), but in its remarkable flexibility. If no annulment had been sought, Mr. and Mrs. M might conceivably have remained married.[19] Marriage is a bar, it seems, that transsexuality variously hurdles over or limbo-dances beneath, but in either case fails to measure up. To me, this points less to law's homophobia and more to the obviously ambiguous and unstable categories marriage tries to render "natural" and clear-cut. In this case Mrs. M's body is not inscribed as homosexual. Rather, the problem is Mrs. M's potential to disrupt the imagined naturalness of sexed and (hetero-)sexualized dimorphism. The representation offered is that if the marriage were to continue, Mrs. M would "become" a homosexual man *by virtue of* the marriage. In other words, marriage is an organizing framework; it is the (phantom) structure by which imaginary logics of corporeality, sex, and sexualities are rendered coherent and governable. "Homosexualizing" a spouse is thus a convenient exclusionary device, a tactic for expunging that which threatens the "logic" of marriage's sexed and sexualized categories.

Ultimately, homosexualizing transsexual or transgendered spouses does not necessarily reflect judicial homophobia. In his influential book *The Case For Same-Sex Marriage* (1996), law professor William Eskridge "retrieves" a number of transgendered unions—some of which have "passed" as heterosexual—and positions them as part of a hidden history of gay and lesbian marriage (see also Coombs 1998). Eskridge's aim is to render the "threat" of same-sex marriage familiar and harmless. In doing so he renders some transgender spouses proximate to homosexual practices in precisely the same way that Ormrod and other legal conservatives do. Where the same tactic is put to entirely contrasting ends, it must stand as homophobic and queer simultaneously. Perhaps, then, it is neither.

A Judicial Castration Complex?

Sharpe notes the diminishing relevance of (hetero-)sexual functioning in marriage, building on this to argue first that consummation is no longer legally relevant in matrimonial law, and second that judicial anxiety over transsexuality has shifted its focus from function to aesthetics, or from acts to appearances. I will come back to the relevance of consummation in the final part of this chapter. For now, I want to challenge the accuracy of the shift Sharpe purports to identify.

Sharpe argues that a perceived emphasis on aesthetically rather than functionally "adequate" trans anatomy in recent cases reflects an effort to reduce homophobic anxiety by reducing its potential visibility (2002, 128). Certainly the readiness and certainty with which other people mark a transsexual person as unambiguously male or female seems to matter to courts. In both *Kevin* and *Kantaras*, judges noted with approval that neither man was likely to be misidentified as "female."

But in both of these cases, female-to-male surgical intervention was argued to be sufficiently complete *without* phalloplasty. That is, while both Kantaras and Kevin underwent mastectomies and hysterectomies, neither elected to have surgeons construct a penis on their bodies. In both cases, the possibility of a corporeally coherent but penis-less man sparked intense debate. The danger, expense, and generally unsatisfactory results of phalloplasty were exhaustively detailed. In these cases, it would seem, the more pressing concern was less with an aesthetics of "passing" and more with the logic of definitional exclusion. The point emphasized in *Kevin* was that having undergone mastectomy and continuing hormone treatments, Kevin could no longer appear unclothed as a woman. This demonstrates a (very recent) willingness to concede, perhaps, a degree of admixture between "that which is not-female must be male" and "that which is not-male must be female." The trend seems to be toward stressing the importance of excising whatever is corporeally inconsistent with transsexual person's preferred embodiment rather than reconstructing a simulation of some "ideal-type" genitalia—for female-to-male transsexuals, at least. In other words, a "man" is occasioned in the absence of breasts, reproductive capacity, and various other corporeal markers of "woman" (such as long hair, makeup, and so on).

It is important to remember that while the most extreme excisions are surgical (mastectomy, orchidectomy, and so on), virtually every human being performs at least some smaller kinds of corporeal excision—in the form of cutting or growing hair and nails, depilating body hair, shaping the body through corsetry or exercise, and so on. Such practices are largely self-regulatory, of course, but inevitably mark men and women as distinct from each other. Indeed, precisely these distinctions are then designated "natural" differences—as in the claim that men have more body hair than women, or that men are typically taller than women, for example. In the social relations of conjugality, the fact that some women are taller than some men matters less than the hegemony of couple pairings of taller-man with shorter-woman. Thus Sharpe is right to suggest that "fear of mutability" drives judicial anxiety, and he is right to suggest that this fear dovetails into homophobia. But it is not *merely* homophobia. Perhaps it is coincidental that *Kevin* and *Kantaras* concern transsexual grooms rather than brides, but the apparent willingness of courts to see them as men, however precariously, is consistent with gendered norms in which "woman" is the marked term in the man/woman binary. To become a woman, natal men must mark themselves carefully and expertly; to become men, natal women must stop marking themselves as such. This is an overstatement, of course, but I propose it to illustrate a simple point: transsexual (male to female) women seem always to be marked with the shadow of castration—yet their task is to produce material signs of "natural" corporeal "lack." That this should entail paradoxes and contradictions in law is hardly surprising.

Is Consummation Obsolete?

Sharpe situates his argument that transsexuality is a site of law's homophobia in competition with the view that laws concerning consummation exclude transsexual people. "[W]hile common law rules of consummation precipitate inquiry into the nature and practice of (hetero)sexual intercourse," he says, "it is difficult to account for the exclusion of transgender people from the institution of marriage through reference to these rules" (2002, 91–92). But, as we have seen, it is not an either-or argument. Rather, consummation is a lodestar in a constellation of practices aiming to maintain congruence and coherence in often ambiguous, sometimes fluid, and almost inevitably anxiety-ridden categories of sex, corporeality, and sexuality.

In this context it comes as no surprise that more inclusive definitions of "man" and "woman" in relation to marriage seem to be gaining purchase in those jurisdictions in which consummation has lost most, if not all, of its legal thrust. Where consummation is no longer a conjugal performative, perhaps law no longer needs to be sure of the existence of the corporeal magic wand (the sexually functional penis). But even in Australia and Aotearoa New Zealand, where consummation and sexual capacity play no part in proceedings for the dissolution of marriage (whether through annulment or divorce), consummation remains relevant. I said earlier that consummation finalizes a wedding in the same way that a handshake seals a business deal. As we all know, a handshake does not demand explicit legal conventions to exercise its performative effects. In the same way, even where marriage is no longer legally inscribed as a fundamentally sexual relationship, it remains normatively constituted as such. Moreover, if consummation's force as a sexual performative is in decline, perhaps it is no coincidence that its decline is occurring at precisely the same moment that valid homosexual performatives (in the form of same-sex marriage) loom into legal view.

In some jurisdictions, consummation and annulment remain robust concepts. Irish law, for example, includes a ground for annulment based on "absent emotional capacity." Fergus Ryan (1988) argues that the availability of annulment on this ground could "smuggle in" annulments whose real grounds are incompatibility. Ryan's argument deconstructs claims for annulment in which one spouse's alleged homosexual orientation is what constitutes the absent "emotional capacity." Given that the division of matrimonial property and other ancillary matters are different where a marriage has been dissolved through annulment rather than divorce, these provisions present another means of "punishing" queer people.

It's Only Natural

Rules governing the validity of weddings and marriage pretend to support a natural order—one in which all people are straight(forwardly) "men" or "women." (If this were the reality, there would be no need for the rule.) Sexed categories are, however, fictions. The familiar binaries of "male/female" and "man/woman" are neither exhaustive nor exclusive. Rather, marriage is one of a number of mechanisms that makes them seem to be so. Marriage operates as an axle not just for heterosexism, but also for corporeal and sexed categories. Sometimes these wheels spin in the same direction, but at other times the very instability of the categories marriage attempts to fix sends clouds of legal smoke into the air. Gender dimorphism sometimes serves masculine privilege as well as heterosexism. At times, it serves racist orders, too, as we will see in Chapter 5.

Marriage seems to reflect sex/gender dimorphism but in fact naturalizes it (see Alsop et al. 2002). Marriage laws do not reflect a simple and clear-cut division of all human beings into "male" and "female," but sustain the fiction of an obvious and natural sexual order. This is apparent wherever legal anxieties over sex/gender identity arise, and is especially evident in nullity suits resting on the contention that parties to a marriage are not "male" and "female," or "man" and "woman." Sharpe says that "legal anxiety over 'gay' and 'lesbian' transgender desire/practice represents . . . a completion of a circuit of homophobia in law" (2002, 121). Another way to conceptualize this is where marriage is the privileged, politically preferred terrain, it sustains its privilege by continually defining itself against that which it is not, expunging and disavowing whatever is not-marriage.

Transsexuality is one such disavowal, and homosexuality is another. In this sense, they are extremes meeting: both are the "opposite" of marriage in the same way that both madness and emotion can be said to be the "opposite" of reason, or both "women" and "boys" are "not-men."[20]

Wedding vows are routinely identified as a kind of archetype performative utterance. We have seen how such performatives can fail, or be "unhappy," according to a range of conventions buttressing the conjugal magic that seems to occur in the utterance of "I do." Judith Butler's adaptation and extension of performativity to encompass gender has drawn attention to the fluidity of gender categories, and to the fundamental instability of those categories (Butler 1990, 1993). In analyzing the conventions underpinning the apparent "naturalness" of gender dimorphism in marriage, its sexual-corporeal performatives are similarly exposed. Marriage is not simply gendered; nor does it merely reflect "sex" as a biological given. Rather, marriage produces meaningfully sexed bodies and supplies the conditions for which certain kinds of sex are performative—and therefore "special" (privileged). This is the case not just in making marriage (as we have seen), but also in *maintaining* marriage.

CHAPTER 4

UNION: ADULTERY AND OTHER
SEXUAL PERFORMATIVES

Marriage, according to the white western traditions examined throughout this book, unites a couple as "one flesh." The most extreme and asymmetrical incarnation of such union is the practice codified in English law as *coverture.*

Coverture operated in England into the nineteenth century, and dictated that "husband and wife are one, and that one is the husband."[1] The doctrine meant, in effect, that upon marriage, women entered into a strikingly subordinate relationship: their property, and to a certain extent, their liberty, became subject to their husband's direction. Under coverture, husbands were permitted to beat their wives, could forbid them from going to certain places or associating with certain people, and could even trade a wife at market.[2] When scholars remind us of coverture's heyday, they generally seek to warn against the ghost of matrimony past, or to show how much better contemporary marriage has become.[3] On Scottish matrimonial law, for example, Eric Clive says, "The old law that the wife was bound to obey the husband and that the husband could control her movements and her activities, forbid her to see people of whom he disapproved and, if necessary, administer reasonable corporal chastisement, has now *gone without trace*" (1992, 156; emphasis added).

The argument to be presented here takes a different view. Although the worst aspects of coverture were overturned with the passage of the English *Married Women's Property Act* 1870 (and similar legislation in other places, along with many subsequent reforms), the logic of coverture has never been entirely extinguished. We continue to expect marriage to accomplish a heavily sexed and distinctly corporeal union, and the mechanisms for effecting such a union endure. A specifically heterosexual kind of sex is understood to constitute a necessary precondition of conjugal unity. The corporeal union of what we might call "consummative" sex establishes a conjugal body whose elements are not in any straightforward way the autonomous, disembodied individuals of liberal political theory. Husbands and wives were not compelled to testify against each other in (non-matrimonial) legal proceedings, could not sue each other in tort, and could not be convicted of conspiring with each other—on the rationale that one cannot by definition conspire with oneself (Finlay and Bailey-Harris 1989, 171). Husband and wife continued to be known by one name (the husband's), and a husband could not normally be known to have raped his wife (163). The bodily mechanisms of heterosex constituted husband and wife as one conjugal body—as "one flesh." The consequences of marital union might have become less asymmetrical over time, but its apparatus remains; the ends, not the means, have altered. These means are *sexual performatives*, and through them, governmental and legal inscriptions of heterosexual and masculine privilege are traced onto the body of the population. The sexual performatives of conjugality continue to produce sexed subjects—some of whom accrue privileges through their actions while others are penalized or disadvantaged. The task ahead of us is to review the vestiges of coverture in modern marriage, and to consider the weight and effects of contemporary sexual performatives. The aim, ultimately, is to understand how sexual performatives operate in contemporary matrimonial law—and indeed, to consider whether they are still necessary or desirable.

The main objective of this chapter, then, is to demonstrate that the logic of coverture extended well beyond its purported demise: it was evident well into the latter half of the twentieth century. Whether it has survived the proliferation of no-fault divorce is less clear, and will be considered in Chapter 6. For this reason, the focus (for the time being) is on marriage as it was immediately prior to those reforms, which began to spread throughout many parts of the world—including western Europe, North America, and Australasia— in the 1970s. At this time, the expectation that marriage should be life-long was, for the most part, taken seriously. Legislation like the English and Australian *Matrimonial Causes Acts* (enacted in 1950 and 1959, respectively), along with various statutes in the United States, prohibited consensual divorce (Green, Long and Murawski 1986, 36–40), and in numerous ways penalized the behavior thought to cause marriage breakdown. In judicial rulings on the issues with which matrimonial law was concerned, a clear picture emerges. Twentieth century conjugality is, as we shall see, a union replete with the vestiges of coverture; it is union accomplished through sexual performatives.

As we saw in the previous chapter, wedding vows have long been held up as a prime example of "performative utterance"—when to *say* something is, simultaneously, to *do* something (Austin 1962, 5; Searle 1989, 554; Parker and Sedgwick 1995, 9). Performative utterances are best illustrated by example: one cannot peel a potato by saying, "I peel this potato," but a person is sentenced to prison *as the judge says*, "I sentence you to ten years"; a promise is made as it is uttered; a baby is named as it is christened; and so on (Searle 1989, 535). Naming, betting, declaring, vowing, sentencing—these are all performative utterances. The "I dos" of wedding vows are often presented as the example par excellence of performative utterance; a more telling (if less thematically apt) illustration, though, is the magician's "Abracadabra." As discussed in the previous chapter, when a conjurer says "Abracadabra," things are transformed as if through the power of the utterance. Like all performative utterances, however, its success depends on what's going on underneath the table, or up the sleeve, or how the cards have been stacked. As witnesses to conjuring, we are perhaps more aware that the success of the performative depends on factors apart from the utterance itself than we are as witnesses to many other performative utterances. The illuminating aspect of "Abracadabra," then, is that it invites critical emphasis on the "as if": transformation occurs *as if* through the power of the utterance.

Let us review and recap the discussion of performativity outlined in previous chapters. Judith Butler develops Austin's work on speech acts in her famous exposition of gender performativity, *Gender Trouble* (1990). Butler takes the class of performative utterances as a model for gender. She argues that gender (and its associated identifications of "man" and "woman") is performative: we continually produce and inscribe gender. Performing or "doing" gender *produces*

gender; it is conjured into being in our performative words and
deeds. For Butler, gender can never be a touchstone at the core of
being a man or a woman. Instead, gender is something brought into
being over and over again, a kind of perpetually shifting
"Abracadabra" whose familiar and predictable consequences lend a
feeling of substance and permanence to the effects it brings about.

If gender can be understood as performative, so too can sexual
activity. Some sex acts are performative, they *accomplish* something
by social-legal convention—something additional to bare sexual
behavior. Vows, then, are not the only performatives required to
produce a valid marriage. In the same way that saying "I do" is a performative *utterance*, consummation, for example, is *sexually* performative. In saying "I do," one is wedded; when a marriage is
"consummated," it is confirmed or finalized. The sex act does not
merely describe or communicate consummation, but *produces* it. In
this way, consummation can be understood as performative sex.
Consummation is not the only sexual performative associated with
marriage, it is merely the first and most obvious one. In many ways,
however, consummation serves as an exemplar for a whole range of
conjugal sexual performatives. And, just as gender performativity is
accomplished iteratively (Butler 1990, 145), so conjugal union is
established and reestablished through repeated sexual performatives
whose model is consummation. In Chapter 3, operations of consummation in relation to validity in marriage were explored. In this
chapter attention turns to the way consummation has figured in
divorce proceedings.

There are several kinds of sexual performatives at work in regulations governing marriage and its dissolution, most of them linked to
the notion of matrimonial offense. Until various reforms occurred in
the late 1960s and 70s, divorce remained very tightly tied to notions
of fault, with one spouse (the instigating "petitioner") having to
prove the other's "matrimonial offense" before a decree could be
issued. Matrimonial offenses can be sorted into three sometimes
overlapping categories: absence, crime, and sex. Absence (most
notably, separation and desertion) and crime (and in particular the
ground of "cruelty") will be analyzed more closely in Chapter 6. In
this chapter, however, the spotlight is on sex.

Lynne Halem, in her history of divorce in the United States,
suggests that by the late 1940s, "psychosexual problems" were

understood to be a major cause of divorce. "Despite this," she says, " . . . sexual incompatibility remained conspicuously absent from the list of statutory grounds for divorce" (1980, 181). She goes on to suggest that the relevant institutions "simply were not ready to contend with sexual problems in public forums" (182). The discussion that follows suggests that she is wrong. Halem's use of the phrase "not ready" implies that courts eventually overcame their reluctance to discuss sex, and recalls the popular misconception that since the Victorian era, society has become progressively more relaxed and more willing to discuss sexual matters. As Foucault (1978) has argued, and as court records confirm, the assumption that society moved along a trajectory from repressed silence about sex to the progressive unshackling of inhibitions is inaccurate. "Sexual incompatibility" might not have rated as a ground for divorce as such in the post-war era, but sexual problems and sex rights certainly figured loud and large in divorce cases. Far from being not yet "ready" to discuss sex in public, divorce courts had for a long time been a very real source of public titillation.[4]

Legal discourses—then and now—stipulate that marriage assumes or demands certain sexual obligations. In *Sex Laws*, Tony Honoré describes a three-part conjugal duty, which, for the most part, endures:

During marriage, husband and wife have a duty:

(a) To consummate the marriage by having sexual intercourse at least once.
(b) To develop and maintain a mutually tolerable sexual relationship.
(c) To be faithful to one another in matters of sex. (1978, 16)

The analysis that follows is organized into sections corresponding to Honoré's list, plus one other. The first section deals with consummation and, in particular, the "willful refusal" of consummation. The second part discusses a number of annulment and divorce cases in which one spouse's rejection of sex with the other was pivotal. In the third section, the focus is on adultery, where sexual performatives operate to rupture conjugal union. The final part discusses a bar or defense to divorce: condonation. Under regimes of fault-based divorce, evidence and arguments concerning condonation would arise where one spouse asserted that the other had forgiven them the offense on which the decree was sought. In each section, we see how conjugal sex works performatively in making, maintaining, dissolving, and reestablishing matrimonial union.

MAKING UNION: CONSUMMATION

Consummation, remember, is *vera copula*, or "the true conjunction of bodies" (Hambly and Turner 1971, 96–98). A marriage is consummated when, after their wedding ceremony, the bride and groom have sex for the first time as husband and wife. As a sexual performative, its first purpose is to confirm the wedding ceremony. *Refusal* to consummate is distinguished from the *inability* to consummate. As we saw in the previous chapter, if one spouse was *incapable* of consummative sex (and the other spouse was ignorant of their incapacity at the time of marriage), this offered an opportunity for annulment. Willful refusal to consummate the marriage was a ground for annulment in England, but elsewhere it was more likely to figure as a ground for divorce (Webb and Bevan 1964, 85). In cases concerning such willful refusal, then, the issue is not whether the spouses are *capable* of consummative sex, but whether they perform it voluntarily and adequately. (By "adequately," here, I mean in a manner closely approximating the legal definition of "consummation" rather than the more subjective standard of adequacy one's spouse might hold.) One judge prefaced his decision on a case of willful refusal by defining it as follows: "By willful refusal I do not mean a mere temporary unwillingness due to a passing phase, or the result of coyness, a feeling of delicacy, affected or real, or a nervous ignorance which might be got rid of or cured by patient forbearance, care, and kindness; but a willful, determined, and steadfast refusal to perform the obligations and to carry out the duties which the matrimonial contract involves" (*S. v. S. [orse C.]* 1956, 15)

A relatively straightforward case of "willful refusal" was heard in England, in 1960 (*Jodla v. Jodla*). Mr. and Mrs. Jodla were married in a registry office. Both being Roman Catholics, they knew that their faith did not recognize the civil ceremony. Mrs. Jodla insisted that they neither cohabit nor consummate their marriage until a religious ceremony had also been performed. Mr. Jodla was well aware of

Mrs. Jodla's stipulation that they be married "in the eyes of God" before beginning a sexual relationship. Mr. Jodla agreed to arrange a Catholic ceremony, but never fulfilled his promise. The wife was willing to have sex contingent on the ceremony, and asked her husband several times to organize this, so that they could enter into life "as man and wife in the fullest sense." The husband, however, let the matter rest. He never expressly asked his wife to have sex with him, and they never did. They "drifted apart": he sought a decree of nullity on the wife's willful refusal to consummate the marriage (238). She defended it and cross-petitioned on the grounds of *his* refusal. The husband's unwillingness to organize the religious ceremony, which would facilitate consummation, was held to demonstrate his willful refusal to consummate the marriage. His petition was denied, hers was granted.

It is important to note that willful refusal to consummate, incapacity to consummate, and infertility are clearly distinguished in law. As P. R. H. Webb and H. K. Bevan explain, "sterility and impotence are very different complaints and they must be sharply distinguished. . . . Infertility . . . affords no ground whatever for obtaining a decree of nullity" (Webb and Bevan 1964, 83). As we saw in Chapter 3, neither, apparently, does the use of contraception—at least not on grounds concerning consummation. The conceptual separation of conjugal sex and reproduction is clear. In a 1943 case, it was found that even though a wife had conceived a child by her husband, the marriage had never been consummated (*Clarke v. Clarke* 1943). In this case, the wife's pregnancy occurred *fecundatio ab extra*: "the husband d[id] not enter the wife, but ma[de] her pregnant by having an emission while . . . lying between her legs" (Honoré 1978, 19). Here, the husband came unstuck, so to speak, at a crucial aspect of coitus falling between Winton and Bayliss's two-part test: penetration. As we saw in the previous chapter, penetration (of the wife's vagina, by the husband's penis) is essential to consummative sex. In the similar case of *L. v. L.* (1949), the husband and wife had produced a (biological) child of their marriage, yet the marriage was held never to have been consummated. The wife in this case was said to have artificially inseminated herself using her husband's sperm. It would seem, then, that neither procreation, penetration, nor ejaculation is entirely sufficient in itself to constitute consummation. The (unstated) principle may be that the elements of penetration and ejaculation are equally important—either one without the other raises doubts about the success of consummation—but that they need not occur simultaneously.

At the very least, what these accounts vividly illustrate is that conjugal sex does not have to be procreative to constitute consummation. Even more tellingly, procreative acts between husband and wife do not necessarily amount to consummation. Given that one of the most frequently heard rationales for marriage is its suitability as an environment for offspring, this may come as something of a surprise. The cases discussed previously seem to suggest that corporeal union, coupled with men's (hetero-)sexual pleasure (as far as such pleasure can be hinged to ejaculation) is *at least* as important as the regulation of reproduction. This view is confirmed by a number of cases concerning the regulation of "conjugal rights."

MAINTAINING UNION: "CONJUGAL RIGHTS"

The first hurdle of conjugality is consummation, but the matrimonial steeplechase is replete with similar jumps. Spouses are entitled to expect and tolerate sex with each other. On this, Clive's commentary on Scottish matrimonial law holds true throughout most Anglo-derived legal systems. He says that "willful refusal of sexual intercourse by either spouse over a sufficiently long time may constitute behavior justifying divorce or separation" (1992, 155). This expectation and exercise of continuing sexual relations between spouses is often referred to as "conjugal rights."

While refusal of sex (subsequent to consummation) does not usually figure as a matrimonial offense in and of itself, it is an important element of conjugality. At least until the reforms of the 1970s (and in some places, even since), the obligation to continue conjugal sexual relations could be enforced with recourse to the law. Where one spouse shunned the sex and society of the other, the court could make an order for the "restitution of conjugal rights"—that is, order the spouse withholding sex to return and yield to the other. If the unwilling spouse continued to refuse to return to the embrace of the party making the order, the recalcitrant spouse could be deemed guilty of matrimonial fault and consequently divorced.[5] In many jurisdictions, the period for compliance was relatively short, especially compared to the period of separation required to prove "desertion." This presented obvious opportunities for collusion, and will be discussed more fully in Chapter 6, where the workings of adversarial versus no-fault divorce will be examined. Refusing sex with one's spouse has also been debated in divorce courts as a component of matrimonial cruelty (Skelly 1969), and as partial justification for leaving ("deserting") the marriage, particularly where the absence of sex could be shown to have had a negative effect on the petitioner's health. A number of such cases (as presented in English courts) demonstrate the gender asymmetry of performative conjugal sex.

It is difficult to isolate general rules in these cases; for the most part, they must be inferred. Judges repeatedly assert the desirability of deciding each case on its merits. While this makes identifying general rules tricky, it is no more difficult to determine whether such decisions hold for husbands and wives alike. Tony Honoré suggests, somewhat hopefully, that what is good for the goose must be assumed to be good for the gander, even where the evidence is contradictory. "Refusal of sexual intercourse by a wife over a period and without good reason," he says, "is a breach of marital duty and *despite cases which seem to deny this*, in equity the same must be true of the husband" (1978, 23; emphasis added). As we will see, Honoré's assumption of equity is misplaced. Let us consider, first of all, cases in which wives have brought suits against their husbands for refusing sex.

Husbands' Refusal to Grant Conjugal Rights

In 1964, a wife (Mrs. P.) married for over fifteen years sought to dissolve her marriage on the basis of her husband's cruelty (*P. v. P.* 1964). This cruelty, she argued, was wholly manifest in her husband's almost complete refusal to have sex with her, despite her many requests. Evidence was presented that the husband had always been somewhat indifferent to sexual intercourse, and that his sex drive (in this respect, at least) had never been strong. Though the marriage had certainly been consummated, the couple's mutual sex life ended completely after about two years of marriage. In his deliberations, Justice Harold Brown said, "It is difficult to accept that sexual desire is solely a matter of volition," particularly on the part of the husband, who is "the positive partner in the act and, unlike a wife, more is required of him physically than mere permission" (921). Leaving aside the question of whether "mere permission" is all that is required of women in such situations, the judge determined that the husband's lack of appetite for sex could be held to be neither volitional nor cruel, saying, "[I]n view of his natural disinclination for sexual intercourse, to find him guilty of cruelty is rather *like beating a dog because it will not eat its food*" (925; emphasis added). It is difficult to imagine a time when this comment would not have caused offense and outrage, given that it positions women, metaphorically, as dog food. It is not entirely surprising, then, that despite professing sympathy for Mrs. P., Brown found in favor of the husband and dismissed the wife's petition, denying her divorce.

The notion that wives must be passive and tolerant was also emphasized in *Clark v. Clark* (1958). In this case, Mrs. Clark alleged that after about two years of marriage, her husband refused sex with her without justification, and this constituted cruelty toward her. The couple had married in 1947, when Mrs. Clark was twenty years old and Mr. Clark was forty. Mrs. Clark made her dissatisfaction known to her husband and remonstrated with him over it, but to no avail. There was a further allegation that Mr. Clark exacerbated his wife's frustration and general unhappiness by frequently making her a witness to his masturbation in the bed they shared. In this case, it was held that "the absence of sexual intercourse was not cruelty," and "it was not proved that the husband ever did anything so as deliberately to insult her" (*B. [L] v. B. [R.]* 1965, 924, fn 22). The rationale for this decision was that a man's sexual appetite cannot be altered, and that if a husband's desire falters or wanes, this does not injure or otherwise constitute any hardship for his wife. Mrs. Clark's petition was dismissed, along with her subsequent appeal.

A case similar to *P. v. P.* was heard in 1965. A woman (Mrs. B.) whose husband was almost entirely "indifferent" to sex petitioned for divorce on the ground that his refusal of sex constituted cruelty (*B. [L.] v. B. [R.]* 1965). Her petition was dismissed, but she appealed the decision. According to the evidence presented, the marriage had been consummated on the couple's honeymoon, but after this, "intercourse was infrequent" (265). The wife raised the issue of her dissatisfaction in conversations with her husband, but his reluctance continued. In desperation, the wife had an affair. She confessed this to her husband, insisting that it would never have happened had it not been for his sexual inattention. He forgave her the adultery, agreeing that he would try harder to please her in this respect. However, after a brief period of time, his inactivity resumed. The husband acknowledged that his refusal to engage in sex was deeply frustrating to his wife, and that this was having an adverse effect on her health. He agreed that his behavior was making his wife "nervous, tense, and at times hysterical" (264). More than this, the husband admitted that his behavior was unacceptable. The judges in this case concurred with the decision handed down when the petition was first heard, and referred to the earlier case (*P. v. P.* 1964) noted earlier. Their decision was that Mrs. B's case was even less meritorious than Mrs. P's. They confirmed the original finding that "it is not cruelty for a man to be negligent in sex matters and not to satisfy his wife" (*B. [L.] v. B. [R.]* 1965, 267).

Taken together, these three cases would seem to suggest that if a husband doesn't care to have sex with his wife—and even if he taunts her frustration—this cannot be held to constitute a breach of marital duty.[6] In cases where wives have refused their husbands, however, the story appears to be different.

Wives' Refusal to Grant Conjugal Rights

In *P. (D.) v. P. (J.)*, a husband petitioned in 1964 for a divorce based partly on alleged cruelty by his wife. The couple had been married for about twelve years. The husband contended that for the previous six or seven years the wife had refused sex completely, and that prior to this had allowed only infrequent or "incomplete" intercourse. He argued that his wife's refusal of sex frustrated him and injured his health. The wife denied cruelty, counter-claiming that "any repugnance that she had to the sexual act was due to her husband's sexual excesses towards her and the nature of the practices which he adopted." The husband "admitted certain acts of which she complained" (1965, 457), but the judge presiding rejected the wife's allegations of "perversity." He accepted the husband's complaint that when the couple had tried to have sex, things would "start well but end badly," and that the wife would "freeze up" during intercourse. The judge found, in this case, that the wife's reluctance to have sex with her husband was based on a morbid fear of pregnancy. If the wife had undergone appropriate psychiatric treatment, he said, the couple's difficulties might have been avoided. The husband's testimony showed "how little [his wife] was able . . . to co-operate in the sexual act" (460). The judge decided that "this wife was consistently depriving her husband of the amount of intercourse which she ought really to have been affording," and that "the husband should not be called on to endure it" (463).

Evans v. Evans presented a similar case the following year. This couple had been married for over twenty years, until the husband petitioned for a divorce on the ground of the wife's cruelty in refusing sex. It was argued that after thirteen years of satisfactory marriage, the wife had "suggested that they could in future live together without sexual intercourse" (1965, 789). The wife denied this. Her explanation—that her husband no longer wanted "ordinary marital intercourse with her" (791)—was discounted on procedural grounds. In effect, then, Mr. Evans argued that his wife was refusing him sex, and as far as the court was concerned, Mrs. Evans merely denied it. The husband was working nights, and although the court heard evidence that his sleep was regularly disrupted, his health was adjudged to have been harmed as a direct consequence of his sexual frustration, and not lack of proper rest. The decision in this case was that the wife *did* refuse sex with her husband. As she offered no justification for this—which of course she could not do without admitting that it was she and not her husband who was refusing—the judge found that her conduct did amount to cruelty, and so found in favor of the husband.

While it is dangerous, perhaps, to generalize on the basis of these few cases, they do offer some insight into the way that sex figures performatively in marriage. While the judges concerned insist that they treat each case on its merits, it is clear that the duties and obligations of conjugal sex are different for men and women. If a husband's desire is minimal, or wanes, the wife is expected to endure this. Even where there is no question of the husband's capacity to perform the mechanics of sex (as in the *Clark* case), it seems that the husband is allowed to refuse, or, at least, the wife is expected to tolerate her husband's refusal, even if this damages her well-being. (Wives, it seems, must take what they can get.) On the other hand, if a wife's desire is lacking, she is expected nonetheless to "submit" to sex. (Wives, it seems, must take what they get, whether or not they want it.) A husband's lack of sexual appetite is beyond his control and not subject to discipline, but wives are expected to "adjust" their will for sex. There is no suggestion that a *husband's* poor libido should be addressed through psychiatric intervention, but wives are expected to seek "treatment" for their "frigidity" (understood, in this sense, as an illness). Women's sexual frustration does not indicate any sufferance of cruelty, but men's does, even where there are competing explanations for his anxiety or depression. If conjugal sex is performative here, it is reasonable to suggest that the more definitely performative subject—the actor—is the husband. His decisions, appetites, and actions are understood to be much more autonomous than those of the wife: if his desire is strong, so be it; if his desire is weak, so be it. The husband sets the sexual agenda and is not expected to endure anything he might find distasteful or alien to his own needs. Conjugal rights, it seems, are men's rights.

Sex operates performatively in the regulation of conjugal rights. Just as gender is iteratively inscribed (Butler 1990), so matrimonial union is reinforced through iterative acts of sexual union. Moreover, just as Butler locates potential gender subversion in its improper or imperfect repetition, so fissures in conjugal unity can be opened through a number of "improper" sex acts. Chief among these (in terms of being frequently cited and widely available as a ground for divorce) is, of course, adultery.

BREAKING UP: ADULTERY

Adultery is, perhaps, the archetypical ground for divorce. In his history of English marriage, O. R. McGregor concludes that "[i]n England until 1937, adultery was the only type of offence legally recognized as cutting at the root of the marriage relationship and warranting its dissolution" (1957, 34). In the state of New York, adultery was the *only* ground for divorce as recently as 1966 (Jacob 1988, 7; Day 1964, 518). In many jurisdictions, adultery continues to figure as a key concept in divorce law—whether as a ground for divorce in its own right, or as evidence that a marriage has irretrievably broken down. Its tensions and substance are familiar to anyone who goes to the movies, watches television, or reads novels. In fact, anyone acquainted with popular culture understands something of the social meaning of adultery. "Adultery" is the voluntary commission of a sexual affair by a married person with someone other than their spouse. The apparent simplicity of adultery as formulaic drama belies its many complexities. In some places, common law has distinguished two different actions for adultery: "alienation of affections" and "criminal conversation" (Rasmusen 2002, 82–84).[7] The differences and similarities regarding the two are many, but for present purposes, it is enough to note the following.

"Alienation of affections" is a tort (that is, a civil action): it is a remedy available to the wronged spouse (the plaintiff) against a third party's malicious interference in the plaintiff's marriage. At first sight, it seems to be a legal remedy against a third party's seduction (or attempted seduction) of one's spouse. Significantly, the action is not brought against one's spouse, but the "interfering" third party. A tort of "alienation of affections" need not necessarily be linked with an action for divorce, and does not require proof of a sexual relation between the third party and the plaintiff's spouse. It is conceivable, in fact, that a suit for alienation of affections might be brought against a third party who interferes with and breaks up a marriage without attempting to redirect those "alienated affections" toward him- or herself (for example, where a mother- or father-in-law who is unhappy with their child's match contrives to wreck the marriage). In effect, then, the action of "alienation of affections" rests on a norm of non-interference: marital relations are figured as properly and fundamentally private. The tort remains available in several U.S. states (Jones 1998, 70n80). Elsewhere, although the tort of "alienation of affections" might seem archaic and obscure, the norm of non-interference it endorses remains strong.

"Criminal conversation" is the matrimonial offense (or ground for divorce) of adultery, and is an action leveled primarily against one's spouse. It arises where one spouse voluntarily has sex with a third party.[8] "Criminal conversation" and alienation of affection can occur in isolation from each other. A married man who buys sex services, for example, may be an adulterer, but the sex worker he hires could not reasonably be accused of interfering in his marriage. Or, if a woman were to form a sexual relationship with a married man without knowing that he was another woman's husband, she could not be construed to have willfully or maliciously alienated his affections. Evidence of sexual intercourse must be admitted or shown to have occurred where one spouse accuses the other of adultery in a divorce suit. "Falling in love" with another person and choosing to associate with them in preference to one's spouse falls significantly short of adultery, and seems nowhere to have been a matrimonial offense (see *Cooper v. Cooper* 1955, 115). Since sex is the focus of this chapter, I will set "alienation of affections" torts aside, even though the distinction is sometimes useful. From this point on, I use "adultery" to mean criminal conversation as a ground for divorce.[9] However, even when we are dealing with this ostensibly clearer category of adultery as a matrimonial offense, historical and continuing ambiguities are rife.

William Blackstone (and of course others following him) defines adultery as "criminal conversation *with a man's wife*" (1773, 139, emphasis added). The inference to be drawn here turns on a fulcrum of sexual asymmetry closely linked to coverture. Blackstone does not mean that only men can be adulterers. Rather, the implication is that husbands commit adultery only when their lover is another man's wife. A husband might have sex with a single woman—most obviously (historically) an employee, servant, or sex worker—without offering his wife grounds for divorce. Married women, on the other hand, (being, by definition, men's wives) commit adultery regardless of whether their extra-marital lover is married or single. The logic of this asymmetry is clearest in coverture, and is strikingly resonant with Carole Pateman's famous account in *The Sexual Contract*. Pateman argues that marriage is a central, hidden part of political stories concerning the origins and rationale of democratic society. The *sexual* contract (crystallized in marriage), she says, underpins the mythical *social* contract in which men exchange their "natural" freedom (as competing patriarchs) to govern and be governed as fraternal political subjects. The parallels are simple: rather than competing for the sexual attentions of any number of women, men agree to respect an arrangement whereby each man is permitted to marry only one woman (at a time). In like fashion, rather than competing anarchically for power or resources, men agree to abide by a number of ostensibly egalitarian rules. By this logic, men commit adultery only where they impinge on another man's rightful dominion.[10]

While marital coverture is archaic, its legacies in respect of adultery are relatively recent. In many places, an overt double standard of adultery has applied. According to the provisions of the English *Matrimonial Causes Act*, for example, husbands were offered grounds for divorce on the basis of a wife's single instance of adultery. Wives, however, had to show grounds in addition to adultery or repeated instances of adultery on the part of the husband (McGregor 1957, 18–19). The English Act was passed in 1857 (and in England applied only until 1923 [29]), but in the colonies the rule continued to apply even into the 1950s (Scutt and Graham 1984). In some U.S. jurisdictions, the situation was similar: a wife could petition for divorce on the ground of adultery only if her husband *lived* in adultery, while a husband could petition on the basis of a single adulterous sex act on the part of his wife (Green, Long, and Murawski 1986, 18). While we might like to think that the consequences and meanings of adultery are now gender-neutral, the nuances of the double standard have not entirely vanished, even though they are no longer so overt. The fable presented in *Fatal Attraction* (1987), for example, would carry different weight if the gender tables were turned. In this movie, Michael Douglas plays Dan Gallagher, a married man who has a brief affair with an apparently disturbed woman (Alex Forrest, played by Glenn Close). The consequences are predictably terrifying: as Forrest forms an unrequited attachment for the flawed hero, her actions become more and more sinister. In effect, she stalks and terrorizes the lover who spurned her. In *Fatal Attraction*, women's power is dichotomized as either sexual magnetism or wifely service. Sexual power is baldly negative, fearsome, unpredictable, selfish, illegitimate, and destructive, while wifely service is represented as diametrically opposed to it in every way. In the end, though we might think him foolish, our sympathies are directed toward the married man (and his wife). *Fatal Attraction* is, in this sense, less about the husband's commission of "criminal conversation" as it is about the adulteress's misguided attempt to alienate the husband's affections. The story would play differently if Forrest (the adulteress) were married. Similarly, it would be an entirely different story, I suspect, if the adulterous spouse were the wife and not the husband—that is, if Dan Gallagher was the wronged, faithful spouse. To work as tragedy (of the Hollywood variety, at least) the film requires us to judge the married man's affair with an unmarried woman less harshly than other permutations of adultery.

Fatal Attraction would also be a very different movie if its hero's lover were another man. Adultery has, at times, been defined as "the voluntary act of sexual intercourse committed by a husband or wife with some person *of the opposite sex* other than the wife or husband" (Joske 1969, 308; emphasis added; see also Callahan 1967, 116). This does not mean that sex with a same-sex partner did not constitute a matrimonial offense—there were, in most jurisdictions, separate grounds for divorce in such cases. Where a married man had an affair with another man, his offense was more likely to be prohibited under criminal codes, or as an "unnatural act"—a ground for divorce that lumped together rape, sodomy, and bestiality.[11] Where a wife had an affair with another woman, the situation was different. The idea that lesbianism was unthinkable and therefore invisible is sometimes cited as a rationale for the lack of overt legal prohibitions against lesbians. This is, at best, a partial explanation. The erroneous inference is that because lesbianism has not been subject to the same sorts of penalties and prohibitions applied to men's homosexuality, it remained in a "safe" location, beyond legal reproach. This is, unfortunately, far from the truth. Sex and sexualities will be addressed more completely in Chapter 8, but for the time being, it should be noted that although an affair by a married person with a same-sex partner historically offered the other spouse a ground for divorce, it was not generally understood to be *adultery*.

At first sight, adultery's gendered double standards and heterosexually blinkered purview seem to suggest that its prohibition is a technique for policing paternity. This is the view presented most famously in Engels's 1884 classic, *The Origin of the Family, Private Property and the State*, and has been echoed in popular accounts ever since.[12] Grossly truncated, the argument runs like this: women are always painfully certain of their relatedness to their offspring, but men (prior to the advent of blood and DNA testing, at least) could rarely be so sure. The Darwinian and capitalist logic of competitive survival and material accumulation dictates that no man would choose to bequeath his property or care for a child not conceived by him. It follows, then, that marriage (and, crucially, its prohibitions against adultery) must be regulated to ensure that a husband can be confident that he is the father of any child born to his wife. The law, according to this rationale, should equip husbands to exercise power to this end. The argument is, in sum, that the law's concern with wives' adultery is, above all, a technique for policing paternity.

This rationale is not entirely convincing. As with consummation, adulterous "sexual intercourse" is by no means defined solely with reference to its procreative aspects. Consider the following definition of adultery:

1. For adultery to be committed there must be the two parties physically present and engaging in the sexual act at the same time. 2. To constitute the sexual act there must be *an act of union* involving some degree of penetration of the female organ by the male organ. 3. It is not a necessary concomitant of adultery that male seed should be deposited in the female's ovum (*MacLennan v. MacLennan* 1958).

This definition comes from a Scottish case of 1958, in which a husband petitioned for divorce on the ground of his wife's adultery. The court heard that the wife (Mrs. MacLennan) had become pregnant during her husband's protracted absence. Ordinarily, this would be prima facie evidence of the wife's adultery (Joske 1969, 316), but in this case evidence was presented that Mrs. MacLennan had conceived her pregnancy through self-administered artificial insemination. The sperm she used had come from an anonymous donor. Lord Wheatley found that although the wife's behavior was "a grave and heinous breach of the contract of marriage," she had *not* committed adultery. He said, "[I]n the eyes of the law surrender of the reproductive organs [that is, ovaries and womb as distinct from vulva and vagina] is not necessary to consummate the act of intercourse. . . . [I]mpregnation per se cannot be a test of adultery" (*MacLennan v. MacLennan* 1958). A wife's pregnancy to a man other than her husband, then, does not necessarily make her an adulterer.[13]

This raises the question—as with consummation—of exactly what constitutes the sexual element of adultery. Commentators generally agree that the "standard" was similar to (or even stricter than) the way that rape was defined (at the same time) (Honoré 1978, 17). However, in criminal courts the standard of evidence offered must be such that guilt "beyond reasonable doubt" can be established. Divorce courts, on the other hand, will find that an offense has been committed if the evidence suggests "on the balance of probabilities" or "to the reasonable satisfaction of the court" (*Matrimonial Causes Act* 1959, §96[1]) that it has.[14] What counts as "sexual intercourse" for the purposes of adultery seems to have been historically much more flexible than for rape and somewhat more flexible than for consummation. In a 1956 Australian case, for example, a woman was granted a divorce on the grounds of her husband's adultery (*Locke v. Locke*). It was alleged that the husband was "interrupted" in a parked car with a woman in circumstances inviting an inference of adultery. In a successful appeal against the decision, the court was presented with evidence that the female "intervener" in the steamy sedan was, in fact, a virgin. The appeal judges determined that she could not have been a party to adultery and overturned the decision. While the appeal was upheld, it was asserted a number of times that the fact that the "intervener" presented indicia of *virgo intacta* did not mean, in itself, that she had *not* committed adultery (see also

Thompson v. Thompson 1938). Moreover, in an earlier case in the South Australian Supreme Court, it was found that where a man had ejaculated in the company of a woman, but had done so without effecting penetration, this *did* amount to adultery (*McKinnon v. McKinnon* 1942). The somewhat unsettling state of affairs in which a "virgin" can be a party to adultery is mirrored in judicial determinations concerning the types of act which might count as adulterous "sex."

When former U.S. President Bill Clinton famously asserted that he did not have sexual relations with Monica Lewinsky, he was, perhaps, defining adulterous "sex" as penis-in-vagina intercourse, consistent with Lord Wheatley's definition (see also Holmes 2000). Cases, however, present a far less straightforward picture. "Sex" in adultery is a relatively flexible category: what counts varies according to the situation of the parties and the weight of evidence presented. In an Australian court, the concept of adultery has been defined as including "[a]ny conduct by way of sexual gratification that involves the juxtaposition of the sexual organs of a married person with those of a person who is not his or her marital partner, even though there be no penetration" (*G. v. G.* 1952, 406). In *MacLennan v. MacLennan*, it was found that in order to prove adultery, there must be evidence of "physical contact with an alien and unlawful sexual organ" (1958, 14). Precisely how one might recognize any such "alien and unlawful sexual organ" remains regrettably unspecified. However, as Honoré notes, "even when sex outside marriage is not a crime it is not 'lawful' . . . Sex outside marriage is not necessarily a crime, but marriage is the only relation in which sex is positively lawful" (1978, 10). While penetrative, penis-in-vagina-sex is the standard model of such "juxtaposition" and "physical contact," other varieties of sex acts have been held, albeit tenuously, to constitute adultery. There is no doubt that penetration *matters*, but sexual gratification and an "element of mutuality" have also been held to be important characteristics of adulterous sex (Joske 1969, 308).

While both penetration and ejaculation are usually (though not necessarily simultaneously) required to constitute consummation, in adultery it seems that *either* element will usually suffice. In an English divorce case of 1954, a husband (Mr. Sapsford) petitioned for divorce on the grounds of his wife's adultery (*Sapsford v. Sapsford* 1954). The court heard evidence that Mrs. Sapsford and her co-respondent (that is, the man alleged to be Mrs. Sapsford's lover, Mr.

Furtado) admitted to enjoying an affectionate and intimate relationship, but they denied ever having committed adultery. Mr. Furtado was an elderly man with a heart condition. His doctors testified that "ordinary" coitus would likely be very dangerous for him—and possibly even fatal. Mr. Furtado admitted that Mrs. Sapsford had, on several occasions, given him "manual satisfaction,"[15] and that they had enjoyed mutual caresses of a sexual nature, which neither led to nor amounted to intercourse. The judge in this case found that, although mutual masturbation did not constitute adultery by itself, and even though there was no firm evidence that "ordinary intercourse" had ever been completed or attempted, Mrs. Sapsford and Mr. Furtado *had* committed adultery. In this case, at least, even an enfeebled "alien and unlawful sexual organ" could produce performative effects.

While consummation and continuing sexual relations between spouses iteratively constitute and endorse matrimonial union, adultery is its prohibited counterpart. In adultery, as in consummation, there is little or no distinction made between procreative and nonprocreative acts. Sex does not have to be procreative to be consummative or adulterous, and conception can occur without consummation or adultery. In law as in life, marriage and reproduction are not necessarily concomitant. Judgments concerning conjugal sex distinguish *incapax copulandi* (sexual impotence) from *incapax procreandi* (infertility) (see *G. v. G.* 1952, 403) In these determinations, the continuing *sexual union* is usually protected and preferred; it is continuing heterosexual union that matters more than procreation or the potential to procreate. What we see in the various cases described earlier is a kind of corporeal performativity: law and legal subjects inscribe and reinscribe a particular kind of sex as meaningfully privileged. What's more, the actors with the greatest share of performative panache are men.

This is especially clear in the operation of condonation as a bar to divorce. So far we have seen that sex works performatively in a number of ways. In making a marriage, consummation is all-important (Chapter 3). In maintaining a marriage, the continuing duty to reperform consummation is likewise instrumental, and sex remains crucial to divorce proceedings in a number of ways, particularly in petitions citing adultery. To obtain a divorce under adversarial systems, one party to the marriage had to accuse the other of one or more matrimonial offenses. There were several bars to divorce, however, one being the "condonation" of the matrimonial fault constituting the ground for divorce.

MAKING UP: CONDONATION

As a bar or defense against divorce, condonation "involves three elements. A matrimonial offense is condoned when the innocent spouse (1) with knowledge that a matrimonial wrong has been committed, (2) forgives or remits the matrimonial offense, and (3) reinstates the offending spouse in the matrimonial relationship" (MacDougall 1966, 295). This is, perhaps, the simplest definition. The elements constituting condonation—knowledge of offense, forgiveness, and reinstatement—are consistent across most jurisdictions, but different permutations and weightings of these elements are evident, especially in the United States (Clark 1968, 526). In all cases and places, however, condonation is most frequently effected through sex. The sexual element is sometimes obscured under the coverall phrase "marital rights": whether this is euphemistic or not is debatable. The relevant part of the California Civil Code, for example, states that "restoration of the offending party to all marital rights" is a required for condonation to have occurred (California Civil Code § 116). However, there is no charter, as such, of "marital rights." Given that the similar phrase "conjugal rights" is synonymous with marital sex, it is fair to assume that it would also be the chief (if not the only) "marital right" referred to in the California code.[16] It is apparent, in any case, that marital sex after the discovery of a matrimonial offense always *implies* condonation, and often suffices *as* condonation. In many (if not most) cases, a single act of conjugal intercourse constitutes condonation.[17] An American judge encapsulates the rationale of sex as condonation neatly when he states, "[T]his court does not feel that parties should be allowed to maintain sexual relations and at the same time seek a divorce as the two acts are completely incompatible" (*Huffine v. Huffine* 1947, 764)

In effect, condonation works like this: if a woman were to discover that her husband had been having an affair, the wife could petition for divorce on that ground. If, however, at any time between her discovery of her husband's adultery and the case being decided in court, the wife were to have sex voluntarily with her husband, she would be said to have *condoned* her husband's adultery—that is, to have for-given him the offense and to have reinstated him as her husband. That single act, that moment of corporeal merger, reconstitutes or repairs conjugality.[18] Condonation of this specifically sexual type is a sexual performative. Like other performatives, condoning-sex accomplishes something more or besides its "face value" (Warnock 1973). According to the relevant social-legal conventions, having marital sex after the discovery of a matrimonial offense assumes a meaning additional to or apart from the everyday meanings having sex might usually bear. Where conjugal sex amounts to condonation, it is as if broken matrimonial union is mended by re-performing sex modeled on consummation.

In 1960, the English Court of Appeal decided a case that, as well as illustrating the nature of condonation, is relevant to our discus-sion of spouses' continuing obligation to have sex with each other. In this case, the husband sought a divorce on the grounds of his wife's cruelty (*Willan v. Willan* 1958). His wife, he said, "badgered him" for sex "when he did not wish to have it, obliging him to con-form to her wishes by indulging in various types of violence in order to bend his will to hers" (*Willan v. Willan* 1960, 625). Mrs. Willan pulled her husband's ears and hair, kicked him, called him names, and interrupted his sleep, "pester[ing] him far into the night to have sexual intercourse, so that eventually he was compelled to comply as the only means of getting his rest" (625). Finally, the morning after just such an incident—the last of many, apparently—Mr. Willan kissed his wife goodbye, left for work, and never returned. Instead, Mr. Willan visited his solicitor to lodge his petition for divorce. The divorce court judge agreed that the wife's behavior did constitute cruelty. However, because Mr. Willan had, albeit reluctantly, had sex with his wife just prior to leaving her, he was held to have condoned her cruelty, and his petition was denied. The husband appealed this decision. The main issues to be decided in the appeals court were (1) whether the act of intercourse in question could really constitute condonation where it was part of the very cruelty complained of, and (2) whether the husband's participation in the relevant sex act occurred under duress.

The three appeal judges had little difficulty in coming to their decision. They agreed that the husband's case "confuses the actual act of sexual intercourse, which constitutes the evidence of condo-nation, with the prior conduct complained of on the part of the wife, whereby she induced the act of intercourse." In other words, the cruelty involved could only include the wife's badgering, pinching, and so on. A wife's engagement in sex with her husband, according to Lord Justice Willmer, could never be understood as cruel. The first part of the appeal was dismissed. As to the second part, the court found that "in the case of a husband the fact of having intercourse with the wife, with full knowledge of the matrimonial offense of which complaint is made, is conclusive evidence of condonation by the husband of the wife. It is conclusive evidence because it is the best possible way of showing that the wife has been reinstated as a wife" (*Willan v. Willan* 1960, 628).

As this case suggests, the ways in which marital sex was measured to decide whether it did in fact amount to condonation differed for men and women. In the United States as elsewhere, "condonation is not as readily inferred or presumed against the wife as against the husband" (*American Law Reports* 1953, 126). As *Willan v. Willan* demonstrates very clearly, for the husband, there could be no allowance made for any misunderstanding or compromise of (his own) consent. According to Willmer L J, "It might be otherwise in the case of a wife; but in the case of a husband who has sexual intercourse it can only be said of him that what he does he does on purpose" (1960, 629). If a man were to have sex with his wife after discovering her matrimonial offense, this sex inevitably amounted to unambiguous condonation (MacDougall 1966). A husband's consent to intercourse, it was argued, could not be compromised by duress, and only very rarely could it be compromised by fraud.[19]

For women, on the other hand, a single act of sexual intercourse did not always amount to condonation: a wife's consent to sex could be more readily vitiated due to duress, for example. This is especially apparent in petitions alleging cruelty on the part of the husband. It is recognized, in such cases, that women might "submit" to intercourse in order to preserve their own safety or that of their children. In such cases, there is legal acknowledgment that a wife might resume sexual intercourse with her husband without its implying her forgiveness of his matrimonial offense or her reinstatement of him as her husband. The law recognized that a woman could be forced to submit to her husband's embraces because of his physical intimidation or abuse of her, or because he denied her the resources required to effect an escape. John MacDougall puts it succinctly: "Where the innocent wife resumes sexual intercourse with her husband the resumption raises a presumption that she has condoned his wrong but this presumption can be rebutted by evidence that she was not 'her own mistress'." (1966, 297). However, the very fact of *being a wife* could be understood as subjection to a kind of ongoing duress. Given that wives were clearly expected to "submit" to their husbands' sexual proclivities (and, conversely, to "tolerate" their own sexual frustrations), we might question whether married women were normally "their own mistress" or whether they continued to be subjected (by degrees, perhaps) to their husband's direction. Theoretically, at least, a wife's consent to condoning sex could be compromised simply *because* of her position as a wife. That a wife was often—or arguably, was *normally*—"not her own mistress" conveys in one simple phrase how the law recognized and constructed a complex unity of husband and wife in marriage. This was a unity called by the name of the husband and "directed," generally, by him—a kind of coverture, in fact.

THE CONJUGAL BODY POLITIC AND SEXUAL PERFORMATIVES

The conjugal troubles discussed here were not frequent occurrences. Cases concerning consummation, conjugal rights, adultery, and condonation might not be typical experiences of conjugality, but they are nonetheless telling. The picture they paint is of matrimonial union accomplished through sex acts. In making and maintaining marriage, breaking up, and making up, sex accomplishes a kind of corporeal fiat regulated and validated in law. The bodily mechanisms of *vera copula* heterosex constitute husband and wife as one conjugal body—as "one flesh." While some aspects of sexual behavior are expressly prohibited (such as the matrimonial offense of adultery), others have been directly or indirectly prescribed as conjugal "duties" or "rights." In this way, the matrimonial markings of heterosexuality are not merely inscribed as prohibitions operating on otherwise passive subjects, but are iteratively performed through sex and its legal meanings. In this sense, conjugal bodies are intimately governed— not through technologies shaping the will or soul (see Rose 1989), but through a much more literal government of the body.

The conjugal body of modern marriage is a complex unity of husband and wife constituted as compulsorily heterosexual but not necessarily procreative. As a number of cases make plain, consummative and adulterous sex acts need not be procreative, and conception can occur even in the absence of consummative or adulterous sex. Moreover, standards of sexual behavior or activity figure differently for wives and husbands. In cases concerning consummation and conjugal rights, wives' activity in heterosex is often elided. What is described in legal commentary as each spouse's duty to accommodate the other's ("normal," hetero-)sexual proclivities turns out to be a heavily gendered prescription. In fact, the "one flesh" of conjugality is a corporation directed, in the main, by husbands. Although adversarial divorce has been largely replaced by "no-fault" systems, the legacies of coverture might yet endure in a common heritage of assumptions about what marriage is and does.

I said at the beginning of this chapter that performatives are like the magic word, "Abracadabra"; startling effects are conjured, apparently, from the exclamation itself. While we might marvel and enjoy the show, we know, at heart, that these effects are accomplished not by magic, but by other, more pedestrian means: stacked decks, smoke and mirrors, trick sleeves. The sexual performatives of conjugality operate in similar fashion: they depend on conventions for their effects. As Butler argues, the conventions buttressing gender operate to reward those who perform it "correctly" and to police those who resist. The conventions facilitating conjugal sexual performatives work in a similar fashion. If we understand sex as performative, it follows that heterosexual privileges are not simply "possessed" or held so much as enacted or performed. Politically preferred sexual subjects—heterosexual spouses and especially husbands—exercise privilege not as a corollary of a deep, core, "true" sexuality, but as a consequence of performative conventions attached to marriage. Heterosexual privilege, then, should not be understood as merely ancillary to marriage, but neither should marriage be understood as a kind of fringe benefit of heterosexuality. Rather, conjugal sex is synecdochical of marriage itself: sexual performatives are simultaneously part and whole parcel of conjugality.

Performative effects flow from conjugal sex. Union is established through consummation, reiterated through the exercise of conjugal rights, ruptured in adultery, and reestablished in condonation. In each case, these performatives aim to produce "one flesh"; they construct a corporation of bodies through sexual proximity. While it might be tempting to understand conjugal performatives as romantic magic, in this chapter we have explored and exposed the social-legal conventions that underpin their success. These conditions are socially inscribed—they are not biological imperatives demanded by our reproductive capacities, nor are they fixed in time and place. However, in each of the aspects discussed here, men's performative potential is significantly greater than women's. In the performative magic of conjugality, it seems, the penis is a corporeal wand. Performative power is certainly sexed and sexual, but other factors also play a part in how the conjugal cards are stacked. In the next chapter, one such factor, "race," will be examined. We will see, there, that the cloud of magic smoke accompanying sexual performatives is inevitably *white*.

CHAPTER 5

MARRIAGE "BEYOND THE PALE": "MIXED" MARRIAGE, "MISCEGENATION," AND ASSIMILATION

Marriage most obviously regulates and polices sex/gender boundaries and behaviors. Marriage is a focus for sex, gender, and sexuality studies, but until recently these rarely attended to the ways racism has figured in marriage law. However, a flurry of new research has begun to consider marriage's recent and shamefully rich history as a mechanism for policing "race" and protecting white privilege.[1] As a whole, such research aims to illustrate the particular threat interracial marriage has posed to racist societies. Until this upsurge of interest in marriage and racism, there were very few analyses of the intersection of racism and sexism in contemporary marriage. Instead, attention has been focused much more consistently on colonial times and Indigenous cultures, producing a number of fascinating and sometimes profound histories and ethnographies of marriage.[2] The best of these endeavor to connect past and present, but too often the explicitly racist rules and prohibitions that shaped marriage before the late 1960s are presented as if they had no continuing effects—as if marriage's racist past has been entirely undone.

Against the collective emphasis on historical and cultural otherness, one relatively recent case concerning an "interracial" marriage is frequently cited. In the 1990s (and since), many scholars have seen fit to consider the U.S. Supreme Court's ruling in *Loving v. Virginia*, a case that overturned remaining bans against "mixed-race" marriage in a number of U.S. states in 1967. However, although the case is often cited, such citation usually occurs in debates about same-sex marriage rather than in analyses of marriage and racism (Wallenstein 2002, 241; Mumford 2005, 526). At a conference marking the thirtieth anniversary of the *Loving* decision, for example, most contributions focused not on racism, but on the viability (or otherwise) of same-sex marriage.[3] Whether the repeal of laws prohibiting mixed "race" marriage offers an analogy for same-sex marriage is a difficult question, and forms a part of my concern in this chapter. More broadly, I want to review marriage's racist history for several additional reasons.

In the first place, attending to the historically racist elements of marriage law helps guard against seeing marriage as a fixed and permanent institution. In the past, lawmakers have believed it perfectly appropriate to regulate marriage according to "racial" categories. This flexibility in the "content" of marriage underscores its place as a social construction whose meaning varies dramatically over time and space. Examining some of its historically racist rationales exposes the folly of insisting that marriage is an institution whose traditions should be immune from criticism. This is, modestly, the usefulness some gay and lesbian thinkers have drawn from *Loving*. A broader view—one that takes account of the particular situation and consequences arising in different times and places—demonstrates the threats as well as the potential promises in *Loving*.

Secondly (and relatedly), few commentators investigating marriage and racism bring any critique of marriage as such into their analyses. The (properly unchallengeable, incontrovertible) view that one person should not be prohibited from marrying another on the basis of either party's racial identity slides, too often, into an assumption that marriage is merely a badge of love. Marriage remains, in such accounts, a self-evidently benevolent institution, undisturbed and unchanged by its racialization and deracialization. Narratives of interracial love tend to present the repeal of prohibitions against interracial marriage as a metaphorical opening of the store doors to all comers. In the celebration of access, it is easy to forget that marriage is not just another product in the supermarket of life but shapes both the construction of the place itself and the way we behave inside or outside the store. As Nancy Cott (2000) has demonstrated so convincingly, the issue is not simply who has access to marriage (often expressed as a right to marry) but how marriage itself is shaped as a creation of the state through such regulation. As Cott reminds us, people have never enjoyed the right to marry whomever they please, exactly, but only to marry according to a range of regulatory schemes.

It is important, then, to consider the historical and continuing effects of marriage laws. Statutes forbidding "interracial" marriage might have been repealed, but to consider that this is where the story ends is to situate marriage as the proper subject of fairy tales rather than scholarship. Regulatory frameworks of antimiscegenation have been dismantled, but—even forty years later—"interracial" marriage remains relatively unusual (Ross 2002, 269n64; Jacobson et al. 2004). In the United States, for example, the number of couples entering into "mixed race" marriage did not dramatically escalate in the years immediately following the repeal of bans. By contrast, at the introduction of no-fault divorce, the number of couples seeking to dissolve their marriages rose almost immediately in most jurisdictions.[4] Interracial marriage's continuing infrequency indicates the need to consider the impact of regulation relative to what people tolerate, celebrate, or care less about. In this respect, the Australian story of Gladys and Mick Daly will be especially germane. At various points, their case shifts under different kinds of regulatory scrutiny: some aspects of their relationship draw the gaze of ostensibly (color-) blind justice, while others are deliberately ignored.

This chapter explores the historical prohibition of interracial or "mixed-race" marriages through two case studies occurring more or less simultaneously in the late 1950s: Richard and Mildred Loving in America, and Gladys and Mick Daly in Australia. I consider these cases not to equate them, but to show how virtually identical situations were governed very differently. While *Loving* case is widely known and cited, and similar provisions operating in South Africa under apartheid are regularly acknowledged, it is not widely known that Australia also forbade certain kinds of "mixed" marriage—albeit as part of a bureaucratic rather than legislative regime. The Australian government's steadfast reluctance to acknowledge and redress its shameful history in race relations justifies bringing the Dalys' case back into the spotlight. Despite the different demographic and geopolitical configurations of the two cases, in both places marriage has served as a vehicle for the protection of white privilege and the subordination of non-white others. More than this, in both nations, marriage was an instrumental component in the production and maintenance of white privilege. This chapter, then, presents an opportunity to reconsider the regulatory impact of marriage at the intersection of sex and race.

Before beginning to consider scholarship on the Lovings' case, I would like to offer a note on terminologies of "race" and racialized categories. Where I discuss the work of others writing about racial categorization, I generally follow their terminology. Where I draw on research by or about particular non-white peoples, my preference is to conform with the terminology those peoples employ. Thus I refer to Indigenous Australians rather than "Aborigines" in Australia.[5] I also refer to "white" and "non-white" people. I do this despite the risk of reinstating "whiteness" as whatever non-white others lack. My reasoning is similar and sympathetic to Richard Dyer's (1997, 11). "Black" can be understood as exclusionary and arguably resubstantiates a black/white binary whose boundaries are in reality less fixed and more permeable than the binary pair suggests. "Colored" is more inclusive but lets rest the inference that "white" is not a color or race category, that "whites" are not raced—an assumption that must be challenged. Like Dyer, I harbor a hankering to fracture the false unity of "white" into pink, olive, grey, and (I would add) beige (44). The linguistic unwieldiness of such a move exposes the heavily dichotomous nature of the black/white binary. In that "color" and "black" can both be understood as polarized responses to their privileged linguistic partner "white," we see extremes meeting. "White" remains stable, unremarked, and often undisturbed by virtue of its (unearned, invisible) privilege. In this way, the linguistic discomfort and risk of embarrassment or offense some of us feel in testing alternatives to racialized categories of color might, in fact, be instructive.

RACISM AND MARRIAGE

In the past, interest in interracial marriage has often been personal (or even prurient) more than intellectual (Ross 2002, 258–59). There are a number of interesting autobiographical accounts of interracial marriage, including Rajkowski (1995), Camfoo (2000), Hoffmann (2005), and Mathabane and Mathabane (1992). A perennial talk-show topic (Perry and Sutton 2006, 894–95), popular interest in interracial relationships is perhaps best characterized as a genre of (political) romance—in films like *Jedda* (1955), *Guess Who's Coming to Dinner* (1967), *Jungle Fever* (1991), *Japanese Story* (2003), or *The Bodyguard* (1992), for example. Indeed, some of the most interesting recent work on interracial relationships focuses on cultural representations of "race."[6] Sociological and psychological analyses drawing from interview or survey data are also useful, though in different ways.[7] In social studies, a flurry of publications on "race" and marriage has appeared, including books by Phyl Newbeck (2004), Peter Wallenstein (2002), and Renee Romano (2003).

Romano's *Race Mixing* (2003) is the best of these—partly because her focus on the postwar period brings the issue of interracial marriage into contemporary view, and partly because it is analytically richer than other treatments. While Newbeck and Wallenstein chart the progress of the *Loving* case as, more or less, a tale of love's triumph, Romano explores the numerous tensions posed by interracial relationships not just for racist states but also for civil rights activists and black solidarity. More than others, Romano interrogates the shape of marriage as both a producer and product of racism. Using an interdisciplinary historical framework, Romano discusses the threat of intermarriage as a diluter of solidarities rooted in racial identity; she examines intermarriage not merely as an effect of love, but also as an assimilatory force. This element of her analysis is useful beyond the American context, as we will see.

One might expect the recent resurgence of interest in interracial marriage in general—and in *Loving v. Virginia* in particular—to be tightly connected to current debates about same-sex marriage. However, despite the fact that the case looms large in this context, this appears not to be so. While such connections are made in Randell Kennedy's (2003) book, neither Newbeck (2004) nor Romano (2003) considers the same-sex analogy at all; Wallenstein considers it only briefly. Similarly, although Newbeck, Romano, and Wallenstein all note that the major concern for anti-miscegenists was "the coupling of white women with black men, not that of white men with black women" (Newbeck 2004, 26; Romano 2003, 87; Wallenstein 2002, 3), none sees this as an analytical fissure inviting the use of a *feminist* lever. All three books detail the heavily sexualized nature of anti-miscegenist racism, but none indexes "feminism," "sexuality" or even "heterosexuality." This suggests that for each author, what marriage is and does is largely self-evident.

And perhaps it is: "marriage," in these accounts, stands for the normal arrangement of intimate relationships in America. Even more simply, perhaps "marriage," in these accounts, is merely a sign of love. But, given that marriage is also self-evidently a gendered arrangement, the reluctance of scholars to engage with feminist ideas in relation to marriage and racism is disappointing. Works such as these begin to fill a very big gap, but even taking these social-historical accounts into consideration, the literature on racism and marriage is far from complete. Before considering these lacuna and the various spaces *Loving v. Virginia* is sometimes asked to fill, let me recount their story.

LOVING V. VIRGINIA

In June 1958, Richard Loving and his fiancée, Mildred Jeter, left their home state of Virginia to be married in Washington, D.C. In Virginia, their marriage was prohibited. Under the Virginian *Racial Integrity Act*, marriage between white and non-white parties was not merely void, but also amounted to a felony punishable by one to five years imprisonment (see Wadlington 1966, 1200). Statutes of the Code of Virginia further prohibited interracial "elopement": that is, where parties left Virginia to be married in a state that did not prohibit interracial marriage, returning to live as husband and wife in Virginia was an equivalent crime, attracting the same penalties. It was in this social-legal climate that Richard Loving, a white man, eloped with Mildred Jeter, a black woman who (using the language of the time) described herself as "part negro and part Indian" (*Loving* 1963; as cited by Newbeck 2004, 136).

Legal scholar Robert Pratt grew up a few streets away from Mildred Jeter's family home. As a family friend, he recalls Richard Loving as a quiet and decent man (Pratt 1998). Unusually, according to Pratt, bricklayer Loving worked for a black boss, and perhaps developed associations and friendships with black people as a consequence. The small town of Central Point has been described as "a place of surprising racial harmony for that era, a harmony perhaps due to the fact that residents of all races were equally poor" (Newbeck 2004, 21). In any case, Richard and Mildred became childhood sweethearts. He was eighteen and she just twelve when they met; they were twenty-four and eighteen when Richard asked Mildred to marry him (Pratt 1998). Knowing that their marriage in Virginia would be prohibited and invalid, the young lovers "eloped" to Washington, D.C., where they were lawfully married. Returning to Virginia, they lived with Mildred's family for a time—until, by Mildred's account, they were awoken one night by police in their bedroom (Newbeck 2004, 11; Romano 2003, 189; Wallenstein 2002, 216). The two were arrested and eventually convicted. After pleading guilty, both were sentenced to one year of imprisonment, but this was suspended on the condition that the couple leave Virginia and not return together for twenty-five years. Faced with the choice of banishment or prison, the Lovings returned to Washington. When they eventually defied the order of exile and came back to Virginia some five years later, they returned with a legal challenge to the ruling against them. When the Virginia court upheld the decision and an appeal, the Lovings took their challenge to the U.S. Supreme Court. The rest, as they say, is history. Virginia's racist marriage laws—and similar laws that existed in fifteen other states—were repealed, and the Lovings were free to live happily ever after.

In *Loving v. Virginia*, the U.S. Supreme Court ruled that marriage is a fundamental right. This aspect of the judgment is referred to over and over again—particularly in arguments supporting same-sex marriage, where the freedom to marry a person of a different race is frequently presented as analogous to freedom to marry a person of the same sex. Whether the analogy holds is a matter of compelling debate, to which we will return in due course. For the time being, we need to consider the more immediate effects that anti-miscegenation statutes like the Virginian code produced.

In 1967, Virginia was one of sixteen American states in which it was still illegal for a white person to marry a non-white person.[8] It was not illegal for people of different non-white ethnicities to marry each other, but any marriage between (for example) a white man and an African American woman, or a Native American man and a white woman, was void *ab initio* (Destro 1997, 1207n1). Categorizations of race were calibrated as a kind of haemomathematics in which the appearance of "color" and a number of other corporeal characteristics were understood to be the physical manifestation of some fraction of inherently racialized blood (Dyer 1997, 24; Wadlington

1966, 1196; Lombardo 1988). The language of the day supplies the impression that differently raced blood is somehow readily detectable—that strands of racialized identity course through our veins like colored threads of eight ply wool, or that a little "black" blood might sit in "white" like oil on water. Indeed, the racialized properties of blood were so thoroughly ingrained that in Louisiana, regulations required white patients to be notified should blood to be received in a transfusion come from a non-white donor. Presumably, the choice to be countenanced by a white patient was whether death would be preferable to becoming the recipient of "black" blood (for discussion, see Wadlington 1966, 1203). It is difficult, today, to imagine a couple obliging the county clerk or marriage registrar by declaring their race-ancestry in quarters, eighths, sixteenths, and even sixty-fourths. Most people today are unlikely to be able to name their eight great grandparents, let alone their sixteen great, great grandparents.[9] However, the spurious logic of "blood" and its corporeal evidence must have been reasonably well accepted among whites at that time.

The determination of race-ancestry such that even a drop of "black blood" makes one black is termed "hypo-descent" (Omi and Winant 1986, 60; see also Dyer 1997, 25).[10] Such regulations construct blackness as supernaturally powerful in order to incite fear as a rationale for racism. At the center of this fear was the starkly unlikely threat of white obliteration. Using the eugenicist arguments that dominated the hearts and minds of a number of white supremacists, Virginia's lawmakers determined, by amendment in 1924 to laws arguably dating back from 1691 (Wadlington 1966), that miscegenation, or inter-racial procreation, would spell disaster for civilization as they knew it. Prohibiting marriage between whites and non-whites was, they reasoned, a crucial defense against miscegenation and its ruinous consequences (Lombardo 1988).[11]

The implications of the repeal of prohibitions on interracial marriage at the time they occurred are fairly obvious. Given that the Lovings' case offers a narrative in which gender and "race" clearly intersect, and given the longstanding appeal of marriage as an arena of feminist inquiry, one might expect the case to have attracted attention from feminist theorists and particularly those feminists interested in "race." That it has not—and that, in fact, interracial marriage more generally has *not* been an object of significant interest in feminist thought—is surprising, and demands explanation.

SISTERS-IN-LAW?
FEMINISM, MARRIAGE, AND RACISM

Thanks largely to the willingness of black feminists like bell hooks[12] to engage critically in feminist theorizing and pedagogy, feminism has in recent years become haltingly adept at acknowledging its racism, and tends at least to gesture toward the ways that sexism and racism intersect and diverge (Phelan 1997, 85; Weedon 1999; hooks 1982). Indeed, one of hooks's most significant and enduring contributions to theories of oppression is her warning to analogize racism and sexism only with a wary eye to the exclusions such analogies produce (hooks 1982, 8; see also Dyer 1997, 5; Grillo and Wildman 1991). Conversely, many same-sex marriage lobbyists analogize sexuality and race in a relatively unsophisticated manner. My suspicion is that if advocates of same-sex marriage paid more attention to (a) feminist critiques of marriage and (b) feminist theory's (imperfect) sensitivity to racism and theories of ethnicity, they would cite *Loving* much more carefully. This is not to suggest that feminist analyses of marriage have developed any definitive or even adequate account of racism. But feminist theory almost routinely considers how white women's privilege might be shored up at the expense of black women and (sometimes) black men. To state the minimal case: while feminist thinkers might not necessarily address their analyses to racism directly, many no longer ignore the contradictions and difficulties raised by considerations of difference, racism, and white race privilege.

Why, then, is feminist interest in interracial marriage so lackluster? One contributing factor may be that (for a change) white feminists have attended to the level of importance given to the topic by non-white women. The reluctance of feminists of color to devote time and energy to issues associated with interracial marriage is understandable, perhaps, given that there are so many more urgent matters on the agenda.[13] Violence against black women is one such matter. However, looking at the connections between marriage regulations and sexual violence exposes marriage as something other than a declaration of love between two people.

In the United States and elsewhere, prohibitions against miscegenation and "mixed" marriage went some way, in effect, toward granting white men impunity to rape non-white women. This is not to deny that there were any number of loving relationships between black women and white men. Rather, it is to highlight the way that anti-miscegenation legislation acted as a kind of amulet for white men's sexual activity with black women—in which he could "have" her, but would never have to "keep" her. Such laws protected white men against the (heavily stereotyped) "damaging temptations" offered by black women. Prohibitions against "mixed-race" marriage marked black women as "not for marrying" (by white men) in the same way that "whores" are "not for marrying." (In reality, of course, many sex workers are married—the mark is symbolic.) As hooks notes, the positioning of black women as providers of sexual services for white men has a long history (1982, 25). It is not accidental that marking a woman as "not for marrying" simultaneously marks her as "unrapeable." Again, the mark is symbolic: sex workers and black women are all too frequently raped, but those who rape them are rarely charged or convicted of the offense. In this sense, an "unrapeable" woman is a subject whose complaint of rape is unlikely to be heard. Thus, as Angela Davis observes, so long as they are "[v]iewed as 'loose women' and whores, Black women's cries of rape . . . necessarily lack legitimacy" (Davis 1981, 182; see also Romano 2003, 236).

The positioning of black women as "not for marrying" and "unrapeable" subjects is a counterpart to the "black man as rapist" stereotype. Complicating hooks's assertion that the myth of the black rapist weakened even as the myth of black women's hypersexuality prevailed, Davis notes that the two constructions reinforce each other: "The fictional image of the Black man as rapist has always strengthened its inseparable companion: the image of the Black woman as chronically promiscuous" (Davis 1981, 182). The effect of such stereotypes is to make white women the proper subjects of white men's "protection" (Fine 2004; Daniels 1997, 93), while subjecting black men and women to outrageous denials of liberty. In the absence of these racial stereotypes and their provision of an impetus for (white) moral panic, anti-miscegenation statutes simply make no sense. After all, the white assumption was always that interracial sexual attraction is "unnatural" in and of itself.

Whether for these or other reasons, relatively few black women are personally involved in interracial marriages: nearly three-quarters of black-white interracial marriages in the United States involve African American men marrying white women (Perry and Sutton 2006, 892; Wilson and Russell 1996, 125; Romano 2003, 5). In the

United Kingdom, the figure is comparable: Perry and Sutton observe that in Greater London, "twice as many black men as black women are in an interracial relationship" (892). In their book *Divided Sisters* (1996), Midge Wilson and Kathy Russell present interracial marriage as an issue of unfair competition between white and non-white women. Documenting the relative scarcity of men as marriage partners for black women, they say:

> by the age of thirty, three fourths of all White women are married, but by the same age, fewer than half that number of Black women are. And by the age of forty, the statistics are more *grim*. As few as one in ten White women has never been married, but nearly one in four Black women who reaches the age of forty has never been married. The situation is *even worse* for college-educated, successful African American women, perhaps because there are fewer suitable Black men for them to marry. (1996, 125; my emphasis.)

Wilson and Russell assert that black men are in short supply and white men are in slight oversupply due to the tendency of relatively affluent black men to marry white women. Instead of seeing this as an opportunity to investigate an intersection of class, race, and sex/gender, Wilson and Russell invite black women to see white women as appropriating black men. Though it might have some popular and intuitive appeal, this analysis is troublesome—not least because it reinforces that stereotype of black women as demanding, possessive, and controlling. Even more worrisome, it invites an assumption that unmarried women are (unanimously, obviously, necessarily) unhappy with their marital status, and leaves unexamined the notion that, for women, not marrying is a sign of personal failure. In Wilson and Russell's ostensibly feminist account, there is no sign of feminism's long, nuanced, and above all *critical* understanding of marriage.

Renee Romano addresses similar issues throughout her book, but in a more thoughtful and useful way. Even so, Romano's analysis does not draw heavily or explicitly on feminist analyses of marriage, even though her own work is clearly influenced by black feminism. Romano's argument, in sum, is that interracial marriage presents a number of tensions across lines of racial and sexual identities, which are not easily resolved. Interracial marriage, she says, was never at the top of the civil rights movement agenda partly because it remained socially unconscionable even as other prejudices fell by the wayside. As a form of political protest, displays of interracial affection could be dangerous not just for the couple concerned but for others beyond the relationship (Romano 2003, 180; Wallenstein 2002, 125; Perry and Sutton 2006). The "final question" for racist whites was, "But would you want your daughter to marry one?" (Romano 2003, 212; Wartenberg 1994). This question illustrates how interracial marriage was simultaneously "beyond the pale" and informed by patriarchal family formations: no one asked white (or black) mothers, "But would you want your son to marry one?" Rather, the question was always pitched at white fathers relative to their "baby girls."[14] The idea that girls (and infantilized women) require protection justifying the most extreme forms of violence against non-white men is no doubt familiar (in several senses of the word) and need not be rehearsed here.

In any case, Romano's compelling conclusion is that interracial marriage came to be tolerated less as a result of activism and more as a side-effect of battles won against racism in other domains. Miscegenation lurked in these other arenas (particularly in schools, but also in other social realms) as a specter to be dismissed rather than as a cause to be fought. *Race Mixing* avoids representing interracial marriage as the triumph of love over white racism in order to explore more difficult aspects of interracial relationships. This exploration includes the idea that intermarriage might be resisted not only by those interested in preserving white privilege, but also by black men and women trying to resist cultural assimilation. It is this aspect that the case of Gladys and Mick Daly dramatically illustrates.

GLADYS AND MICK

Richard and Mildred Loving married in 1958. In 1959, a case whose broad features bear an uncanny resemblance to the Lovings' made headlines in the popular press on the other side of the world. In July of that year, two white men—Mick Daly and his brother Stephen— were droving cattle across western Australia into the Northern Territory. They employed a number of laborers and assistants, among them, an Indigenous couple—Gladys Namagu and Arthur Julama.[15] Gladys and Arthur were "a couple," but they did not have a certificate of marriage. Along the way, Arthur Julama left the droving party, thus ending his relationship with Gladys, who remained with the drovers. Consequently, Gladys Namagu and Mick Daly entered into an intimate relationship with each other. When a welfare officer visited the drovers' campsite (to investigate a matter concerning the working conditions of their Indigenous employees), that officer made a report to the local police that Daly was illegally cohabiting with Namagu. Daly was arrested and eventually brought before the local courthouse.

Daly had committed an offense under the Northern Territory's *Welfare Ordinance* (1953). According to its provision, Gladys Namagu was considered to be a "ward." The ordinance defined wards as people unable to manage their own affairs or take adequate care of themselves (Northern Territory of Australia 1953—henceforth 'N.T. *Welfare Ordinance*'—sections 14–15). The territory pretended to believe that it did not discriminate on the basis of race or skin color; Indigenous wards were so declared, it was claimed, due to their incapacity to manage their own affairs in a proper manner, and not simply *because* of their indigeneity.[16] However, Indigenous Australian people were *routinely* declared wards. In December 1957, it was estimated that 15,598 Indigenous people were living in the Northern Territory. Of these, 15,276 (98 percent) had been declared wards (N.T. Administration, Welfare Branch 1958, 11). In theory, one was not a ward until evidence of one's lifestyle was submitted to the Administrator or Director of Welfare, who then made a declaration of wardship. In practice, however, the onus of proof was the other way around; to gain a certificate of exemption from these provisions, applicants had to pass rigorous assessments of character and lifestyle.[17] There was no provision at all for a person to appeal a declaration of wardship (Hughes 1965); having already been deemed incapable of managing one's affairs, how could such a person contest the fitness of any such decision?

When Gladys Namagu entered the Northern Territory from Western Australia, she automatically became a ward for the purposes of the *Welfare Ordinance*. These purposes were, ostensibly, to promote the welfare of wards, and endowed the director of welfare with powers to take wards into custody, transport and confine them to reserves or institutions, take possession of their land or personal possessions, forbid them engaging in certain activities, and generally manage any ward's affairs. The ordinance also specified that no ward was to be married without the director's written consent (N.T.

Welfare Ordinance 1953, sections 8, 17, 67). Because Australian regulations concerning miscegenation were detailed in bureaucratic euphemism rather than as clear federal laws, Australia is generally excused from critical investigation into anti-miscegenation laws.[18] While it is true that provisions relating to race were never part of Australian *federal* law on marriage, the nation managed the subjection of Indigenous people in marriage nonetheless.

The N.T. *Welfare Ordinance* made it an offense for non-wards to engage in certain activities with wards: a person was not to have transactions of value greater than £10 with a ward, for example, nor supply a ward with any alcoholic beverage. The offense that Mick Daly was alleged to have committed is detailed under section 64, which states:

A male person, other than a ward, shall not —

   (a) habitually live with a female ward to whom he is not married;
   (b) habitually consort, keep company or associate, with a female
       ward to whom he is not married;
   (c) between the hours of sunset and sunrise, be in the company of a
       female ward to whom he is not married, except with lawful
       excuse;[19]
   (d) cohabit with, have or attempt to have sexual intercourse with, a
       ward to whom he is not married; or
   (e) invite, persuade, or attempt to persuade a ward to whom he is
       not married to have sexual intercourse with him.

(1953, section 64)

These provisions, and the euphemistic language used to discuss them, mirror prohibitions against interracial "cohabitation" in the United States. However, interracial "cohabitation" was not treated everywhere as an offense equivalent to marriage. Phyl Newbeck notes that "although 41 states prohibited interracial marriage, only 22 banned interracial sex . . . [and] only eight states prohibited interracial cohabitation" (Newbeck 2004, 27). Peter Wallenstein confirms that American laws "generally targeted sustained relationships rather than episodic encounters" (2002, 125) and that it was where relationships were marriage-like, even if not marriage in fact, that anxieties arose (Robinson 2003, 49; Ross 2002, 260, 263).

This raises interesting questions about marriage and its meanings, and supports the contention (asserted throughout this book) that marriage occupies a place additional to and apart from (although certainly related to) sex and reproduction more generally.[20] In Australia, even casual sexual encounters were subject to the Welfare Department's scrutiny, but this seems to have been an unpoliced (and possibly unpoliceable) rule.

In any case, before a Northern Territory courthouse, Mick Daly claimed that he had not known that his association with Gladys Namagu was illegal, and, in front of the magistrate and police, made a dramatic proposal of marriage to her. The magistrate, undoubtedly hoping that they would all live happily ever after, enjoined Mick to request Gladys's hand officially, and stipulated that reports on their matrimonial progress be presented to the court in due course. Daly immediately wrote to the director of welfare, Harry Giese, seeking permission to marry. To the great surprise of all concerned, Giese's reply came back in the *negative*, and Gladys Namagu was removed to a "native settlement" at Warrabri. The very "novelty" of a white man's desire to marry an Indigenous woman had seen the case reported in the Australian press, but this new turn of events caused something of a furore. Dick Ward, a lawyer and member of the Northern Territory parliament, took up the star-crossed lovers' case, and there began a legal and bureaucratic correspondence that saw letters and telegrams flying to and from the federal parliament, the Welfare Department, the press, and even the United Nations (Hughes 1965).

The white Australian attitude to Indigenous peoples in the 1950s was encapsulated in a word: *assimilation*. Assimilation policies implemented white hopes that Indigenous peoples would eventually be thoroughly and seamlessly absorbed into the white population. The policies were genocidal in that they promoted the physical and cultural invisibility of Indigenous people and practices (Tatz 2001), and endorsed standards for Indigenous people that were directly counter to those thought to be in the best interests of white people. Chief among these was the tactic of removing Indigenous children from their families, fracturing communities, and retarding (if not completely halting) the transmission of cultural knowledge from adults to children. These policies were considered by the white government to be appropriate for Indigenous peoples, even as the importance of maintaining robust family structures was being affirmed in the federal Parliament. The parliamentary rhetoric, which applauded the value of strong (white) families in the process of nation-building as it dispersed black families, was clearly racist. This racism, however, was largely invisible to white Australians because it was usually unmarked. Parliamentarians did not extol "white" families as such but instead referred to a supposedly generic entity: "the family." What they meant (but did not say) was "the *white* family." Similarly, the policy of dispersing Indigenous families and communities was never directly juxtaposed to the very different political attitude to "the (white) family." The disastrous and divisive effects of this double standard are well-documented (Australia, HREOC 1997) and are still being felt today (Bird 1998; Cuthbert 2000; Edwards and Read 1989).

Abandonment of a range of Indigenous marriage practices in favor of white, Christian marriage was seen as an important step toward assimilation (Bell 1988; *cf* Cott 2000). More controversially, "racially mixed" marriage (according to the rules of the non-Indigenous model) was described as a necessary step toward "ultimate assimilation" (*Northern Territory News* 1959; see also Romano 2003, 87). Given that marriage (of itself) and assimilation were both promoted in Australian politics as productive and proper—as being, in various ways, constitutive of the public good—why was the marriage of Gladys Namagu and Mick Daly vetoed by the Northern Territory administration? In the mobilization of marriage as a metaphor and strategy of assimilation, what went wrong?

In the Welfare Branch's discourse about marriage, it was generally assumed that, given time and "training," Indigenous women would come to prefer the white Australian construction of marriage rather than the "tribal" model, which was usually represented as complete subjection to an allotted husband (Jebb and Haebich 1992, 30). (In fact, Indigenous Australian marriage practices are many and varied, and "love matches," as opposed to "arranged" unions, are a routine feature [Bell 1980, 1981].) In the marriage of a non-Indigenous man to an Indigenous woman, it was assumed that the Indigenous woman's status would inevitably be elevated. The white husband's elevation of his non-white wife is assumed to occur in the fact of (white) marriage, rather than by his treatment of her, or by the conduct of their relationship in general. In this sense, marriage can be understood as a metaphor and strategy of assimilation (Cott 2000).[21]

In the troubled engagement of Gladys Namagu and Mick Daly, various factors were identified as spanners in the matrimonial works—all of them pertaining to Gladys. The Northern Territory authorities defended their decision to forbid the marriage on two major fronts: they presented evidence from a celebrated anthropologist suggesting that Gladys was already "tribally" married to Arthur Julama, and raised doubts about the validity of Gladys's consent to marry Mick (Berndt 1961; Hughes 1965). Proposing that Gladys was already married "under tribal law" invited the inference that any subsequent marriage would be morally, if not legally, bigamous. Given that, at this time, customary Indigenous marriage practices were not recognized as lawful unions (Australia, LRC 1986),[22] the Welfare Department's tactic demonstrates a certain desperation. Popular tracts of the time emphasized the "exotic" and polygynous aspects of (some) Indigenous marriage practices, and by highlighting customs such as infant betrothal and polygamy in a particularly distorted manner, portrayed customary marriage as sexually perverted and unproductive (Telfer 1939, 197; Gsell 1956). Infant betrothal is not infant *marriage*; betrothal arrangements generally mark an infant girl as a merely potential wife, subject to various conditions unfolding as she matures (Goodale 1971; see also Bell 1988; A. Hamilton 1981). A betrothed infant girl is not a "wife" as such any more than a baby whose name has been placed on a "waiting list" for a prestigious school is an alumnus of that school. However, white society was horrified by betrothals arranged between adult men and infant girls because the discursive stability of "marriage" as the term was governmentally used demanded a systematized (hetero-)sexual relation between the married parties. Some traditional Indigenous marriages, then, were erroneously seen to be dependent on a "perverted" or pedophilic sexual relation between adult men and infant girls. This misconception is a fine example of the kind of sexualization that Josephine Ross (2002, after Foucault 1978) suggests is a mechanism for a particular kind of subordination or oppression.

Ross argues, in sum, that analogies between the prohibition of mixed "race" and same-sex marriage hold. In both cases, she says, the affective and affectionate emotional bond we call "love" is denied legitimacy as it is thoroughly sexualized. A "sexualized" relationship is one "viewed as essentially sexual, and is not seen to be about commitment, communication, or love" (Ross 2002, 256). Setting aside Ross's argument as it concerns same-sex marriage, her

characterization of interracial relationships as sexualized is persuasive. Non-white peoples were heavily sexualized in general: non-
white men as rapists and perverts (Messerschmidt 1997, 23),
non-white women as sexually insatiable, supernaturally or precociously alluring.[23] Thus, in the case of particular marriage traditions
observed by some Australian Indigenous peoples, relationships that
were not sexual *at all*, but rather mapped a social order of kinship,
responsibilities, and reciprocity, were sexualized.

The suggestion that Gladys Namagu and Mick Daly's proposed
marriage might be bigamous helped substantiate doubts raised by
the Welfare Department concerning Gladys's consent to marry. In a
complicated and highly unusual move, the Department argued that
Gladys's wishes in the matter of her own marriage were irrelevant.
The contrast they drew was of "tribal" marriage as a union not
requiring the bride's consent, as opposed to white marriage in which
consent is pivotal and defining.[24] Figuring Gladys Namagu as
"already" married privileged an Indigenous model of marriage only
as a mechanism for silencing Gladys's clearly stated preference to
marry Daly rather than "return" to her alleged "tribal husband."
The man said to have been already married to Gladys Namagu,
Arthur Julama, insisted that he had no matrimonial interest in her,
but the Welfare Department insinuated that his expression of disin-
terest might have been feigned under duress. At every turn, then,
Gladys's position is doubly subordinated: her femaleness subjects her
to an all-encompassing masculine "tribal" authority; her "lack" of
whiteness prohibits her from contracting a consensual marriage.
Like Shakespeare's Portia, she could neither choose a husband for
herself nor refuse a suitor she disliked.

The Department's desperation to rationalize its prohibition of
Gladys and Mick's marriage demonstrates the lengths to which it
was prepared to go in order to position the problem as Aboriginal.
In fact, as documents from the Australian government archives
reveal, the *real* problem it wrestled with was not Gladys and her consent, but Mick.

Though by his own admission he had never done anything "really
bad" (Hughes 1965, 310), Mick Daly had certainly felt the displeas-
ure of the Welfare Branch prior to his appearance in court. The complaint that led to Daly being charged with "cohabitation" had been
raised by a former employee, an Indigenous man by the name of
Frank Clements. According to the welfare officer investigating the

problem, Clements's complaint was that "Daly had continually abused [Indigenous employees] during the [droving] trip, particularly when under the influence of liquor. Frank [Clements] said that he objected strongly to being called a fucking black fellow in the presence of his wife" (Australian Archives 1959). Daly's authority to employ wards (at their extremely cheap rates) was revoked by the Welfare Department, but his brother simply hired the labor instead. When a Tennant Creek welfare officer visited the Daly camp to investigate Clements's complaint, he reported in a memo that there were empty and half-empty bottles scattered around the camp. He noted that Daly "was very drunk . . . and became abusive when I refused to drink with him"(Australian Archives 1959). It is clear that the Welfare Branch did not consider Daly "a fit and proper person" to employ—let alone marry—a ward. "Mick Daly," they alleged, was, "not a person who should be permitted to associate with wards. He is a hard-drinking man and has a rather violent temper. It would not be in the best interests of the girl [sic] to allow her to marry Daly even if she were willing to do so" (Australian Archives 1959).

This information concerning the dubious character and less than saintly behavior of Mick Daly was not made public.[25] Where marriage is conceived as an assimilatory strategy, the non-Indigenous husband of a black woman must wear the white hat of a "good-guy": he must be positioned as offering his wife a step *up* the social ladder, even at some possible cost to his own position. For the Welfare Branch to acknowledge that Daly's knight's armor might have been somewhat tarnished would have resulted in two significantly embarrassing discrepancies.

Firstly, it would upset the "approved" roles of white "teacher" directing black "child" inherent in the idea of "mixed marriage" as an assimilatory strategy. It is no accident that the regulatory "success stories"—or at least the cases that seem to have garnered significant public support—concern the pairing of white *men* with black *women*. Secondly, if Daly's inadequacies to take on the role of the proverbial white knight are accepted as mere marks of human frailty, another set of complications arises. In this case, the construction of conjugality as a public good—that is, of marriage as a "sound and strong" foundation of social life—must come under scrutiny. If Daly's violence and drinking prevented the Welfare Branch from being persuaded that the marriage of Mick and Gladys would "succeed," the director was obliged to rule that the marriage ought not to take place. The immediate difficulty here is that many—or even most—marriages, regardless of their "racial" makeup, likewise did not measure up to the discursive ideal of conjugality. Would it not be in the public interest similarly to police these other marriages? The effect here would be to disrupt the director's paternalistic concern with Gladys's welfare in marriage, and to question whether the department could properly deny her the opportunity to embark upon a "dangerous" romance. The popular appeal of such *liaisons dangereuses* is, of course, as old as the hills. There would be (and was) great public sympathy for the outback Romeo and Juliet, especially where the "forbidding father" was an already unpopular bureaucrat. It was easier, therefore, for the director to sustain his objection to the marriage as bound up in Gladys's and not Mick's situation. In the end, the Northern Territory authorities succumbed to public pressure and, citing a technical difficulty, stepped back from their opposition to the marriage (Brook 1997). Gladys and Mick were married on New Year's Day, 1960 (*Pix*, 1960).

Where marriage was mobilized as a strategy and metaphor for the assimilation of Indigenous Australians, its intelligibility depended on figuring the white party as endowed with the power to rehabilitate and render productive the non-white party. The governmental expectation was that Mick Daly, as a white man, should experience marriage as vigorously productive, regulated by consent, and as a prerogative of his adult citizenship. Gladys Namagu, on the other hand, was implicated in a discourse of marriage as radically unproductive, sickly, perverted, and decayed—a relationship bound by custom and subjection rather than consent, and reflective of a "primitive" or juvenile social order. In an assimilatory marriage, the white model of marriage would be expected to rehabilitate the Indigenous model: in the union of Indigenous and non-Indigenous spouses in a conjugal body politic, the non-Indigenous is sovereign. That the N.T. Welfare Department was prepared to protect white men's matrimonial interests even as it struggled to "protect" Gladys Namagu presents a patently astonishing picture of racialized and sexualized relations.

OF MISCEGENATION AND MEN

Gladys and Mick Daly's case is both similar to and very different from that of Mildred and Richard Loving. The cases were resolved in different ways—bureaucratically for the Dalys, judicially for the Lovings—but their immediate effects were arguably similar. Both were popularly represented as the triumph of ("color-blind") human love over regulatory obstacles; both were romantic victories for the couples concerned. But neither represents a straightforward defeat of racism—especially not for black women, whose experience of racism intersects with (but is not reducible to) sexism.

In Australia, the model of Indigenous marriage held up as "tribal" was figured as the absolute subjection of the wife to the husband. It was assumed that Indigenous women would elect to "elevate" themselves by entering into the more "civilized" style of marriage modeled by the colonists. This presents something of a paradox in comparison to the United States experience. In the United States, it has been suggested that one of the reasons black men marry white women in greater numbers than black women marry white men is that white women are *more* submissive than black women, and that the gender skewing of interracial marriages reflects the exercise of men's power *as men* (Romano 2003, 87–89). The social formation offered is that black or Indigenous women try to avoid wifely subjection, while white women embrace it. In fact the logic of both constructions is appallingly consistent. The object of these constructions is not "women" but "wives of black men." Both discourses position black men's wives as resignedly servile and sexually obsequious. Both discourses elevate the white-colonial model of marriage over alternative arrangements, reinforcing a racialized and sexualized hierarchy that privileges both whiteness and maleness. One effect of this is to position women as competitors for men—a competition in which, to restate Wilson and Russell's (1996) complaint, white women are vested with unfair advantages.[26]

Black women are, of course, acutely aware of the racialized dimensions of the logic of beauty pageants (Romano 2003, 221–34), and it is little wonder that critiques of racist "beauty" are an important element of black feminism. Similarly, it is hardly surprising that some black women have expressed a kind of resentful dismay over the "defection" of a significant number of black men to white marriage partners. Given the continuing history of white men's sexual (and other) violence toward black women; given white women's complicity in racism; and given that racism and sexism combine to form an oppression greater than the sum of its parts, black women continue to face obstacles to personal happiness that neither white women nor black men must negotiate. In this context, marriage is not a neutral framework to which individuals bring only their own personal history, but a framework whose shape is thoroughly immersed in racist and sexist social histories. It is not that white women steal potential husbands from black women, then, but that black women are unfairly positioned as having to compete with white women for marriage partners in a system that consistently favors whiteness and men, and thus doubly privileges white men. No wonder, then, that black women have opposed intermarriage more intensely than either white women or men (of any "race") (Root 2001, 77).

Despite their similarities, the legacies of the *Loving* and *Daly* cases are quite different. In the United States, *Loving* has come to represent the right to marry. The case presented a test, of sorts, of the constitutional guarantee that Americans have a fundamental right to pursue happiness (Brinig 1998; Wardle 1998). In this way, *Loving v. Virginia* established a precedent: the state of Virginia prohibited marriage between people whose happiness conceivably depended on being not so prohibited, and so the ban was overturned. In Australia, by contrast, the Dalys have been all but forgotten. Their case was an ephemeral "human interest" interest story in its day, but not beyond. Its chief legacy was dully administrative; it established a right to appeal certain decisions (Hughes 1965). Australian advocates of marriage rights for gay and lesbian couples do not cite Gladys and Mick's story. As it occurred, their case was represented as a "right to happiness" tale, but the untold back-story was less rosy.

Both cases, however, demonstrate that the regulation of marriage could be used as a racist strategy. In the United States and Australia, marriage was prohibited between whites and targeted "others." The point of such segregation was not so much to ensure "racial purity," but to protect white privilege—and, in particular, to absolve the rich from any responsibility for the consequences of their exploits. Since there was no shortage of black women bearing "mixed-race" offspring, and no effort at all to ensure that white fathers contributed to the welfare of such children, it seems unlikely that miscegenation as such—that is, the production of "mixed-race" offspring—was ever the *real* threat. "Secret" miscegenation flourished, after all. To suggest that such relationships were inevitably violent or desperate[27] erases (again) the possibility of black women's rational sexual agency even as it points to white men's relative power and privilege, but in so doing conceals other orders of oppression.

It is significant, then, that both Richard Loving and Mick Daly were easily identifiable as working-class men. White upper-class men's relationships with black women—whether illicit or legitimate—have never been subject to equivalent scrutiny, just as their sexual assaults have gone largely unpunished (Davis 1981, 199). It is not unreasonable to suggest that "interracial" marriages have been historically troublesome partly because they constitute an arena of class antagonism as much as any other kind of "problem." Just as the contraceptive pill is regularly figured as a catalyst for and trophy of women's liberation rather than as a mechanism for the (targeted) control of particular (poor, non-white) populations, so the repeal of anti-miscegenation stands as a victory against racism. This is not to suggest that there is no cause to celebrate such inventions and events. There can be no doubt that the eventual marriages of Gladys and Mick Daly and Mildred and Richard Loving were literally and metonymically right. Public support for both couples centered on the rights of lovers to contract a lawful marriage if they so desired, and the justness of such capacity was and still is incontrovertible. However, it is not necessarily accurate or useful to see these marriages as stations on an unambiguously progressive line.

In Australia, where "assimilation" was official government policy, the assumption was that in the union of marriage, the "stronger" part of the binary pairs man/woman and black/white would "naturally" direct the union. If, to paraphrase Blackstone, in marriage husband and wife are one, and that one is the husband; in an assimilatory marriage, black and white are one—and that one is white. Mick Daly was a white man, but his "natural" fitness to direct a marital union by virtue of his white-maleness was scrutinized and found wanting, yet could not be admitted. The Northern Territory, and white Australians in general, could not openly countenance the possibility that a young Indigenous woman might be more decent—and more fit to govern her own life—than her white fiancé. The "problem" in the partnership was thus shifted to Gladys Namagu, where it became instantly more familiar and less threatening to a white population firmly convinced of its own superiority.

Indeed, the repeal of anti-miscegenation statutes (in Australia as well as in the United States) remains, primarily, a story about whiteness. As noted at the beginning of this chapter, ending various bans on "mixed" marriage has never been an especially high priority for feminist activists, despite feminism's substantial and still growing literature on racism. Wilson and Russell's claim that the proportion of racially mixed marriages in the United States nearly tripled between 1970 and 1990 sounds impressive and significant (1996, 124), but the percentage of such marriages remains less than half of one percent.[28] My view is that the repeal of anti-miscegenation laws has operated more as a salve for anxiously "tolerant" white consciences than as evidence for substantial anti-racist change.

Further, unless analyses of anti-miscegenation laws and their repeal take account of the ways that racialized subjectivities are also thoroughly embroiled in sex-gender systems, we will only ever see half the picture. It is worth noting that when *Loving* first started being cited in the same-sex marriage literature in the mid-1990s, reference was rarely, if ever, made to the sex-race configuration of the couple. I remember reading at least a dozen articles by different authors citing the case before I could ascertain that Mr. Loving was white and Mrs. Loving was black. Would it have made a difference if the Lovings and the Dalys had been black man/white woman pairings? Undoubtedly. Both the Lovings in America and the Dalys in Australia conform to a model of conjugal assimilation in which white "rehabilitates" or incorporates black, and in which male contains or incorporates female. The fact that the vast majority of "interracial" marriages today are composed of black husbands and white wives tells a different story. It suggests that a complex undertow of sexualization continues to pull—sexualizing "women" in general even as it reinscribes racialized class boundaries between us, perhaps.

In the end, can we understand Mildred Loving or Gladys Namagu's marriages as episodes in black women's history of resistance? The question is difficult and complex. If the gendered dynamics of racism and the racist dynamics of sexism render Mrs. Loving and Mrs. Daly less than clearly resistant, and render their marriages less than absolute triumphs (structurally rather than personally), then we need to think about exactly what manner of analogy the repeal of bans against interracial marriage can sustain. If the repeal of anti-miscegenative marriage legislation is assimilatory above all—appeasing white consciences, allowing white racism to assuage its guilt even as it fails to address the problems and issues identified by those experiencing racial oppression—then marriage will probably not be the remedy for homophobia and heterosexism that gay and lesbian activists may be hoping for. Intermarriage was never a straightforward project for the civil rights movement: as

Kevin Mumford observes, "African Americans never waged a campaign for the right to marry whites" (Mumford 2005, 527)—and neither the Lovings nor the Dalys were civil rights activists. Instead, as Romano shows, prohibitions against miscegenation were overturned in the wake of a tide of other social reforms. Importantly, while the lawfulness of interracial marriage and social responses to it have undoubtedly shifted, racist hierarchies remain. So what place does marriage occupy—what role has it performed—in the structure and exercise of racism? Marriage is neither merely a cause nor an effect of racism, but both: it is a conduit for shaping relations between states and their gendered, racialized subjects. It also remains, of course, a marker of love between two people. But love, unfortunately, does not conquer all.

So far, in the regulation of marriage through sexed, gendered, and racialized frameworks, we have witnessed a style of government "from above"—the rules governing what constitutes acceptable behavior in marriage are determined by governments and judiciaries and are simply applied. This is sometimes described as the "rule of law": certain activities or behaviors were proscribed, and anyone committing a proscribed offense (such as adultery under various matrimonial laws, or "cohabiting with a native" under the provisions of an Australian government department) could find themselves subject to a legal judgment concerning their guilt or innocence as charged. With the enactment of divorce reforms in the 1970s, something very much resembling the shift Foucault describes in his "Governmentality" essay (1991)—a shift from "rule of law" to "governmentality"—occurred in the regulation of marriage. Today, marriage is not what it was when the Lovings, the Dalys, or any other couple married over forty years ago. I will map and explore this dramatic change in the following chapter.

CHAPTER 6

S/HE DONE ME WRONG:
ADVERSARIAL VERSUS
"NO-FAULT" DIVORCE

The rules and regulations governing the dissolution of marriage build a legal framework. While we might inhabit the place in various ways, the structure itself is at least partly determined by our rules for dismantling it. In this way, divorce defines marriage. For those of us growing up in a time and place in which "no-fault" divorce has always been available, the historical character of divorce as a judgment or punishment seems archaic. The notion that divorce might be shameful or scandalous is almost laughable today, yet the availability of unilateral, no-fault divorce is barely a generation old. Things have changed. Indeed, the increased incidence of divorce over the last thirty years or so is often claimed to be a particularly poignant sign of our times. However, the operation and effects of different divorce rationales are rarely examined in any depth. Adversarial divorce is generally assumed to be more "difficult" than no-fault divorce, but in what sense, and with what effects? Does a more flexible procedure for the dissolution of marriage construct a more flexible institution? This chapter explores the broad, large-scale transition from adversarial to no-fault divorce. Until the mid-1970s, most nations whose legal traditions are English allowed divorce only where one spouse wronged the other. Only the wronged spouse (the "innocent" party) could launch a suit for divorce. Beginning in the 1960s, the effectiveness and appropriate-ness of existing divorce laws began to be questioned. By the middle of the 1980s, most white western nations allowed their citizenry simply to separate and divorce without "trying" one another. Either spouse could secure a divorce without having to prove that the other had committed some wrong. No-fault divorce became a defining feature of the matrimonial landscape, and a defining feature of con-temporary social relations in general.

It is not necessary, however, to track the repeal of fault-based rules and their replacement on a comparative level here.[1] In the first place, there are a large number of jurisdictions to consider, and the large-scale transformation from adversarial to no-fault divorce occurred over many years. In the second place, it is not always a sim-ple matter: many jurisdictions already included one or more "no-fault" clauses in their fault-based divorce systems, and many systems did not entirely abolish fault (Biondi 1999; Caldwell 1998; Woodhouse 1994). In some places, no-fault provisions were added to existing fault grounds (Swisher 2005, 243; Biondi 1999, 614). Small differences in the way that fault and its repeal have been inter-preted complicate matters further. Some no-fault regulations specify that a marriage must be "irretrievably broken down" before a decree can be issued, others prefer the language of "irreconcilable differ-ences" or "incompatibility" (Schoenfeld 1996). Evidence of break-down differs across jurisdictions too: under some no-fault systems, separation is the only relevant evidence, while others allow adultery or cruelty to stand as evidence—perhaps thereby smuggling fault back into divorce proceedings (Swisher 2005; Woodhouse 1994). Despite the degree of variation in no-fault provisions over time and space, meaningful generalizations can be made. The main aim of this chapter is to consider the implications of the transition from fault to no-fault divorce in general, paying particular attention to its gen-dered effects.

In the first part of this chapter, the ordinary operation of fault-based divorce will be described and discussed. Three broad cate-gories of matrimonial offense will be identified, and each will be explored using grounds pertinent to the broader category. Fault-based divorce systems were challenged on a number of fronts from the 1960s onwards; some of these will be explored in the second part of this chapter. In the third and final section of this chapter, the effects and legacies of no-fault divorce will be surveyed. Throughout,

I will argue that the movement from adversarial to no-fault divorce constitutes a very important political transition—typifying a shift from juridical to governmental power that had especially significant consequences for women. These consequences are most apparent in the interconnection and cleaving of the matrimonial fault of cruelty, collusion as a bar to divorce, and the more recent regulation of domestic violence as criminal.

ADVERSARIAL DIVORCE

Where a system of divorce is described as "adversarial," a legal contest between the divorcing husband and wife takes place. One spouse must charge the other with disrupting matrimonial harmony; one partner must be guilty of an offense to the other or to the marriage, causing it to break down. The range of behavior that might amount to such offense is codified as a number of grounds for divorce, which typically include adultery, the commission of certain crimes, cruelty, and desertion. In an adversarial system, the divorce court assesses whether the behavior of the errant spouse constitutes a valid ground for divorce. Only an "innocent" spouse might initiate (by "filing" or "petitioning" for) divorce. The terms "petitioner" and "respondent" are loaded. "Petitioners" are those who have been done wrong and who initiate legal proceedings against their spouse; the "respondent" is the "wrong-doer"—the partner being held accountable for the break-up. Divorce suits might be defended or unopposed, and an accused spouse might cross-petition the accuser. However, if both spouses are found to have wronged each other, the court is required to deny them a divorce (Wheeler 1974, 16).[2] Only when one spouse is found to have offended against an ostensibly innocent other can a decree of divorce be issued. As Norman Katter observes, in such divorce proceedings, "[f]ault . . . involves a quasi-criminal approach whereby conduct is seen as breaching a code of behaviour and for which . . . [the] offender ought to be punished" (1987, 5). Adversarial divorce is a system that clearly invites the apportionment of blame: the petitioning spouse seeks redress against the offending spouse, who is in effect punished. The nature of such "punishment" is largely social, but also extends to provisions for the continuing maintenance of one spouse by the other. A "guilty" husband would be required to continue to support his former wife, while a "guilty" wife would lose "any right to income from her former husband" (McGregor 1957, 131; see also Biondi 1999, 616).

Matrimonial offenses—or "grounds for divorce"—are historically various. In 1970, there were fourteen grounds for divorce in Australia, fifteen in Canada, and four in the United Kingdom. Across the United States, where divorce is governed at the state level, there were around forty recognized grounds for divorce in 1963, many with competing definitions of pertinent elements such as "cruelty" or "desertion" (Chester and Streather 1972, 706). In Australia, by far the most frequently proven offenses involved single or dual grounds of desertion, cruelty, drunkenness, and separation (Australian Bureau of Statistics 1967–1974). In Canada, just prior to the introduction of no-fault divorce, the grounds of cruelty, separation, and adultery accounted (in close to equal measure) for 97 percent of decrees (Bissett-Johnson and Day 1986, 16; da Costa 1970). Although certain grounds were infrequently cited, they nevertheless play a significant part in constituting the social meaning of marriage. Perhaps the infrequency of their transgression can be read as some indication of the depth of their significance. In any case, the meaningfulness of the frequency with which various offenses are cited also differs according to the range of grounds available. Although they vary across time and space, most grounds can be grouped for convenient analysis into three overlapping categories: offenses against "public order" or society in general, offenses against one's individual spouse, and offenses by absence or neglect. Each of these will be considered in turn.

Crime and Other Matrimonial
Offenses Against Public Order

Grounds for divorce that might be categorized as offenses against public order include frequent convictions or long-term imprisonment, rape, sodomy and bestiality (sometimes grouped together as "unnatural acts"), and habitual drunkenness or other intoxication.

In post-war public-political discourse, marriage was routinely invoked as a mark of civilization, a sign of national maturity, and a productive duty and pleasure of proper citizenship. Marriage—in all its corporeal splendor—is, in this sense, one of the chief pleasures forfeited by those who fail to conform to the established rules of law; that is, convicted criminals. Significantly, in many places, any person serving a long sentence of imprisonment (usually five years or longer) also forfeits their suffrage. In this way, breaking the law can be understood as simultaneously breaking (up) social and sexual contracts. As one Australian politician made plain, in the immediate postwar period, "good citizens" did not divorce: "Show me a divorced couple and I will show you one person, and in some cases two people who are intolerant, selfish, mean, immoral or unfaithful—people who are not prepared to make concessions to each other in order to keep their home going; people who are not in the true sense *good citizens*"[3] (Australia, House of Representatives 1959, 2709; my emphasis). Grounds for divorce relating to criminal conviction illustrate the way that conjugality and citizenship are sometimes aligned. Crime in general is not compatible with the duties and (debatable) pleasures of marriage. In addition, certain crimes were singled out as matrimonial offenses in themselves.

We already know that in some jurisdictions, adultery was historically considered a crime. It is not so surprising, then, that rape, sodomy, and bestiality have also been matrimonial offenses and thus grounds for divorce. Sometimes rape, sodomy, and bestiality are grouped together as "unnatural offenses," and are almost inevitably described as among the gravest matrimonial offenses. Sodomy is defined rather imprecisely by one leading legal scholar as "the unnatural connexion of the respondent with a man" (Joske 1969, 437). P. E. Joske's definition is imprecise in its almost coy avoidance of the nature of such a "connexion." The "unspeakable" nature of homosexual sex is apparent here: there seem to be no similar qualms in detailing precisely how (heterosexual) consummation is accomplished. It is ambiguous, too, in that Joske goes on to state that the commission of sodomy as a ground for divorce includes "sodomy with a wife against her will" (437)—and as we have seen, a wife cannot be a man. However, it is reasonable to read the matrimonial offense of sodomy as the commission of consensual anal sex by either husband or wife with another person.

In some places (Canada, for example), not just sodomy but *any* "homosexual act" was also included in historical provisions against "unnatural offenses" (Bissett-Johnson and Day 1986, 6n32). However, homosexuality was not always specifically proscribed as a matrimonial offense. (Remember, of course, that in many jurisdictions, homosexuality was in any case prohibited at criminal law.[4]) Evidence of a husband's homosexuality might see a petition drawn

on the ground of sodomy, while lesbianism in a wife has been categorized as matrimonial cruelty (Smart 1984, 44; Selby 1960, 244).
Petitions on these grounds were extremely rare, no doubt due to the
scandal and stigma that would accrue to both parties as the details of
their case were reported. The grounds of sodomy and bestiality—
"bestiality" being sex with animals or, to use Joske's quaint but consistent phrase, "[unnatural] connexion with an animal" (1969,
437)—existed, albeit in a clumsy way, to reinforce "correct" conjugality as heterosexual, penis-in-vagina sex.

As we saw in Chapter 4, such provisions foreground the arena of
marriage as the scene of specifically lawful sex. To recall Tony
Honoré's observation, "[E]ven when sex outside marriage is not a
crime it is not 'lawful' . . . Sex outside marriage is not necessarily a
crime, but marriage is the only relation in which sex is positively lawful" (1978, 10). Indeed, sex acts that might ordinarily be understood as criminal in their day seem to have lost some of their
scandalous overtones when committed within a marriage. Hearing
an appeal against the criminal court's sentence of a man convicted of
(consensually) "buggering" a woman, an English judge said, "There
have been various cases[5] when in the matrimonial bed a husband,
possibly a drunken husband, has done something of this sort to his
wife, and such offenses have been treated with great leniency" (*R. v.
Harris* 1971). In different divorce cases, opinions were aired as to
whether incest between a man and his daughter by a previous marriage constituted matrimonial cruelty against the current wife (*Boyd
v. Boyd* 1955), and whether the conviction of a man for the indecent
assault of his daughter amounted to grounds upon which the wife
could petition for divorce (*Cooper v. Cooper* 1955).[6]

In legal commentary on post-war marriage, rape tends to be discussed alongside adultery rather than with the "unnatural acts" of
sodomy and bestiality. Though it is taxonomically linked to these
other offenses, rape is not usually positioned as an "unnatural act,"
but is constructed more as a kind of "special case" of adultery.
"Rape, as distinct from adultery, is in the [Australian *Matrimonial
Causes*] Act a specific ground of divorce . . . [But, where a married
man rapes] a woman other than his wife, he will also commit adultery" (Barwick 1961, 430). Thus, rape is usually also adultery. This
seems to hold despite adulterous sexual intercourse being explicitly
defined as "'voluntary,' 'willing' and 'consensual'" (Tarlo 1963, 12).
Perhaps the suggestion is merely that for the married rapist (who in

raping "consents" to his own sexual involvement), rape is also, simultaneously, adulterous (Barwick 1961, 430).[7] The need to posit rape as a subclass of adultery seems alarmingly anachronistic—even in the 1950s and 60s—yet the distinction is consistent with the discursive coherence of matrimony. Whether a married man rapes or has consensual sex with a woman other than his wife, his *matrimonial* offense is essentially the same: he has disrupted the corporeal unity of conjugality.

If a married woman is raped, however, she does not commit adultery (Hambly and Turner 1971, 136n3). "Consent" to sex is, of course, the axle around which allegations of rape turn. The absence of consent implies rape, but as prosecutors know all too well, it is often difficult to prove the absence of something as intangible as consent. Consent is similarly crucial to marriage proceedings (as we saw in Chapter 3). Until the advent of no-fault divorce (and arguably since), a person's consent to marry was also held to imply consent to sex with their spouse (see Chapter 4). Honoré describes the assumption that wives consent to sex with their husbands as "pure fiction" (1978, 23). He also notes that a "husband . . . is not deemed, even by a fiction, to consent to intercourse with his wife at all times and in all circumstances" (33). The fiction of wifely consent, however, had very real effects. Under the kinds of matrimonial regimes in place in the 1960s, a wife could not ordinarily be understood to have been raped by her husband (Hasday 2000; Bergen 2004). However, events that today might be described as "marital rape" were sometimes acknowledged in divorce courts as instances of "cruelty."

Cruelty and Other Offenses
Against One's Spouse

A number of historical grounds for divorce could be classified as offenses against one's spouse. Again, these vary by jurisdiction, but typically include adultery, refusal to grant conjugal rights, and cruelty. Sometimes attempting to murder or inflict grievous bodily harm on one's spouse were considered offenses apart from (or additional to) cruelty. Adultery and refusal to grant conjugal rights have been considered at length in Chapter 4, so discussion here will be mostly limited to "cruelty" and associated grounds for divorce.

As a matrimonial offense, definitions and interpretations of what constitutes "cruelty" are many and various. In 1967, an Australian judge summarized the prevailing rationale by which charges of cruelty should be ascertained:

> [I]n matrimonial causes, before a spouse can be found guilty of cruelty, certain elements must be present. They may be listed as follows: 1. The conduct must cause injury or reasonable apprehension of injury to the health of the other party, irrespective of whether such result was intended. 2. The conduct which is alleged to constitute cruelty must be grave and weighty. 3. The conduct, viewed as a whole in the light of all relevant circumstances, must be capable of bearing the description of cruelty in the generally accepted use of that word. (Hambly and Turner 1971, 207)

Despite the requirement that "cruelty" be "grave and weighty" before a divorce might be granted, all manner of behavior—from laziness to lesbianism—has been alleged to constitute matrimonial cruelty. Over time, it seems, the ground became more elastic.[8] Writing in 1969, one judge remarked, "As recently as 40 years ago, for a wife to convince a court that she had suffered sufficient cruelty to justify a divorce . . . required her to prove conduct which was practically diabolical. Gradually . . . much less serious conduct became acceptable as sufficient cruelty" (Barber 1969, 72).

As the range of behavior amounting to cruelty expanded, some jurisdictions distinguished between "physical" and "mental" varieties (Glendon 1989, 191). In England, for example, it was recognized that there could be "cruelty without violence, and a wide range of non-violent behavior has been held to be potentially cruel" (Chester and Streather 1972, 707). As one judge observed, physical violence is not necessarily more serious or damaging than other kinds: "there can be words which would be much worse than blows with a saucepan" (*Le Brocq v. Le Brocq* 1964). Indeed, even "nagging" has been held to constitute matrimonial cruelty (*Atkins v. Atkins* 1942; *King v. King* 1953). This kind of cruelty drew something of a fine line: to avoid an inference of connivance, the complaining spouse was sometimes required to remonstrate—that is, to seek a negotiated change in the "cruel" spouse's behavior—but excessive remonstration might constitute "cruelty" in itself.

Typically, however, matrimonial "cruelty" involved the infliction of violence against one's spouse. In some places, isolated instances of violence were not sufficient grounds for divorce. In Australia, for example, one party had to be found to have "during a period of not less that one year, *habitually* been guilty of cruelty to the petitioner" (Australian *Matrimonial Causes Act* § 28[d]; emphasis added). Not surprisingly, grounds of cruelty—with or without additional grounds—were cited much more frequently by wives than husbands (Chester and Streather 1972, 708). It is no coincidence that prior to the introduction of no-fault divorce laws, domestic violence and spousal rape were rarely treated as criminal offenses. Matrimonial law offered, in effect, the only avenue to any kind of judgement and redress against a violent spouse.

In adversarial divorce systems, offenses against one's spouse stress the nature of marriage as a *union*. Husbands and wives are bound together by the behavior of each other rather than simply as an effect of their wishes. That is to say, the conjugal union of this kind of marriage really is binding: a wife might not divorce her husband unless he offers her grounds; similarly, a husband might not divorce his wife without her behavior offering him cause. Offenses, however, are not limited to violent occurrences—particular kinds of absence also offer grounds for divorce.

Desertion and Other Offenses by Absence or Neglect

Historically, various kinds of conjugal absence or neglect opened pathways to divorce. Adversarial divorce systems demand a conjugal body whose constituent husband and wife ordinarily live together, and whose cohabitation is figured as sexual, physical, economic, and emotional. This is evident in provisions detailing physical desertion and the withholding of money or necessities as matrimonial offenses. We might also consider the grounds of a spouse's "mental incapacity" or "insanity" here, along with petitions brought on the grounds that one's spouse is presumed dead. Although they are rarely identified as such, these last grounds cannot properly be understood as fault-based. A person lost at sea, missing in action, or mentally ill can hardly be accused of any deliberate breach of matrimonial unity.[9]

In Aotearoa New Zealand, the inclusion of a spouse's insanity as a ground for divorce at the beginning of the twentieth century was hotly debated. As Roderick Phillips (1988, 35–38) notes, it seemed, to some, to reverse the roles of "innocent" and "guilty" spouses. After all, did not marriage partners agree to stand by each other "in sickness and in health"? It was argued that loyal husbands and wives should care for their partner regardless of illness: there was no provision to divorce a spouse confined to hospital—indeed, most people would find such a notion unconscionable. Why should it matter

whether illness was of mind or body? According to Phillips, the availability of this ground prefigured divorce based on the *fact* of marital
breakdown rather than identifying and stigmatizing the cause of that
breakdown. My view is rather more cynical.

Precisely what counts as "insanity" or "mental incapacity" varies
enormously—not just across time and space but according to other
markers of identity such as class and sex/gender. In *The Feminine
Mystique*, Betty Friedan argued, in effect, that psychiatric knowledge
was a highly gendered disciplinary force (1963). The "problem that
has no name" was that intelligent, capable women were repressed by
a society more or less forcing women to "underachieve" as wives and
mothers in an entirely domestic realm. American (and other) women
in the immediate post-war period were subject to diagnoses defining
gender deviance—and even mere dissatisfaction—as mental illness.
Recalcitrant wives and sexually "deviant" women were likely to be
understood as "maladjusted" or otherwise mentally abnormal in
ways that were much less likely to be applied to men (Russell 1995).
"Sexual deviance" was not confined to the predictable persecution of
lesbians, but extended to include others—white women involved in
relationships with black men, for example (Romano 2003, 68–69).
Illustrations of women's "madness" were sometimes thoroughly
mundane: if a woman showed insufficient interest in housekeeping,
for example, she might be understood to be experiencing a problem
of marital adjustment. "Adjustment" was used (in popular as well as
psy-discourses) as a kind of cover-all term indicating a need for self-
disciplinary change in one's behavior or demeanor in order to stabilize some temporary relational difficulty (Friedan 1963).[10] In this
sense, discourses of marriage and divorce construct sanity in especially gendered ways. The *work* of "marital adjustment"—of making
a success of one's marriage—fell largely to women. If a wife failed to
labor to repair or "save" her marriage—or even if she avoided assuming responsibility for her husband's happiness—she risked being
diagnosed as "maladjusted."

Desertion and Constructive Desertion

Before discussing the distinction between desertion and separation,
let us consider how desertion operates, ordinarily, as a ground for
divorce. Desertion is one of the less scandalous grounds for divorce,
but it is also, historically, one of the slowest (McGregor 1957, 45).
The duration of absence required to prove desertion varies. In 1970,

English, Australian and Canadian law required three years, while in New Zealand it was two years. In the United States, the period differed from state to state. Desertion might be said to occur where one spouse abandons the other—that is, where husband or wife permanently moves out of the matrimonial home. Elements required to prove desertion typically include "intention to desert, the fact of living apart for the required period; lack of consent to the separation, and no just cause for the separation" (Bissett-Johnson and Day 1986, 9).

Sometimes the person leaving the matrimonial home would accuse the remaining spouse of desertion. In such cases, the petitioner might argue that the respondent made home life so intolerable that the petitioner was forced to leave. These circumstances came to be known as "constructive desertion." For example, in a case whose detail is comical by today's standards, an English wife refused to give up her many cats. When her husband (who did not care for cats) issued his wife an ultimatum, she opted to keep the cats. Given that the husband found his wife's pets intolerable, the wife was understood to have forced her husband to leave her—and was thus guilty of constructive desertion (*Winnan v. Winnan* 1949). A number of cases explore the significance of *intention* in constructive desertion. In a case whose details are particularly brutal, an Australian man (Mr. Lang) who habitually beat his wife claimed that his behavior was carried out with the intention of retaining rather than alienating his wife. Mr. Lang admitted raping and torturing Mrs. Lang, but this, he said, did not amount to constructive desertion, but rather reflected advice he had received from a psychiatrist friend to try "caveman stuff." The case was referred to the English Privy Council, where the husband's appeal was (thankfully) dismissed (*Lang v. Lang* 1955).

THE WRONGS OF (MATRIMONIAL) WRONGS

Under fault-based divorce, the law could be understood as properly righting a wrong, as "giving relief when a wrong has been done" (Australia, HR 1959, 2681). Central to this understanding of matrimonial law as retributive were three absolute bars to divorce: condonation, connivance, and collusion. Condonation has been considered at length in Chapter 4 and so will not be revisited here, except to note how some advocates of divorce reform criticized it.

One of the primary rationales for fault-based divorce was its rein-
forcement of matrimonial unity. Governments sought to "protect"
and "strengthen" marriage by ensuring that it could not easily be
dismantled. As the push to reform divorce gathered momentum, it
was argued that some aspects of fault-based divorce law worked
against this principle. It was suggested that the bar of condonation
could discourage parties from attempting reconciliation. If, while
establishing the required period of separation on the ground of
desertion, a petitioner and respondent attempted but failed to
achieve a reconciliation, their cohabitation could be interpreted as
condonation, resulting in their having to begin the waiting period all
over again. Some jurisdictions attempted to address this inconsis-
tency by excluding short periods of cohabitation in the interests of
reconciliation from inferences of condonation, but such provisions
are awkward, and subject to difficulties of interpretation, qualification, and quantification.

Connivance and Collusion

Under adversarial systems, connivance and collusion were also bars
to divorce. Connivance is "the guilty promotion of adultery of the
other spouse or the wilful refusal to prevent the continuance of adultery already occurring" (Bissett-Johnson and Day 1986, 8). The bar
of connivance meant that someone who committed a matrimonial
offense at the bidding of their spouse, or with their spouse's consent,
could not be divorced. A husband who, for several years, tolerated
his wife's adultery, for example, was found to have been "wilfully
blind" to her matrimonial offenses. When, eventually, he filed for
divorce on the basis of her admitted adultery, his petition was denied
(*Rumbelow v. Rumbelow and Hadden* 1965). The bar of connivance
is certainly strange: it suggests that for a spouse to be deemed
"offended against," he or she must be seen to have sustained some
injury; he or she must present to the court as an *injured* party (and
not merely one wronged). If a spouse were indifferent to a matrimonial offense committed against him or her, that spouse would by
the letter of the law be denied a divorce on that ground.

Collusion involves the fabrication or suppression of evidence in
order to deceive the court. The bar of collusion applied "where the
parties concocted a false case by, for example, pretending one party
had committed a matrimonial wrong simply to obtain a divorce"
(Eekelaar 1991, 146). The bars of collusion and connivance operated

to rule that in the absence of at least one matrimonial offense, husband and wife could not simply agree to divorce each other (see McGregor 1957, 132n1; Wheeler 1974, 7). If the matrimonial fault charged against the respondent was proven to have been fabricated, their petition would be dismissed (*Heffernan v. Heffernan* 1953).

It is widely acknowledged that despite the bars of collusion and connivance, many couples did in fact agree to divorce (Pearce 1969; Brinig and Crafton 1994; Wicks 2000). In some jurisdictions, collusion was thought to be almost ubiquitous, and while judges and lawyers acknowledged its undesirability, they were, it seems, largely resigned to it (Wicks 2000, 1575n67; Wheeler 1974, chap. 1). According to an American judge, "Every day . . . the same melancholy charade was played: the 'innocent' spouse, generally the wife, would take the stand and, to the accompanying cacophony of sobbing and nose-blowing, testify under the deft guidance of an attorney to the spousal conduct that she deemed 'cruel'" (*McKim*, 1972).

Legal historian Lawrence Friedman suggests that collusion was especially rife in those jurisdictions whose divorce laws were strictest, such as New York, where adultery was the sole ground for divorce until 1966 (Friedman 2000). However, the connection between limited grounds for divorce and collusion may not be causal. Collusion in New York was possibly no more prevalent but merely more obvious than in jurisdictions with a wider range of grounds. If couples decide to stage an offense, it follows that their theatrics are likely to be less conspicuous where they choose the script from a range of options (see McGregor 1957, 131–40).

The high number of perfunctorily or completely undefended divorce cases also suggests that collusion was rife. Under Canada's adversarial system, for example, "in 95 percent of cases the parties agreed that their marriage had broken down" (Bissett-Johnson and Day 1986, 7). Prior to the 1987 introduction of no-fault divorce in Canada, less than one percent of divorce petitions were rejected (15). The figures are similar across very different geopolitical situations—from Moscow to Sydney to Los Angeles, few divorce cases were defended, and even fewer failed (Field 1998, 606; Glendon 1989, 156, 188; Friedman 2000, 1523; Wheeler 1974, 4). In as much as adversarial divorce courts resemble criminal proceedings, not defending a divorce suit is a little like pleading guilty. However, mere admission of fault was not supposed to be sufficient reason in itself for the court to grant a divorce: the matters were required to be proven at trial (Bisset-Johnson and Day 1986, 8). Nonetheless, as one judge noted, "More and more the evidence received in uncontested divorces appears to be minimal, if not negligible, yet the decree *nisi* is usually granted." (Glube CJTD as cited by Bissett Johnson and Day 1986, 7). Divorce proceedings were becoming mere procedures—a means to an end rather than a mechanism of justice (Friedman 2000, 1524; *cf* Berns 2000). Given that proscribed matrimonial offenses worked as templates for divorce, various degrees of collusion or connivance were probably inevitable. Petitioners and lawyers built their suits around the legal requirements, "satisfy[ing] the letter of the law while violating its essential spirit" (Chester and Streather 1972, 706).

Whether more often breached than observed, bars to divorce are a fundamental component of adversarial systems. They are a legacy of coverture—the legal doctrine that husband and wife are one, that one being the husband—whose effects continue. We can view the examination of "dead" law as a kind of archaeology (as Friedman does), but this should not be understood as the dryly objective examination of historical objects. Rather we should understand such research as archaeology in the Foucaultian sense. That is, I would not suggest that in places where no-fault divorce prevails, marriage law has necessarily expunged all traces of its patriarchal past. On the contrary, while no-fault provisions might replace the adversarial character of their predecessors wholly or in part, the new never entirely supplants the old. Legal discourse is inscriptive, and the body of the law is in this sense a palimpsest—though erased, the imprint of old lettering can still be traced beneath the new. In this way, the heritage of repealed matrimonial legislation nonetheless influences various aspects of legal proceedings today. One of the more obvious arenas in which the legacy of collusion as a bar to divorce can be seen is the extinction of "cruelty" as a ground for divorce, and the concomitant (though not necessarily simultaneous) criminalization of domestic violence and spousal rape.

With the abolition of fault from divorce proceedings, the ground of cruelty disappeared—and with it, in most cases, any judicial remedy against a violent spouse. Although most jurisdictions were slow to address it, eventually—after prolonged and courageous feminist struggle—"wife-beating" was criminalized through domestic violence legislation. In fact, then, we can conceptualize the ground of cruelty as having been cleft: collusive or trivial instances of cruelty were subsumed as "irreconcilable differences" or incompatibility, while the more serious offenses—whether physical or other kinds of cruelty—became criminalized as domestic violence. Criminal sanctions against domestic violence are patently necessary. When one spouse is being beaten by the other—and when such beatings all too often end in death or permanent disability—it is obviously preferable to call the police rather than a divorce lawyer. The movement of husband-wife violence into the more "serious" realm of criminal law, with its associated shame and punishment, represents a significant feminist victory. However, there is widespread agreement that domestic violence laws do not always work effectively. Despite the existence of a large and important literature on domestic violence, its legal ancestry as the matrimonial fault of cruelty is often unacknowledged. This ancestry, however, explains some of the continuing difficulties battered spouses—and especially wives—experience.

Grounds of cruelty in divorce cases were, as we have already seen, subject to broad and often highly inclusive interpretation. Where couples colluded on this ground, it is understandable that they might build a case in which mere incompatibility is presented as cruelty. Further, it is understandable that couples might try to build a *minimal* case in order to protect the respondent's reputation as much as possible, particularly if the husband was never, in fact, violent. Thus constrained by the limited availability of divorce, petitioners (usually women, remember) sometimes represented relatively trivial disagreements as "cruelty" (Chester and Streather 1972, 707). As a Canadian judge complained, "[J]udges are asked to accept evidence which in some cases may appear to the judge to be no more than any one of us experiences in marriage. Sometimes the complaints border on the ridiculous" (Glube CJTD as cited in Bissett-Johnson and Day 1986, 7). It was widely understood, then, that "cruelty" could be real or manufactured, and was thus subject to judicial and popular scepticism. As Michael Wheeler comments, "If there actually are no facts which constitute grounds, cruelty is the easiest lie to tell" (Wheeler 1974, 7).

It is hardly surprising, then, that this scepticism concerning the seriousness and truthfulness of allegations of matrimonial cruelty is now similarly attached to allegations of domestic violence. Today, feminists argue that police, judges, and the general public routinely trivialize domestic violence (James 1995). Women battered or raped by their husbands resist making complaints to the police partly out of fear that they will not be believed. These fears are all too often borne out. In an English divorce case from 1954, the justices openly acceded that where there was a conflict of interest, they preferred the husband's evidence (*Cooper v. Cooper* 1955). Even if we interpret this as a preference for a particular husband's evidence rather than a broader willingness to believe men in general over women in general, it is alarming: in this case, the husband was a man convicted of indecently assaulting his nine-year-old daughter. Perhaps (relatively) appropriate doubt surrounding collusive accusations of cruelty has been transferred as inappropriate doubt regarding the reliability of accusations of domestic violence, and in this way the legacy of fault infects domestic violence law. More surprising, perhaps, is the way that provisions for no-fault divorce have also leeched into understandings of domestic violence.

With the advent of no-fault divorce, separation became the typical route to divorce. While the difficulties of petitioning a violent husband under fault-based systems are fairly clear, the relative "ease" of no-fault divorce (with its unilateral release system) sometimes obscures the difficulties still faced by many women trying to escape a violent partner. As Friedman observes, "If the law before no-fault assumed a wicked husband and a suffering wife, no-fault seems in some ways to assume away the issue of inequality, or rather to ignore it" (2000, 1534; see also Fineman 1994, xiv). If today the obvious response to the problem of wife-beating is to ask, "Why doesn't she just leave?" (Hirsch 1994, 6; Hosking 2005), perhaps this is because separation and divorce are now represented as being "easy." It is as if, in fact, the remedy for spousal violence is still expected to lie in matrimonial and not criminal law.[11] The theoretical contours of this (and related) problems have been explored in feminist research on the public/private split (Fineman and Mykitiuk 1994; Landes 1998).

Within this large body of work on the public/private split, some feminists suggest that the shifting of wife-beating from matrimonial to criminal law illustrates an (incomplete) but desirable movement from "private" to "public." Jocelynne Scutt advocates pushing further in the same direction: domestic violence, she says, should be treated no differently from other kinds of assault; marital rape should be treated as identical to any other incidence of rape (1995). Scutt's argument is appealing, but seems unlikely to solve the problem. As Scutt observes, judges have resisted treating marital rape and domestic violence as they would any other instance of sexual or other assault. Conviction rates for violence against women are notoriously low, not simply because such violence typically occurs in the domestic sphere, but because women often expect (correctly, as it turns out) their testimony to be discounted as evidence. Typically, the exercise of justice in cases of marital rape involves assessing different accounts of events rather than material forensics. As such, the contest might revolve not so much around public/private divisions as a number of other binaries, including science/language (the "truth" of DNA tests versus different witnesses' accounts) and abstraction/materiality (considering logic and truthfulness versus bloodstains and fingerprints).

In a similar spirit, Isobel Marcus (1994) offers a provocative "reframing" of domestic violence. She suggests (writing before the events of 9/11) that violence against women in their homes should be understood as terrorism. The parallels she draws between the two are compelling: in both cases, the violence is unannounced, psychological as well as physical, and creates an atmosphere of intimidation. Further, both tend to occur in "mundane" environments—environments normally assumed to be safe. The usefulness of her analysis is its provocative stance: there is something shocking about even comparing terrorism and domestic violence, let alone finding them similar. For all the persuasiveness of the comparison, however, it is unlikely to overcome the kinds of problems already noted. Violence against women in their homes might be considered terrorism, but it is unlikely to be understood as terrorism *unmodified* (*cf* Marcus 1994, 26). Just as domestic violence is iteratively distinguished from other forms of violence, so *domestic* terrorism is likely to be distinguished from other forms of terrorism. This is not to suggest that reframing domestic violence as (even modified, "domestic") terrorism would not be useful. It seems to me that "terrorism" is a more accurate and telling term for wife-beating than either "cruelty" or "assault" for precisely the reasons Marcus offers. We know, in the twenty-first century, that "terrorism" is a term subject to fierce contests of meaning. Where "terrorism" is the violent resort of the weak against the strong, it tends to be vilified as a most heinous crime. Where *governments* promote fearfulness or otherwise "legitimately" intimidate populations, identical activities are far less likely to be named "terrorism." Given the historical legitimacy and acceptability of domestic violence as a strategy for the intimidation and control of "the weak" (women) by "the strong" (men), the rejection of Marcus's reframing by non-feminists seems assured. Finally, it may be salutary to consider how governments have *responded* to terrorist threats and acts. What kinds of defenses against terrorism have been mobilized? How have states and populations moved to prevent terrorist attacks and capture those responsible for attacks? If these strategies have not guaranteed people's safety, and if they are unlikely to find domestic applications or parallels, the shock value of recasting wife-beating as terrorism is likely to be short lived.

It may be useful to compare more thoroughly the way that cruelty operated in matrimonial law against the operations of domestic violence in criminal law. It seems to me that while the matrimonial offense of "cruelty" was (in some times and places, at least) too easily proven, the crime of domestic violence is too difficult to prosecute. Perhaps, then, feminist jurisprudence should focus on advocating for changes in the consideration of evidence regarding domestic violence by judges and juries. If the range of domestic offenses were attached to a wider range of penalties, perhaps some cases could be decided on the balance of probabilities rather than on proof beyond reasonable doubt. Alternatively, if wife-beating continues to stand as a modified, lesser imitation of other crimes more readily recognized and condemned, perhaps the feminist effort to render "private" violence "public" should be abandoned as a lost cause. Regardless of the names we assign to it—"habitual cruelty," "domestic violence," "assault," or even "terrorism"—wife-beating sturdily resists the censure of equivalent offenses. Perhaps, then, feminists might continue to theorize the relationship of domestic violence and the public/private division from the other side of the split. "Private" responses to "private" violence against women might take a variety of shapes. These would not necessarily be more individualized or less radical than "public" approaches. Indeed, some *very* radical suggestions have been mooted.[12] There are obvious risks with these strategies too, but, given that the current situation is unacceptable, we need to continue to think through alternatives and potential solutions.

Whether or not we pursue reforms such as those proposed by Scutt and Marcus, the fact that the legislative seeds for the criminalization of domestic violence came not from laws concerning other kinds of violent assault, but from the matrimonial offense of "cruelty" must not be forgotten (Siegel 1996). If nothing else, the somewhat malleable nature of the boundaries between matrimonial and criminal law (in relation to both cruelty/domestic violence and crime as a ground for divorce) allows a limited traffic of offenses from matrimonial to criminal law. This traffic suggests that marriage is deeply implicated in the production of (sexed and sexualized) citizen-subjects.

SEPARATION ANXIETIES: THE END OF FAULT

Separation is a key concept in no-fault divorce. In most jurisdictions today, separation is not a ground for divorce as such. Rather, it constitutes evidence of "irretrievable breakdown" or "irreconcilable differences" in a marriage. In some places (including Australia and Sweden), such separation is the *only* admissable evidence of breakdown, while in many other places, alternative or additional evidence—such as adultery or cruelty—may be presented. It is easy to see, then, that vestiges of "matrimonial offense" continue to apply in some places. Less obviously, it is also the case that many jurisdictions have allowed separation as a ground for divorce *within* an otherwise fault-based system. Under fault-based divorce, the period required to establish that breakdown had occurred through separation was usually considerable: in Australia, a seven-year period was required; in England and Wales, parties had to have been separated for five years in the case of a unilateral petition, or two years for a joint application (Fine and Fine 1994, 252–53). Given that divorce reform was being vigorously debated throughout the 1950s and 60s, one might expect no-fault grounds (and particularly separation) to have been popular where they were available within otherwise fault-based systems. However, separation as a ground for divorce was very infrequently cited. The main reason for its relative lack of popularity is probably related to the lengthy time frames required, as previously noted.[13] The social stigma attached to divorce and its grounds might be another factor; where discriminatory attitudes prevailed, perhaps ex-spouses preferred to avoid the ambiguity of guilt/innocence attached to a no-fault ground. Similarly, where adversarial divorce was the norm, conforming to its requirements might offer unnecessary, but nonetheless reassuring, certainty of dissolution to divorcing spouses.

In any case, the point here is that in the early 1970s, no-fault divorce was not necessarily novel; it already existed as an infrequently used ground within many fault-based systems. What was new was the acceptability of the idea that a married couple might agree to end their marriage without apportioning blame; what was new was the establishment of no-fault grounds as the *norm* for divorce.[14] This shift (beginning in the late 1960s and continuing into the mid-1980s) is important because its consequences were far-reaching. In the ascendance of no-fault divorce, we see major changes in the government of conjugal relationships, from outlawing offenses to recognizing breakdown; from prohibiting behavior believed to *cause* divorce to managing the *effects* of breaking up; and, most important of all, a shift from rules to norms in the rationale of governing conjugality. These changes recast marriage from a relationship characterized by (legal-corporeal) *union* to a relationship characterized as *consortium vitae* (or "togetherness").

Foucault characterizes the rise of governmentality as a historical shift from sovereign law to more managerial and tactical concerns (1991). It is easy to see that under adversarial systems, divorce law operated in sovereign manner. The courts handed down verdicts of guilt or innocence—granting or denying dissolution—against a number of expressly proscribed offenses. With the advent of no-fault divorce, courts no longer sought to apportion blame in the dissolution of marriage, but adopted a more managerial role. The shift from adversarial to no-fault divorce echoes Foucualt's precisely. But Foucault explicates the rise of the art of government as confined to a particular historical epoch long preceding the changes to divorce law under discussion here. Why would the government of relationships lag so far behind other arenas of regulation? Foucault claims that, as a corollary to the rise of governmentality, the family no longer served as a model for government (1991). However, as feminists rightly insist, models of the family continue to shape women's political subjectivity. Perhaps, then, the rise of no-fault divorce signals a real improvement in the constitution of women as political subjects.

If we adopt this Foucaultian approach to the construction of identities and political subjectivities, we could expect the politics of wifely subjectivity to change as the governance and regulation of marriage changes. In this way, we take up aspects of Gatens's theorization of subjectivity—in which the subject is *not* presupposed, but emerges, chameleon-like, as it is governed (Gatens 1996, 58). The subject who becomes a wife under adversarial constructions of divorce, then, is *not the same subject* as one who marries where no-fault divorce prevails, regardless of whether that subject is one and the same *person*. Where marriage is understood as a fixed, sexual contract, it implicates women in relations of corporeal subjection. But where marriage becomes a governmental exercise and is regulated through disposing things rather than through the rule of law, the sexual subjectivities of husband and wife change, and the "contractual" (that is, fixed) image of marriage slides away—to a certain extent, at least. Let us consider the gendered impact of this more governmental approach to conjugality across its most significant features.

From Offense to Breakdown: Governing Effects

No-fault divorce laws do not address the *causes* of marital breakdown at all. Rather, the matters to be governed are the *effects* of broken marriage. An English law commission paper compared the proposed role of the new Family Court judge to that of coroner, saying, "The role of the court . . . [is to acknowledge] that the marriage is dead and fulfil its official function by virtually issuing a death certificate in respect of the marriage" (cited in Australia, House of Representatives, 1975, 1157). In Australia, one politician was prompted to characterize the new Family Court as undertaker, saying, "If the marriage is dead, the object of the law should be to afford it a decent burial . . . It should not merely bury the marriage, but do so with decency and dignity" (Australia, HR, 1975, 907). The divorce court's objective, then, was no longer to identify the cause of a conjugal body's death (let alone to pronounce the person or persons guilty of its demise), but to recognize that marriage could "die a natural death" (913). Under no-fault divorce, the problem to be governed was not the identification of a guilty party, but rather the *disposal* of a relationship.

As the push for divorce reform gathered pace, the need to accuse one spouse of having caused the break-up—even in the absence of collusion or outright fabrication—seemed to be an increasingly futile exercise. During a 1975 debate on divorce reform in the Australian parliament, the then Attorney General, Kep Enderby, said, "Ninety-five per cent of divorces are undefended. Ninety-five per cent of divorces are for practical purposes by consent. Ninety-five per cent of divorces reflect that the marriage has broken down but the parties are obliged to go through this cruel ritual of saying: 'I have never done anything wrong. It is all your fault. You have been sleeping with someone. You have been bashing me, picking your nose or farting at the breakfast table'—whatever it happens to be" (Australia, HR, 1975, 322). Enderby's comments do not imply that adultery and nose-picking are equivalent matrimonial offenses, but accuse the fault-based system of judging them as such. Along with many others, he suggests that it is farcical to lay the entire blame for a marriage breakdown on one spouse—let alone to one event. Proscribed matrimonial offenses were positioned as mythical keystones in the institution of marriage: cruel, adulterous, or neglectful behavior was thought to cause the whole structure to collapse. It was widely understood, however, that few marriages really did break down in this way—the process was more often akin to mutual, gradual erosion rather than collapse (Katter 1987, 32).

The UK Law Society expressed a similar view when it argued that "[t]he conduct of the apparently "innocent" spouse can often turn out, on close investigation, to have been quite as destructive as that of the "guilty" one though in less obvious ways" (1979, 19). The idea that the ostensibly "innocent" spouse might not be so innocent after all was well established in the popular imagination. The unloving husband who drives his wife to seek affection in an affair and the wife who "deserves" ill treatment were almost stock dramatic characters. Wives petitioned for divorce more frequently than husbands (Friedman 2000), but this is not necessarily an accurate reflection of the facts of marriage break-up. Ending the allocation of fault in divorce law would also end the chivalrous fiction that demanded a token from men (often to "be divorced" by their wives rather than to act as petitioner themselves, regardless of the facts of the case), even while women copped the social blame for broken marriages. This fiction was necessary because of structural disadvantages women faced as divorced respondents. Not only were wives typically dependent on their husbands, their wages were lower and their job opportunities more limited than men's. Moreover, it was the policy of many companies and organizations (including schools and government departments) not to employ divorced women. A woman with dependent children faced an even bleaker economic future. Few women, then, were in a position to allow themselves to be the respondent in a divorce case—with obvious corollaries on wives' conjugal behavior.

While public debate tended to illustrate the threats inherent in abolishing fault with reference to errant and irresponsible husbands ("playboys," "tom cats," and "casanovas"), the work of preventing such a husband from the temptation to stray from conjugality rested with his wife. Even while "cruelty" was becoming a more and more flexible ground for divorce, judges did not always interpret petitions generously. A woman seeking a divorce on the ground of her husband's cruelty, for example, could be denied a divorce if the court believed that she "provoked" his wrath (Marcus 1994, 22). In 1961, one judge said, "The court will not grant relief to a wife if she could have ensured her own safety by an alteration of her own conduct by being dutiful, restraining her outbursts of temper and exercising self command"(Burbury 1963, 291; see also Selby 1960, 240).

There is no gender symmetry in this state of affairs. Under adversarial divorce, those wives understood to have "provoked" their husbands' beatings could be left destitute or find their petition denied, and were in many other ways subject to stringent scrutiny. As Scutt and Graham explain:

> Because fault and guilt remained central to action for separation or divorce, the law reinforced the idea that women had to live up to an ideal of womanhood, wifehood and motherhood. After divorce, a woman's right to be maintained had no relationship to her property or income. It had everything to do with her chastity, purity, and womanliness—as determined by male judges, in male courts, on evidence and cross-examination drawn from witnesses by almost exclusively male lawyers. If the woman had been wronged, and her husband a gross adulterer, physically brutal in the worst terms, or in some heinous way had severely violated gentlemanly standards (despite her perfection as a wife and mother), then she might be granted maintenance . . . But the definition of men's wrongs to their wives would be cast in male terms: if a man committed adultery or was brutal to his wife, the assumption was that the woman must have done something wrong; she must have "driven him to it," or "done something to deserve it." (Scutt and Graham 1984, 98)

The chivalrous fiction arising from these double standards was that a "decent" man would shoulder the blame for his divorce by not contesting the charge against him. (Even if he had committed offenses, then, the respondent husband was positioned as possibly "innocent.") Women rarely had the means to do the same: most "wronged" wives' options were limited to "allowing" or "denying" their husband a divorce. Remember that if an "innocent" party chose not to act on their spouse's offense, there was next to nothing that the "offending" party could do about it—except try to make their spouse as miserable as possible. As previously noted, in some places, there was provision for divorce by separation but the duration of separation required could be as long as seven years. Where the "offending" party had no means to leave the marriage, and where the "innocent" spouse refused divorce, the "guilty" party remained trapped. Again, it is obvious that such provisions limit wives more than husbands. Shifting the rationale for divorce from adversarial offenses to simple "breakdown" began to transform not just the collusive and farcical allocation of blame but also the gendered double standards it both produced and supported (Biondi 1999).

From Rules to Norms: Governing Conduct

The abolition of fault in establishing grounds for divorce introduced a new rationality of government in the regulation of marriage. By repealing the list of matrimonial offenses available as grounds for divorce, marriage became much more overtly *self*-regulating. As Chisholm and Jessep (1981, 58) put it, "[t]he law now provides no code of behaviour for married persons: the obligations of spouses can only be spoken of in a very limited sense" (as cited in Katter 1987, 5). The new law modernized divorce law by more closely approximating a purported shift in public attitudes on marriage. Divorce was no longer premised on the crime-like commission of particular matrimonial offenses, but was seen rather as the failure of both spouses to negotiate a happy life together (Kay 2002, 33).

Opponents of no-fault divorce describe the government of marriage as properly concerned with outlawing behavior that (in their eyes) could be seen to promote matrimonial discord and divorce. Under adversarial systems, the problem requiring governance was a complex of sexual, economic, and personal relationships expressed as rights, responsibilities, and offenses. Under no-fault provisions, the defining motif of marriage would not be vested in the uttered and sexual performatives reminiscent of coverture, but would be understood as a much more flexible mutuality, or *consortium vitae*. "Togetherness" came to be understood as a range of normative performances whose indicia included living together, mutual support and society, care of children, division of labor, and, importantly, sexual relations. The presumption of conjugal unity would not disappear entirely—marriage continued to be understood as a unification of husband and wife—but elements of wives' subjection to their husbands were significantly eroded.

With the advent of no-fault divorce, the sexual operations of consummation and condonation (discussed in Chapters 3 and 4) were dismantled such that their transformative potential was eroded if not eradicated. Sex between separated spouses no longer negated the matrimonial offense standing as the ground for divorce, but could nevertheless compromise the fact of separation. As one judge warned, "a man who maintains that he is living separately and apart from his wife but nevertheless returns to her in the nuptial bed, does so at his own risk" (Parker et al. 1994, 415). Above all, however, wives' vulnerability to divorce (and the threat of divorce) as a kind of matrimonial punishment was defused. This amelioration by no means amounted to complete alleviation, but did mean that the double standards of matrimonial blame were to some extent disabled. With grounds for divorce whipped out from beneath its institutional feet, the basis of conjugality was radically destabilized. Each spouse's consent to marriage was no longer conditional and contingent on the behavior of the other, but was a matter for each to decide. What constitutes a "happy" marriage could be determined in a hundred different ways by a hundred different couples. In effect, either spouse could initiate a divorce at any time, and for any (or even no) reason.

Given that separation constituted evidence of marital breakdown, its definition became crucial. According to a key Australian judgement:

> "[S]eparation" means more than physical separation—it involves the destruction of the marital relationship (the consortium vitae). Separation can only occur . . . where one or both of the spouses form the intention to sever or not to resume the marital relationship and act on that intention, or alternatively act as if the marital relationship has been severed. *What comprises the marital relationship for each couple will vary.* Marriage involves many elements some or all of which may be present in a particular marriage—elements such as dwelling under the same roof, sexual intercourse, mutual society and protection, recognition of the existence of the marriage by both spouses in public and private relationships.
>
> When it is asserted that a separation has taken place it may be necessary to examine and contrast the state of the marital relationship before and after the alleged separation. Whether there has been a separation will be a question of fact to be determined in each case. (*Todd* 1976; emphasis added)

Because marriage was now based on togetherness rather than union, and governed in a self-regulatory fashion through norms rather than rules, it became subject to more or less continuous operations of

consent. A person could no longer be forced to remain in an
unhappy marriage (Fine and Fine 1994, 253; citing Sundberg
1975). The activation of consent in this fashion had crucial consequences for women in particular. It meant, in the first place, that
consent to sex and consent to marriage could no longer be equated.

If remaining married was to be conditional and could be unilater-
ally challenged, it followed that there could be no assumption of
consent to sex, fictional or not. In effect, the legal unity of the conjugal body constructed in adversarial systems was cleft. This move
complicates Carole Pateman's assertion that the "contractual" trap-
pings of marriage merely disguise the subjection of wives to their
husbands. In *The Sexual Contract* (1988), Pateman argues that a
wife, as she promises obedience to her husband, enters a slave-like
relation of subjection, which cannot be rescinded of her own volition. Marriage, she says, is not truly contractual at all, but rather, in
its *naming* as contract, assumes a semblance of voluntarism. A rose
by any other name would smell as sweet, but Pateman's analysis of
contract as liberalism's arsenal of oppression suggests that women
are lured into marriage by its contractual perfume.

Leaving to one side the question of whether marriage is or is not
contractual as such, Pateman's critique cannot be upheld against
marriage as it is constructed under no-fault divorce law.[15] While the
performative utterances of the wedding do establish a particular legal
relationship between husband and wife, the terms of the marriage
"contract" are now highly flexible, if not entirely self-regulated.
Pateman's conception of marriage is a "fixed terms" model. Her
analysis of marriage as a sexual contract offers a reasonably good fit
with marriage before no-fault, where each party's obligation to
remain married is bound up in the conduct of the other. However, it
takes on a decidedly anachronistic flavor against the reforms of the
1970s and beyond, where remaining married is supposed always to
be a mutual negotiation. This is not to suggest that men and women
or husbands and wives are now in a position to contract with each
other as equals. Rather, it is to suggest that, in spite of their varying
capacities and privileges, the legal positioning of husbands and wives
relative to each other is no longer quite so rigid.

In this respect, Carol Smart's contention that the liberalisation of
divorce law did *not* significantly change the institution of marriage
must also be challenged. On reforms to divorce law in the United
Kingdom, Smart says:

Easier divorce offered only a spurious sense of permissiveness and lib-eralisation. Although it might provide freedom from a relationship with one individual it did nothing to alter the institution of marriage or its structural effects.

. . . What might otherwise be understood as a "reform" or a break in previous practices, can in consequence be seen as a continu-ation of modes of regulation over sexual and reproductive relation-ships through the agency of marriage. (1984, 56)

To suggest that such fundamental changes as the abolition of fault in divorce have *not* had significant and corollary effects in the con-struction and meanings of conjugality is misconceived. Though the institution of marriage has remained identifiable as such, its struc-ture and shape have shifted dramatically. Since marriage figures in the construction of political subjectivities, and since the operations of matrimonial legislation vary, changes in the *government of mar-riage* necessarily transform its sexual-political subjects. For exam-ple, under adversarial regulations, adultery was a "punishable" matrimonial offense—a charge against which one might be found "innocent" or "guilty." Under no-fault regulations, adultery might still "cause" a marriage to break up, but is now read as sympto-matic of the "irretrievable breakdown" of that relationship. Where adultery is understood as the failure to measure up to a conjugal norm (of sexual exclusivity) rather than as the commission of one of a list of prohibited matrimonial offenses, the "adulterer," too, is differently constructed and interpellated. To be sure, adultery as such remains a problem of sorts, and might continue to disappoint and infuriate husbands and wives. But, as Judith Butler might say, its iteration *as* a problem is articulated differently, and this different articulation has important consequences. Of course, this shift occurs *throughout* governmental discourses of marriage and not just in relation to adultery.

CONTEMPORARY OPPOSITION TO NO-FAULT: CHALLENGING "DIVORCE ON DEMAND'

No-fault divorce is now well established, but continues to provoke debates about social stability and personal happiness.[16] Wherever no-fault divorce supersedes adversarial divorce, the number of dissolutions seems to rise.[17] For many, this is a source of high anxiety. National divorce rates are sometimes viewed as a kind of barometer of social health—the higher the rate, the greater political concern over the future of "the family." The view that a high divorce rate is inherently bad may be waning, but many conservatives—especially religious conservatives—continue to argue that the availability of divorce promotes the breakdown of marriages (Wicks 2000, 1578). Economists Antony Dnes and Robert Rowthorn, for example, argue that a "badly designed divorce law may undermine the fabric of trust upon which stable marriages depend. . . . *[T]he law itself may stimulate divorce* and contribute to a great deal of human misery" (Dnes and Rowthorn 2002, 2; emphasis added). They and others imply, but rarely state baldly, that many marriages ending with "easy" divorce are unions that would otherwise prosper.[18] Their twofold assumption is that divorce is patently miserable, and that an undissolved but unhappy marriage is not.

Accepting the first part of this assumption, some jurisdictions have interpreted high rates of divorce as high rates of social unhappiness that would otherwise not exist, and build on this premise a rationale for reconsidering the place of fault in divorce law (see Schoenfeld 1996). Divorce is rarely a happy occasion, of course. The optimism and joy with which we celebrate marriage is not usually mirrored in the finalization of a decree nisi. That is not to say, however, that unhappy but undissolved marriages are preferable to divorce. While it is reasonable to suggest that "easy" or more accessible divorce laws might spike an increase in rates of divorce, it is by no means the case that "easy" divorce prompts marital breakdown (as distinct from divorce). Whether no-fault divorce increases the rate of divorce seems to me to be beside the point; the more salient issue is not divorce as such but the management of marriage breakdown. It is appropriate, then, to understand divorce as a necessary adjunct to the usually undesirable but sometimes inevitable breakdown of marriage. Most advocates of no-fault divorce recognize this, and argue that the connivance and collusion that flourish under adversarial systems damage the social repute of marriage. Similarly, the farcical maintenance of marriages that have ended in all but their legal status can be seen to undermine public confidence in marriage (Finlay 1969, 13). To extend the metaphor so often favored by divorce law commentators, undissolved but "dead" marriages ought not to be left rotting in the streets.

The rise in divorce has also enabled second and subsequent marriages to be contracted more frequently. If divorce were not so readily available, there would be fewer opportunities for people to end an unhappy marriage in order to "try again" (Ellman 1997, 221). In the absence of such opportunities, a significant avenue to happiness (albeit a heavily sexed/gendered kind of happiness) is foreclosed. A number of commentators argue, however, that more *restrictive* divorce laws promote personal happiness. Elizabeth Scott, for example, makes the trebly oxymoronic argument that "easy" divorce has restricted spouses' freedom to bind themselves (2002). Her argument is specious: the capacity of spouses to agree to persevere in an unhappy marriage is not negated in no-fault divorce law. Where marriage is largely a self-regulated arrangement, spouses might agree to restrict each other's behavior more or less as they please. That such agreements might continue only with the mutual consent of the parties is hardly an imposition.

The rise of no-fault divorce has had important consequences for women (Kay 1987). In the first place, the refiguring of marriage as "life together" rather than "union" positions wives and husbands as bound together by consent rather than by the behavior of each to the other. Under adversarial systems, marriage is a knot binding husband and wife that neither can legitimately untie for him- or herself: only the husband can free the wife; only the wife can free the husband. Given that the social and economic situation of men and women has never been symmetrical, adversarial divorce carries greater risks for women than men. In the past, its troublesome power differentials were dealt with, in part, through paradoxically chivalrous fictions that positioned women as victims of men's matrimonial offenses even as the prevalence and danger of domestic violence was obscured. While the social and economic situation of men and women is still very different, the operations of no-fault divorce represent a step away from the traditions of coverture.

It is a step that some would prefer to retrace. In a number of jurisdictions, governments have endorsed moves to "strengthen" marriage by "tightening" or restricting divorce (Wicks 2000; Bradford 1997). Such moves have been inspired, in part, by the political influence of anti-feminist men's groups like the Promise Keepers. The Promise Keepers advocate a particularly chauvinistic model of Christian fundamentalism, and blame no-fault divorce and an inferred bias against men in family law for all manner of social ills. One of their particular irks is that divorce is available even where one spouse would prefer to remain married. Usually presenting their arguments around the need to "protect" the abandoned wife who wishes to "save" her marriage,[19] while in fact protecting the proprietary husband, these groups attempt to revive the view that marriage should be more binding. Casting their arguments in the language of nostalgia, they advocate a return to the "chivalry" of earlier times—and in doing so, re-endorse women's subordination in marriage (Bradford 1997, 142n61). As we have seen, chivalry is in effect the notion that men should exercise their power and privilege nobly, and disguises women's disadvantage by deflecting attention from questions concerning the justness of the existence of such power in the first place. Advocacy of more restrictive divorce is most pronounced in the United States, where the abolition of fault in divorce is arguably less complete than in other similar places.[20] In Louisiana, a form of "covenant" (or "lifelong") marriage has been introduced, inviting parties to enter into a more binding form of marriage. Elsewhere, proposals to allow divorce only by mutual consent are being mooted (for example Parkman 2002; others are identified by Ellman 1997). While such "reforms" reflect dangerously backward thinking, they are unlikely to displace the acceptability of no-fault divorce. As long as such provisions are offered as optional alternatives to no-fault systems, they are likely to constitute nothing more than a kind of unpopular and sanctimonious moral high ground in conjugality.[21] There can be no doubt that the move from adversarial to no-fault divorce was and is progressive and just (Biondi 1999; Brook 2004). In fact, as we will see in Chapter 8, moves to "strengthen" and "protect" marriage usually reflect sexist and homophobic anxieties.

In a number of ways, no-fault divorce refigured the conjugal body politic. Under adversarial systems, husband and wife were grafted as a conjugal body replete with the vestiges of coverture. Their unity was rule-bound, and was directed for the most part by the husband. The conjugal body of no-fault divorce is much more a subject of governmentality: the rationale for its governance deploys tactics for disposing things rather than the administration of justice through rule of law. The court's decisions and awards now generally concern economic disposal and management rather than the wrong and redress of moral justice. Married couples have become much more self-regulating: each couple can decide for themselves what constitutes "marriage" in terms of the irretrievable breakdown of their own relationship. The defining motif of marriage is no longer so vested in the sexual performatives of coverture, but is understood as "life together." The presumption of conjugal unity did not vanish entirely—marriage is described as a (singular) "life together," not (plural) lives intertwined—but elements of wives' subjection to their husbands have been significantly eroded.

There is much more that could be said about the introduction and operation of no-fault divorce. No-fault divorce was one of a number of relatively radical social reforms introduced during a period of far-reaching social upheaval. It was, most significantly, a *feminist* victory attendant on the women's liberation movement, which flourished in and around the 1970s. It is no exaggeration to suggest that the innovation of no-fault divorce and the governmental shifts it produced represents the single most influential achievement of the contemporary women's movement. This is not to say, however, that with the enactment of divorce reform, feminists packed their kits and marched away from the scene of matrimonial struggles. Rather, new problems arose from the old. For example, the introduction of normative rather than rule-based understandings of marriage brought with it new complications for managing and understanding uncertified, (merely) marriage-*like* relationships. Given that cohabitation outside of marriage is sometimes conceptualized as an expression of feminist resistance to marriage's patriarchal traditions, the shift from union to "togetherness" as the defining characteristic of marriage poses a number of very prickly questions. The theoretical and practical issues attending these questions are the subject of the following chapter.

CHAPTER 7

THE "LIMPING" MARRIAGE:
REGULATING COHABITATION

Cohabitation is an arena of paradox. It is simultaneously romantic and mundane; a scene of potential liberation and regulation. For some, cohabitation is shameful, even sinful. For others, it is a situation arising almost accidentally, out of apathy or convenience rather than by design. For others still, cohabitation offers a kind of non-conformist elopement—a radical rejection of marriage as such. Whichever way we look at it, cohabitation defies easy explanation. Cohabitation tends to be painted as an especially modern way of living, but of course there have always been people who live together without celebrating a valid wedding. The regulation of cohabitation likewise has a long history; in different times and places, living together as husband and wife has constituted marriage as much as having undergone a wedding ceremony (Oldham 2000; Parker 1990). However, it is no coincidence that in many jurisdictions, legislation equating cohabitation with marriage (by degrees) began to be introduced shortly after the divorce reforms discussed in the previous chapter.

Cohabitative relationships are defined and treated in a variety of ways. If what constitutes "marriage" is subject to debate, cohabitation and its difference from formal marriage is even more variously defined (Willmott 1996, vii). This diversity arises partly because while marriage tends to be regulated at the national or federal level of government (except in the United States, of course, where it is a matter for each state), cohabitation tends to be regulated at lower tiers of government.[1] The different criteria used by various authorities to establish the existence of a cohabitative relationship gives rise to the possibility that the same couple might be considered "married" for some purposes but not for others. This is what legal scholar John Wade calls the "limping marriage." But, as lawyer Lindy Willmott notes, no matter what they are called or how they are defined, the substance of what is being referred to is broadly similar (1996, 8). To "cohabit" generally means "to live together as husband and wife, and is usually used [to describe the relationship] of a man and a woman who are not married to each other" (Parry 1993, 1). When we talk about cohabitative or de facto relationships, we talk about *marriage-like* relationships that are *not marriages*. Cohabitation, then, is "marriage." The quotation marks are important: they signify a discursive "as if"; they alert us to the way that the term is being simultaneously likened to yet distinguished from its unqualified counterpart.

A plethora of terms are used to describe what I will call cohabitation or "de facto" marriage, including "common-law marriage," "putative marriage," "informal marriage," "trial marriage," "marriage-like relationships," "living together," "living as a couple," "domestic relationships," and "domestic partnerships."[2] Historically, this range of terms has usually been contrasted with just one: marriage. Nonetheless, cohabitation is routinely treated as a *kind* of marriage, or at least as a marriage-like relationship. Likening cohabitation and marriage may be akin to comparing apples and oranges, but both are conjugal relationships, just as apples and oranges are both fruit. To avoid ambiguity, then, it is necessary also to qualify the more formal conjugal relationship. I avoid the terms "bona fide" and "de jure" marriage because they invite the inference that cohabitation is a less genuinely conjugal relationship than certified marriage. (And if it is, this remains to be demonstrated.) As may already be evident, the qualifier I use to indicate those marriages solemnized with a wedding ceremony is "certified marriage." I prefer this term for two reasons. In the first place, it evokes the assuredness of the union as opposed to the sometimes uncertain status of cohabitants. People who participate in a wedding ceremony do so purposefully, while cohabitative relationships often congeal more slowly into the day-to-day norms of conjugality. Secondly, to speak of certified marriage as such reminds us of an important distinction: certified marriage is registered, while cohabitation is not.

Cohabitation is constituted in its very substance as marriage-*like*. As noted above, cohabitation has been part of the matrimonial landscape for a long time—so much so that in many cultures, cohabitative relationships and certified marriage play an important part in defining each other. Distinctions between certified and de facto marriage are full of ironies and paradoxes, and these present intellectual puzzles not just for thinking about gender and sexualities (important arenas for feminism), but also for thinking more broadly about subjectivities, governmental regulation, and freedom. However, although cohabitation has been a phenomenon of interest to many thinkers across a range of disciplinary boundaries, it is rarely theorized.

The "institution" of marriage is a cornerstone of feminist scholarship, but most feminist analyses of conjugality do not examine the distinction between certified and de facto conjugality. Indeed, while many feminists have theorized marriage, very few have tackled cohabitation. This is probably because we tend to assume that de facto relationships simulate marriage, and that whatever we have to say about marriage will also hold true for de facto relationships. This is, for example, the path taken by Delphy and Leonard (1992). Such conflation of marriage and de facto relationships is not necessarily erroneous: when we talk about domestic labor or rape in marriage, for example, it hardly matters whether we are talking about certified or cohabiting couples. But in fact cohabitation and certified marriage are neither identical nor dissimilar. If we are interested in theorizing resistance to marriage, minimizing cohabitation's difference from certified marriage and subsuming it into analyses of "the institution of marriage" seems inaccurate and inadequate. Treating cohabitation as if it is something entirely other than marriage is not much better. In the context of debates about marriage, at least, the two forms and their relation to each other must be distinguished.

There is a considerable literature on cohabitation, particularly in demography, law, and sociology. In these disciplines, the questions posed are often comparative. Scholarship attends to whether cohabitants and certified spouses organize the division of their household labor differently; are more or less committed or sexually faithful to each other; examine the well-being of children born in each situation; compare the average duration of each type of relationship and their dissolution; and so on. These questions have useful applications: they speak to people's experience of and rationales for the particular conjugal arrangements they pursue. But if we want to better understand how marriage and cohabitation relate to each other, difficulties and gaps remain.

One such difficulty is that cohabitation is regulated in different ways—sometimes even within jurisdictions. Cohabitation is so variously managed that overviews beyond the single-nation survey are scarce. J. Thomas Oldham presents a relatively up-to-date and thorough overview of the kinds of regulations in place in a number of western nations (2000). Oldham's method is to assume (certified) marriage as a uniform entity, and to consider how various laws pertaining to cohabitation differ against that uniform entity. In other words, Oldham compares many (cohabitation) to one (marriage). The problem with his approach is that we know that (certified) marriage is not uniform: different jurisdictions deploy combinations of fault-based and no-fault grounds for divorce, which in turn contribute to the shape of marriage itself. So in Australia, for example, cohabitation provisions exist on a state-by-state basis, and can be fairly easily compared to the model of certified marriage regulated federally. But Australian certified marriage is somewhat different from, say, certified marriage in Alabama or Aberdeen. It gets even more complex: some jurisdictions include same-sex couples within the ambit of their cohabitation laws, while others do not. Moreover, the legislative basis for the regulation of cohabitation is continually in flux as governments reconsider and revise their provisions. The regulatory net becomes finer and finer, and the glass we would need to examine its structure requires stronger and stronger magnification—until, eventually, we see only fibers. This makes it difficult to distinguish cohabitation and marriage in any precise and useful way. However, if we think about cohabitation's general articulation with a variety of debates about freedom, some avenues for exploration emerge.

COHABITATION AS FREEDOM

Some commentators have considered whether the regulation of de facto relationships closes off an avenue of marriage resistance by equating (or virtually equating) certified marriage and cohabitation. Such debates typically polarize the right of persons who wish specifically to avoid marriage and its consequences against those who might be exploited in a relationship whose shape is precisely identical to certified marriage, but which exhibits none of its legal consequences. The key ideas informing debates about the social-political meanings of cohabitation are several. They are, first, that cohabitation presents freedom from the patriarchal weight of institutionalized marriage; second, that legal recognition of cohabitation "devalues" marriage; and, third, that cohabitation offers freedom from state incursions into "private life." Each of these ideas involves complexities worth considering at some length.

Freedom from the Patriarchal Institution of Marriage

Cohabitation is sometimes represented as a specifically *feminist* alternative to marriage, even though few feminists explicitly condone cohabitation (regulated or otherwise). In her beautiful and passionate 1911 essay on "Love and Marriage," Emma Goldman argues that (certified) marriage is a yoke encumbering and enslaving women. Goldman contrasts marriage, "that poor little State- and Church-begotten weed," (1972, 165) with "free love." Her description of a new and better world in which men and women might love each other by choice rather than compulsion rings with an almost evangelical cadence: "Some day, some day men and women will rise, they will reach the mountain peak, they will meet big and strong and free, ready to receive, to partake, and to bask in the golden rays of love. . . . If the world is ever to give birth to true companionship and oneness, not marriage, but love will be the parent" (167). For Goldman, unless marriage could be done away with entirely, and unless women were to turn away from it willingly, relationships between men and women must remain unavoidably, indelibly patriarchal.

Sociologist Sotirios Sarantakos might be thinking of Goldman's "free love" when he claims that cohabitation has historically offered "[l]iberation from the ideology of marriage" and "liberation from oppressive sexist structures embedded in the traditional marriage /family" (1994, 150). He asserts that "[f]eminists in particular presented cohabitation as a way of liberation from traditions and conventions as well as from structures embedded in marriage, an institution believed to openly discriminate against women" (149–50). According to this view, the recognition and regulation of de facto marriage could be understood as an attempt to multiply the regulatory tentacles of patriarchal matrimony to include even those women who consciously choose to organize their intimate relationships outside of marriage. In her celebrated analysis of heterosexuality, Andrea Dworkin seems to express such concern when she asks, "Will intercourse remain the fundamental expression of male rule over women, a legal right protected by the state especially in marriage . . . ? Or will the rights of husbands be legally extended to unmarried men over unmarried women so that intercourse functions as state-sanctioned domination not only in marriage but also outside it?" (1987, 166).

While Sarantakos is right to suggest that feminists like Goldman, Dworkin, and others have criticized marriage, their critiques of marriage hardly amount to an unequivocal endorsement of unregulated cohabitation as an alternative to marriage. Ruth Deech (1980), however, presents exactly this view. Situating her argument as ideologically "individualist," Deech argues that (unregulated) cohabitation is attractive precisely in its presumption of spousal equality. She contends that the differing intentions of cohabiting versus certified married couples must be balanced against the need for equal treatment in identical circumstances. Neither marriage nor cohabitation, in Deech's view, should assume women to be ordinarily in need of protection, economically or otherwise. Indeed, Deech suggests that both marriage and regulated cohabitation are very much like a form of prostitution in which payment is deferred but nonetheless clearly tied to sexual services (1980, 485). Her target is well chosen: since marriage has historically been a site for women's legal incorporation and subjection to husbands, extending those traces of coverture and dependence from marriage to cohabitation would seem to extend the patriarchal grasp. Deech wants to ensure a legal space for women (and men) who reject the "terms and conditions" of marriage but who wish nevertheless to cohabit.

In certain respects Deech's analysis is remarkably prescient. "Cohabitation could only be assimilated to marriage," she says, "if the legal incidents of marriage itself were reduced . . . [M]arriage should become more like cohabitation and not the other way around" (1980, 484–85). I will suggest a little later that this is precisely what has occurred—although not quite in the way that Deech might have hoped. The problem that Deech does not adequately address is that which might be called "marriage creep." That is, while couples might begin a cohabitative relationship with clear ideas and preferences for each spouse to maintain financial and social independence, over time such spousal relationships often begin to leech and bleed. The longer a cohabitative relationship endures, the more likely it is to resemble a marriage in fact (even if not in intention), particularly with respect to financial matters. Ten years after the event, and in the absence of a rigorously detailed (and time-consuming) domestic ledger, who will remember whether the split for a new refrigerator was sixty-forty or fifty-fifty? Who will judge whether the offsets negotiated at the beginning of a cohabitative relationship were fair? Long-term cohabitation thus appears to be better suited to regulation than short-term cohabitation—but defining "short-" or "long-term" cohabitation is obviously hazardous. Should the rights and responsibilities pertaining to a three-year relationship not apply to one that has lasted for two years and ten months?

Rebecca Bailey-Harris raises similar questions in a 1996 article, but settles on a different overall conclusion. Evaluating the different position of married versus cohabiting women in relation to children, domestic violence, and property matters in English law, Bailey-Harris argues that while the legal regulation of cohabitation is neither inherently oppressive nor liberating, it is necessary. Her response implicitly criticizes Deech's notion that individualism serves women well and questions the idea that women always act in straightforwardly self-interested ways.

Thus, despite the qualms expressed by Deech, feminist agitation has figured directly and strongly in various efforts to regulate cohabitation. Legislation that specifically addresses cohabitation has sometimes been enacted partly in response to feminist demands to end the sexual and economic exploitation of women in abusive or unfair de facto marriages. While Sarantakos and Deech criticize such legislation as limiting conjugal freedom, others might see it as extending protections and privileges inhering in certified marriage. Either way, it remains unclear as to how occupying spousal roles in cohabitation "outside" marriage could really accomplish the liberation of women more efficiently than the refusal to adopt traditional roles within it—regardless of whether such relationships are recognized in law or not. This is not to deny that people in de facto relationships might understand their relationships differently than certified married couples (VanEvery 1996a), or that certified marriage might be experienced as qualitatively different from cohabitation. Rather, it is to bring into question the nature of the "freedom" being invoked here.

Freedom to Contract a Different Arrangement

Sometimes, cohabitation is understood to offer opportunities for couples to contract their own conjugal arrangements. However, closer examination shows that "contract" occupies shaky ground in conjugal matters (Pawlowski 1996; Fehlberg and Smyth 2000). In some times and places, contracts between cohabitants have been untenable, while sometimes it has been certified spouses who have been prohibited from contracting their conjugal affairs. Until relatively recently, contracts between de facto spouses were unenforceable in many jurisdictions because cohabitation was understood to be "contrary to public policy" (Foreman and O'Ryan 1985, 56). Wheresoever such understandings remained in place, certified marriage was explicitly privileged and preferred by the state; intimate partners might "contract" a conjugal relationship according to the state's marriage model, or not at all.

The rationale for prohibiting contractual cohabitation was that it implied contracting sexual services—an "immoral consideration." This is precisely the objection drawn by Deech in her case against regulating cohabitation (1980, 485). As Tony Honoré explains, "A contract for which the whole or part of the consideration is sexual intercourse (or any other sexual relation) outside marriage is void, as is a contract which tends to promote unlawful sexual intercourse" (Honoré 1978, 44). Michel Foucault's "sexualization" argument can be usefully extended here. As we saw in Chapter 5, prohibitions against interracial and same-sex marriage operate analogously to sexualize those relationships—that is, to mark them as "about" sex above all. In that Others are thoroughly saturated and overdetermined by their sexualities, sexualization is a subordinating tactic. Extending this contention, it might be argued that (certified) marriage *desexualizes* intimate relationships. Even where a conjugal relationship is characterized and sometimes defined by sex acts, it is rendered as being about other things—national maturity, reproduction, domestic productivity, love, companionship, and so on—precisely *as* it moves into the purview of state-sanctioned "marriage." Thus, contracts between cohabitants are "immoral" only where the nature of any such contract is assumed to revolve around the provision of sexual services (Honoré 1978, 45).[3]

The desexualization theory helps to explain why debates concerning state recognition and acceptance of cohabitation prompt panicked defenses of certified marriage. Where legislation on cohabitation has been introduced, political debates inevitably challenge

the "demeaning" and "downgrading" of certified marriage such legislation is thought to entail. These concerns hardly make sense in the
absence of an account of binarized sexuality as either "marital" (and
therefore legitimate and productive) or "immoral" (non-marital,
and therefore thoroughly or even purely sexual). It also begins to
explain why, in some jurisdictions, contracts between certified
spouses have been invalid (Pawlowski 1996). Where "pre-nuptial"
agreements have been unenforceable (including, until recently,
Australia and the United Kingdom), it is because certified marriage
is a "contract" to be entered into on the *state's* terms. Similarly,
where a state does allow cohabitative or prenuptial agreements, the
limits of such agreements are, of course, determined by the state,
and are rationalized as being about matters other than the exchange
of sexual services (and therefore comprise part of a legitimate conjugality). As we will see later, the chief mechanism for desexualizing
sex acts is to figure them as conjugal performatives.

From State Incursion into Private Life

The idea that cohabitation should be understood as a specifically
private ordering of relationships (and therefore ought to remain
exempt or free from the legislative grasp of the state) appears in
political, legal, and academic discourse. In the United Kingdom,
Michael Freeman and Christina Lyon (1983) argue that regulating
cohabitation forces rights and responsibilities on parties who may be
seeking, specifically, to reject those effects. Recognizing cohabitation in law, they assert, would constitute an unnecessary incursion
into private life. Similarly, when a bill to regulate cohabitation was
discussed in the New South Wales (NSW) parliament, politicians
swung between defending the properness and sanctity of certified
marriage and propounding people's right to do as they please *outside*
of certified wedlock (1984, 2492–493). The NSW bill was eventually passed as the *De Facto Relationships Act* (1984). Sarantakos
argues that with the advent of such legislation, the liberatory potential of cohabitation was obliterated. He opines, "When . . . the state
closed all options for freedom [by passing legislation on cohabita-
tion] the hope for liberating dyadic relationships through cohabitation was lost for ever: cohabitation ceased to be the liberated zone of
dyadic relationships that it [had been] for centuries" (1994, 158).
   There are problems with this view. In the first place, cohabitative
relationships have often been subject to historical regulation.
"Common-law marriage," for example, was well accepted in the

United States at the beginning of the twentieth century, and was treated in most cases as attracting precisely the same rights and obligations as certified marriage (Oldham 2001, 1410; Stein 1969). More importantly, if the personal does not exclude the political, and if lives are regulated through disciplinary ephemera as well as by laws and their police, there is little reason to assume that the absence of legislative regulation imputes or implies any necessary increase in freedom. The division of public and private levels of relationship (where—ostensibly—marriage is public and non-marriage is private) accomplishes little more than to attempt to underline an already problematic and unstable theoretical distinction. As Nikolas Rose has argued, it has been "in the name of public citizenship *and* private welfare [that] the family has been configured as a [regulatory technology]." If, as Rose suggests, "the agonistic relation between liberty and government is an intrinsic part of what we have come to know as freedom" (1996, 37), there is little to be gained in continuing, as Sarantakos does, to treat law and liberty as mutual antagonists. It is neither accurate nor useful, then, to suggest that cohabitation is "free" while certified marriage binds couples with historically sticky patriarchal tape.

NORMATIVE MARRIAGE: SIX DEGREES OF SEPARATION

It is sometimes suggested that cohabitation demands fewer obligations than certified marriage. For this and other reasons, people might deliberately elect to cohabit rather than merely fall under its legal purview. In this sense, cohabitation can be represented as a matter of choice and freedom. But as we have seen, choices regarding cohabitation are limited freedoms. Not just the terms of the contract but also the capacity to contract at all are tightly and sometimes paradoxically constrained. What's more, cohabitation can be a governmental ascription or interpellation as well as (or even despite) a couple's personal preference.

Cohabitation and certified marriage cannot properly be opposed or dichotomized against each other if both are constituted according to the same norms. As divorce reforms came into effect in the 1970s (and beyond), it became necessary to define exactly what constituted marital "breakdown" or "separation," since the means by which a divorce could be contested depended on proving that such breakdown had not occurred. Where no-fault grounds were deployed, "togetherness" had to be normatively defined in order to determine its absence. Such determinations included consideration as to whether parties continued to live together under the same roof, have sex with each other, offer each other "mutual society and protection" (including through the performance and division of household labor), or be interpellated by others as "husband and wife" (Parker et al. 1994, 410–14). The need to define marriage according to such normative criteria invites obvious comparisons between certified marriage and cohabitation. If the *absence* of consortium vitae evidenced the irretrievable breakdown of marriage, then surely the *presence* of such indicia points to the existence of marriage "in fact"—that is, cohabitation or "de facto marriage."

Indeed, indicia of certified and de facto marriage are often virtually identical. Thus, from the socio-legal point of view, cohabitation and certified marriage have come to resemble each other more and more. As Parker, Parkinson, and Behrens observe: "At the same time that unmarried cohabitation has had legal consequences conferred upon it, marriage itself has shed some of them. In practical terms, marriage and cohabitation look as if they are going to meet in the middle. Although marriage is a legal status and cohabitation is not, the results of living in either relationship do not differ greatly for some people" (1994, 299). Barrister George Cho likewise suggests that when we compare cohabitation and certified marriage, we see "a distinction without a difference." In many places, "those who live outside marriage have been given the same legal recognition as those who live together within it" (1991, 33). In his insistence that the two are distinct but not different, Cho argues that "cohabitation" and "certified marriage" are, in effect, different names for the same thing. Where law, legislation, and policy treat cohabitation and certified marriage as identical, the experience of couples in de facto relationships is likely to be very similar to those in certified marriage, but their discursive distinction remains meaningful. This suggests that there *are* differences between certified marriage and cohabitation, even if they are treated as equivalent for most purposes. However, pinpointing those differences and their effects is not as easy as it sounds.

So What's the Difference?

It has already been acknowledged that there may be qualitative differences in people's experience of cohabitation as distinct from certified marriage. Understandings of freedom, commitment, stability, and consent all play an important part in the social meanings of conjugality. But what differentiates cohabitation from certified marriage in public/political terms? The simplest answer is that marriage confers a status, while cohabitation does not (Oldham 2001, 1409). "Status" in this context means a person's legal position or classification. When we are asked on countless forms to check a box for "marital status," we are being asked, "What manner of conjugal subject are you?" Marital status is a matter of interest not just in people's ordinary interactions with each other, but also to the state. (That the root of both "status" and "state" is the same—from the Latin "to stand"—should come as no surprise.) Some of the subtler differences between certified marriage and cohabitation pertain to status.

Financial Support and the Cohabitation Rule

Cohabiting spouses are often said to have no obligation to support each other (though they are generally obliged to support any children they might have), and this situation is often contrasted with the obligation of certified spouses to provide each other mutual support (Oldham 2001, 1411). However, given that most if not all government welfare systems mobilize some version of "the cohabitation rule," the contention that there is no requirement for cohabiting spouses to support each other is debatable. Legal scholar Regina Graycar defines the cohabitation rule as the "shorthand expression which describes the . . . policy of treating unmarried people who live together as if they were a married couple," particularly with respect to social security and/or welfare entitlements (1987, 114). Among other effects, the cohabitation rule "results in the aggregation of a heterosexual couple's assets and/or income for the purpose of calculating rates of pension or benefit" (115). The rule has operated in slightly different ways historically, geographically, and socio-politically, but has been a typical feature of public welfare systems in the various jurisdictions considered in this book.[4] In light of this, it might be posited that, *ordinarily*, cohabiting spouses have no obligation to support each other, but it could be countered that any such obligation does not "ordinarily" arise. Rather, it comes into play only if one party to the relationship looks to the state rather than their partner for financial support. By the same token, in the ordinary course of affairs, a certified married couple might choose to keep their day-to-day financial affairs entirely separate—indeed, (in some places) they might enter into a specific agreement to do so. However, a married couple cannot agree that for the purposes of social security or taxation claims, they will not support each other. The couple's preference in such situations does not matter: the state insists that welfare is a resort for those whose partners cannot (rather than choose not to) support them.

"Opting In" Versus Undertow

An arguably more significant difference between certified and de facto marriage pertains to contract. Each category of conjugal relationship involves a different kind of state/couple relationship. Certified spouses "opt in": they accept, if you like, the state's invitation to become a particular kind of political subject. For cohabiting couples, it is almost the reverse. The state "accepts" or tolerates cohabitative relationships by regulating them. In this way—and perhaps in this way alone—cohabitation retains some vestige of political nonconformity, but it is a nonconformity nonetheless subject to state scrutiny and surveillance. A certified marriage remains a marriage so long as both spouses wish it, no matter how they organize their living arrangements. On the other hand, the existence or otherwise of a de facto marriage is subject to continuing measurement of a couple's behavior against a number of conjugal norms. This produces the ironic situation in which cohabitation can be understood to be regulated in a more detailed and comprehensive manner than certified marriage, prompting the kinds of objections to legislation on cohabitation voiced by Sarantakos, outlined earlier in the chapter.

Bigamy and Divorce

As we saw in Chapter 3, only one certified marriage at a time may be entered into by the same person. Bigamy remains criminal; unless an existing marriage is dissolved through death or divorce, any subsequent marriage is illegal. There are no such restrictions on parties to a de facto marriage. Similarly, while there are restrictions concerning relatedness and other matters pertaining to who can marry whom, legislation on cohabitation tends not to specify prohibited degrees of affinity (and so on).[5] This means that while a certified married spouse is prohibited from marrying a second time (until or unless the existing marriage is dissolved), there is nothing to prevent that spouse from entering into a new or additional cohabitative relationship. Nor is there any restriction on how many de facto relationships a person might enter into simultaneously. However, given that the normative indicia of cohabitation include "living together" under one roof, it could be difficult for a person to sustain more than one de facto relationship at a time, except in the unlikely event that the dual spouses were aware of and willing to live with each other. Conversely, there is no expectation that in order to remain married, certified spouses must live together under one roof. Certified spouses are permitted to live in separate residences—or even in different countries—without bringing their marriage into question, even as separation remains key evidence of any marital breakdown.

Marriage Without Weddings

All of these sometimes subtle considerations point to one overarching difference between certified and de facto marriage, a difference relating to the manner in which the status of marriage is conferred. What distinguishes cohabitative from certified conjugality is precisely that certified (or "registered') conjugal relationships require a conscious moment of enactment—a point at which one signs a paper or kisses the bride. There is no ceremony or certificate of cohabitation, and even if cohabitants were to mark their relationship with some kind of ceremony, this would not ordinarily attract the attention of state authorities.[6] Thus, the sometimes cumulative or accidental nature of cohabitation becomes apparent. "Moving in" together might never even be proposed as such: where one person spends the night with another more and more frequently, for example, at what point can they be said to be "cohabiting"? What constitutes "moving in," anyway? Keeping a toothbrush in the bathroom? Storing clothes in a wardrobe rather than a suitcase? Sharing the cost of food? Doing laundry together? If one cohabitant does not entirely relinquish their own household (but sublets, perhaps), can we say that the two have "joint" household interests? Cohabitants might celebrate their relationship by making vows to each other, they might even seek the support of a community of family and friends to sustain their relationship, but only in certified marriage is conjugal status conferred through certification or registration.

The relationship between wedding and marriage, though conspicuous and direct, is rarely theorized. Dale Spender (1994) argues that the historical connection between weddings and marriage has been completely, happily severed. Women, she says, might have any number of weddings without subscribing to the historical subjection of wifehood. Indeed, the idea that weddings are something very much apart from marriage seems to dominate current thinking. As a topic of research in and of itself, the study of weddings is routinely differentiated from research on marriage (Howard 2006; Otnes and Pleck 2003; Freeman 2002; Ingraham 1999). Vicki Howard, for example, traces the history of what she calls the wedding industry— from costumes and rings to bridal magazines and wedding planners (2006). Her approach focuses on the production of "expert" advice and the popularization of the consumable white wedding. Dawn H. Currie (1993) undertakes a similar endeavor employing different means. Using interview data with contemporary brides, Currie makes the marvelously ironic observation that the division of labor in planning a wedding thoroughly contrasts with the symbolism of the wedding ceremony, yet manages somehow not to compromise, for brides, the significance of that symbolism.

Artifacts of wedding such as invitations, rings, and cakes form a relatively small but important element of marriage research; these kinds of analyses usually focus on the symbolic weight such artifacts bear. Jaclyn Geller's (1999) examination of wedding invitations, for example, positions them as part of a wider discourse of marriage. In Carol Wilson's brief history of wedding cakes, she notes the many ways that the cake has "represented" or symbolized marriage. (That such symbolism is literally consumed—incorporated, if you like— offers a particularly delicious parallel to marriage's corporeal hold.) "Today," she concludes, "there are practically no rules about wedding cakes" (Wilson 2005, 72; see also Charsley 1993). Perhaps the most ambitious reach in recent wedding studies is Cele Otnes and Elizabeth Pleck's (2003) *Cinderella Dreams*. As its title suggests, the authors consider all manner of wedding-related phenomena and paraphernalia, arguing that today's brides seek "to experience unabashed magic in their lives" (2003, 279). Adopting a stance that neither celebrates nor condemns women's enthusiasm for weddings, Pleck and Otnes steadfastly resist connecting weddings and marriage, seeing weddings instead as a kind of "floating signifier" (2006, 124). This suits their task, and produces a wealth of fine scholarship. What interests me in the present context, however, is the frequency with which Otnes and Pleck, along with their informants and sources, appeal to the *magic* of weddings.

The wedding ceremony is most obviously understood as an initiating event offering entry into a new, institutionally-figured status and subjectivity. As we saw in Chapter 3, weddings are fundamentally and thoroughly performative. As such, a raft of conventions underpins and facilitates their performative effects. While these conventions are easily identified and explored, the political subjectivities of wedding and the nature of transformation any (valid) wedding accomplishes are harder to discern. Elizabeth Freeman's (2002) account of the cultural/literary shape and meaning of weddings (again) explicitly disconnects weddings from marriage, yet in the end produces a theoretically sophisticated analysis of their relationship. In considering weddings as fantasies of transformation and occasions for pageantry, Freeman's account suggests that weddings can be reclaimed, even as the historically dominant "institution" of marriage is repudiated. Freeman's book begins (almost in spite of itself) to explain the historical and contemporary relationship between wedding and marriage. This important research goes some way toward showing that, just as laws concerning the validity of wedding ceremonies form part of the raft of conventions supporting and enabling the performatives of marriage, the symbolic artifacts of wedding likewise form part of conjugality's performative backdrop. They are, in a sense, the sparks and smoke accompanying the magician's "Abracadabra," they are the sequins and stage makeup priming us for the performative magic to which we will bear witness. Despite a welcome flurry of new research on weddings (including Boden 2003 and Montemurro 2006), the work of comparing and drawing together the kinds of subjectivities produced in weddings and marriages—that is, the subjective movement from bride to wife and groom to husband—remains unfinished and, in my opinion, urgent. If weddings are a scene of fantasy and magic, what differentiates the subject who embraces such fantasy from the subject whose understanding of marriage is (arguably) more normative?

Some might disagree with the primacy I afford to weddings as the mark distinguishing cohabitation from certified marriage. The introduction of new provisions, in some jurisdictions, for "civil unions" or "registered partnerships" has seen these new arrangements treated by many commentators as varieties of cohabitation rather than certified marriage. I would argue, however, that their performative structures and effects constitute them as "certified" rather than as "de facto" marriage, albeit in a "marked" (and thus inherently subordinate) form. Civil unions and other forms of registered partnership are brought into being with conscious speech acts or discursive performatives: they are signed, sealed, and witnessed and are a form of certified rather than normative or presumptive marriage.

I would also insist, however, that *all* of these forms of relationship—cohabitation, certified marriage, civil unions, domestic partnerships, and so on—should be understood as forms of marriage (or, less ambiguously, *conjugality*). Whether performatively enacted or not, all are conjugal relationships. To treat them otherwise—to treat "civil unions" and "registered partnerships" as varieties of "not-marriage"—is to reinstate the false primacy of "marriage." The effect of such reinstatement is to iterate the distinction between (traditional, heterosexual, certified) "marriage" versus "not-marriage" (namely, anything other than traditional, heterosexual, certified marriage) as the only categorization that matters. If we think about what is happening in terms of the state's response to and interest in intimate relationships, "civil unions" and "registered partnerships" are clearly better understood as "certified marriage" and not cohabitation.[7] Certified marriage confers status in the same way that citizenship does—namely, as a politically preferred subjectivity established performatively.

My view, then, is that in order to understand the political distinction between cohabitation and certified marriage, we need to consider two related aspects of conjugality and its regulation. First and most obviously, we need to theorize the relationship between marriage's performative utterances and the constitution of conjugal-political subjectivities. Secondly, we need to examine the proximate similarity of cohabitation and certified marriage against the social-governmental insistence that they are (discursively, "properly") distinct. The thinker whose work offers obvious avenues of exploration in both these regards is, of course, Judith Butler.

SIMULATION, SPEECH ACTS, AND SEX ACTS

Butler's most enduring contribution to social theory is her account of gender performativity (as outlined in Chapters 2 and 3). For Butler, performing or "doing" gender produces that which it names; *performing* gender *produces* gender. Butler is often accused of being too abstract. It is certainly true that her writing is densely philosophical and can seem removed from reality. But if we bring Butler's ideas into an analysis of conjugality, something very interesting happens: we can begin to see cohabitation as a *performance* of marriage. We know that performative speech acts (the vows and declarations of wedding) and performative sex acts (consummation and so on) play a crucial role in the establishment and reestablishment of certified marriage. But where the continuing existence of marriage is constructed normatively—that is, against a number of typically mundane indicia—conjugality can be understood to be *entirely* performative. That is, if marriage is maintained through norms of togetherness such as sharing an address, having sex, dividing household labor, and socializing as a couple, then one's coherence as a "married" subject—a spouse—inheres in the very act of washing the dishes, kissing, paying a bill, or receiving a joint invitation. Conjugality shifts from being premised on the "special" kinds of performative analyzed by J. L. Austin to the repetitive, cumulative, everyday performatives theorized by Butler. The rise and regulation of cohabitation means that marriage is now brought into being as it is performed; the performance of conjugality brings "marriage" into continued being. What, then, of the specifically sexual performatives identified in Chapters 3 and 4?

We saw, in the operations of consummation, adultery, and condonation, how sex acts could have explicitly performative effects. Cohabitative sex acts do not necessarily connote the same degree of "Abracadabra" transformation, but are performative nonetheless. In Social Security tests pertaining to the cohabitation rule, for example, sex figures more prominently than any other indicator of conjugality, and takes on precisely the kind of iterative weight theorized by Butler as (routinely) performative. In Australia, the body charged with deciding appeals regarding the cohabitation rule is the Social Security Appeals Tribunal. In 1982, the tribunal noted that "to date, there has been no instance where a woman living under the same roof as, and enjoying a sexual relationship of a continuing nature with [to the apparent exclusion of others] a man, has been held *not* in the particular circumstances, to be "living with a man as his wife" (*Tozer v. DSS* 1982, 99).

Taking Australian decisions reported by the appeals tribunal as cases in point, it seems that so long as a mutually exclusive sexual relationship has existed between a couple *at some time*, and as long as that relationship has not been supplanted by a *new* sexual relationship, a de facto relationship will generally be understood to exist. In one case, a couple who insisted that they had not had sex with each other for almost twenty years were nevertheless deemed to be in a de facto relationship (*Hucker v. DSS* 1992, 935–36). Similarly, another couple deemed to be in a de facto relationship had slept in separate bedrooms and forsaken sexual relations with each other for the previous thirteen years (*Gray v. DSS* 1992, 1009).

However, where a couple has *never* had sex with each other, a de facto relationship is unlikely to be understood to exist, despite other evidence to the contrary. For example, a woman appealing a decision to cancel her widow's pension under the cohabitation rule offered evidence to the tribunal that the man with whom she was living was in fact homosexual (*Wieland v. DSS* 1993, 1108). The tribunal noted that the man had named the woman as his dependent spouse on tax returns, and the couple had applied jointly for a home loan. They referred to themselves as "Mr. and Mrs.," and lived together in a caravan. Despite their very intimate living arrangements, their shared expenses, and provision for each other—he went to the local pub most nights and she left his dinner in the oven—the tribunal determined that the two could not be understood to be in a de facto relationship because they had never had sex and probably never would. Even in cohabitative relationships, then, sex acts continue to produce performative effects.

Simulating Marriage?

Where certified marriage and cohabitation share a set of normative indicia, cohabitation can appear to be a copy or imitation of certified marriage. The popular characterization of cohabitation as "trial marriage" suggests this, too. If cohabitants are not married with the certification of the state but are treated as "married"—that is, *as if* they are married—what ramifications do those quotation marks discursively impute?[8] One way to address this question might be to consider whether cohabitation *simulates* marriage.

In his 1981 essay "Simulacra and Simulations," Jean Baudrillard speculates on what he sees as the no longer tenable relationship between objects and their representations, the real and its imitations. Baudrillard is a cultural theorist: his primary interests are located in the world of commodities and consumption, objects and representations. His work is provocative, to say the least, and is rarely (if ever) put to the kinds of purposes I propose to explore here. More often, the kinds of representational fields subject to Baudrillardean analysis are "cultural" in the sense that art and other creative artifacts are cultural, and where "representation" is constituted in imagery and visual projections more than words. The more appropriate question on marriage, for Baudrillard and his commentators, might be whether "reality" television programs like "The Bachelor" or "American Princess" (internationally syndicated shows featuring contestants vying for a real-life marriage proposal from a "genuine" Prince Charming) constitute a form of hyperreal marriage.[9] Such an inquiry might yield interesting responses, but it is not strictly relevant here. The representational field forming the main focus of this book is law and its political supports. My concern is not with the intelligibility of cultural systems of representation and consumption as such, but whether it may be useful in this instance to conceive of cohabitation as a kind of simulated marriage.

Baudrillard opens his 1981 essay on simulacra and simulations with a tale about cartographers drawing "a map so detailed that it ends up exactly covering the territory" (1988, 166). The map is a *simulacrum* of the territory. To analogize: indicia of cohabitation "map" marriage, whose contours range from the organization of laundry to the names on title deeds, to the kinds of personal photographs displayed on a mantelpiece. Baudrillard continues, "Abstraction today is no longer that of the map, the double, the mirror or the concept. Simulation is no longer that of a territory, a referential being or a substance. It is the generation by models of a real without origin or reality: a hyperreal. The territory no longer precedes the map, nor survives it. Henceforth, it is the map that engenders the territory" (167). Certified marriage does not use the normative indicia of marriage described earlier except to determine their absence (and thus a dissoluble, irretrievably broken down union). It is entirely plausible to suggest that the territory of marriage neither precedes nor survives the mapping of its indicia. The map (cohabitation) now engenders the territory (marriage).

Baudrillard brings his consideration of the cartographers' tale to an end with a grieving, almost nihilistic ruefulness:

> But it is no longer a question of either maps or territory. Something has disappeared: the sovereign difference between them that was the abstraction's charm. For it is the difference which forms the poetry of

the map and the charm of the territory, the magic of the concept and
the charm of the real.

> . . . The real . . . is nothing more than operational. In fact, since
> it is no longer enveloped by an imaginary, it is no longer real at all.
> (Baudrillard 1988, 166–67)

This note of mourning seems to be echoed rather precisely by scholars of cohabitation like Sarantakos, who grieves for what he sees as its
lost liberatory potential. Sarantakos, after all, is not bemoaning the
loss of the real (that is, the diminution or devaluation of certified
marriage), but rather the charm of cohabitation as distinct from the
"real" (marriage).

For Baudrillard, simulation is not merely pretense. A person
might pretend to be ill, he says, but someone simulating an illness
actually produces symptoms of that illness. In this way, "simulation
threatens the difference between 'true' and 'false,' between 'real'
and 'imaginary'" (1988, 171). In the same way, cohabitants do not
merely *pretend* marriage, but produce its symptoms, enact its norms.
Butler (1991) suggests that a similar process establishes and re-
establishes a (mythical) origin for "gender." In *Gender Trouble*, she
posits that gender performatives create an illusion of something
more solid. Heavily gendered acts (like crying over a romantic movie
or wearing eye shadow) are mistakenly thought to merely *reflect* or
express some underlying source of femininity. Butler's argument is
that it is the performative references themselves that *produce* the idea
of an "original" source for gender. Gender is not merely expressed
or revealed, then, but actively creates the very divisions and differences it is said to reflect. Gender is, in effect, a simulation with no
"original" referent; it is a baseless simulation.

Combining Butler's analysis of performativity with Baudrillard's
theory of simulation, we can begin to understand conjugal performatives as similarly baseless. If we adopt such a view, neither cohabitation nor certified marriage can be understood as essentially better
(or more liberated, or more repressive) than the other. Certified
marriage and cohabitation constitute performances whose steps and
rhythms are more or less identical. One is biopolitically registered,
the other is not. One is brought into being, in the first instance, with
explicit, instantly transformative speech acts (and sex acts), while the

other tends to congeal as "marriage" over time. But neither is more or less authentic than the other.

If cohabitative and certified marriage entail different kinds of couple-state relationship, the difference is (arguably) subtle. The subject who enters a certified marriage is a subject who promises: a subject endowed with the capacity to produce explicit performative utterances and acts. This subject is, I would argue, characterized less by its proprietary selfhood (as Carole Pateman's [1988] work suggests) and more by its correspondence with a mode of government characterized by rules, laws, and prohibitions. Cohabitant subjects—who do not promise, but whose conduct solidifies as marriage—are subjects better matched to a more governmental style of regulation. If both have become subject to highly self-regulatory, norm-based regimes, perhaps this indicates a shift in the exercise of political as much as conjugal power.

NOT LIMPING, DANCING?

If we understand cohabitation and certified marriage as different regulatory approaches to conjugality rather than as different orders of love or intimacy, a new picture of their significance emerges. Cohabitation as opposed to certified marriage is neither more nor less liberating for women. Rather, the very positioning of cohabitation as something other than marriage brings this "contrast" into being. In that cohabitation is in most places no longer the heavily sexualized zone it once was, its regulation situates cohabiting spouses more or less identically to certified spouses. However, in that certified marriage has itself become increasingly defined according to a range of normative indicia rather than through the transformative fiat of wedding, it is reasonable to suggest that certified marriage simulates cohabitation. Ironically, however, these indicia are referents for regulating certified marriage only in ascertaining their absence. That is, where no-fault provisions govern divorce, the *absence* of indicia of "togetherness" suggests that a marriage has, in fact, broken down. The irony lies in the counter-intuitive but logical progression. Certified marriage is, in itself, a more flexible regulatory construction than cohabitation. The contents of any valid marriage—the corporeal norms and behaviors adopted by those who wed successfully—are not subject to scrutiny in the same way that cohabiting couples can be. It is this uncertainty—the less than assured step with which cohabitants move in the regulatory arena— that keeps cohabitation at the limits of conjugality, simultaneously "like-marriage" and "not-marriage."

CHAPTER 8

QUEER PROPOSITIONS:
SEX AND SEXUALITIES

Until recently, conjugality—in all its regulatory forms—needed homosexuality only as a foil. Gay and lesbian people sometimes accommodated themselves in the available structures by shaping their relationships to "pass" as straight, or by unhappily conforming to marriage norms in other ways. Many, at least in recent times, have found ways to live outside of marriage, and as such are not alone. As we saw in Chapter 3, historically, transsexuals and intersexual people have also been barred from entry to marriage (along with "epileptics" and "lunatics," among others). While such people were prohibited, in effect, from ever trying to enter conjugal territory, others were routinely deported from within it for failing to meet various standards of matrimonial civility—drunkards, criminals, and adulterers, for example. It could be argued that a need to reject the objectionable company kept by gay and lesbian people outside the matrimonial gates has outweighed the questionable desirability of the destination on the other side. Most of these excluded others could, of course, reenter after a time, and in most places are no longer restricted at all. Similarly, while cohabitants also dwell beyond certified marriage, they are nonetheless situated at its edges, and can, if they choose, enter at any time. For many gay and lesbian couples, then, access to marriage is doubly desirous.

If the simple fact of exclusion from something characterized as productive and decent were not sufficient in and of itself to justify queer disquiet, the effects of that exclusion have been manifestly unjust and for some, disastrous. A number of problems arise when lesbian and gay relationships are not accorded any legal recognition. These include matters relating to the injury, illness, or death of a spouse; matters arising when a relationship ends; aspects of criminal law; financial issues; and matters relating to parenthood.

THE RECOGNITION AND PRIVILEGES OF MARRIAGE

Some financial arrangements such as joint ownership arrangements, access to health and other insurance benefits, and welfare and taxation policies privilege marital relationships. Other areas of privilege include concessions attaching to criminal proceedings, immigration laws, and laws pertaining to the adoption and custody of children. Especially relevant are those rights each spouse acquires through marriage to act for the other in matters related to illness and death: hospital visitation, decisions concerning the cessation of medical treatment, and funeral and testatory arrangements. As Jill Sandell has observed, "In the context of AIDS, gay men (and, to a lesser extent, lesbians) vowing 'til death do us part' clearly has its own particular, and poignant, set of meanings" (Sandell 1994, 7; see also Butler 2000). Such matters have been detailed extensively elsewhere (Wolfson 2004; Chambers 1996), and it is not my intention to rehearse them here, especially while the legal situation in various places remains in flux. Indeed, the very currency of controversies marking the recognition and regulation of gay and lesbian relationships make it a difficult matter to address.

Already, debates on same-sex marriage have covered a vast terrain using a variety of vehicles. Some have advanced the case for same-sex marriage by highlighting its historical precedents (Boswell 1994; Eskridge 1996). Others have shown how non-western cultures have allowed and respected "irregular" sex/gender arrangements.[1] Yet another line of argument concerns scriptural and other religious aspects of marriage and sexuality (Boswell 1980, Grammick 1989). Though loudest in the United States, demands for same-sex marriage are circulating in various parts of the world in somewhat similar ways. Same-sex marriage is seen as deeply provocative, and speculation as to its potential effects varies widely. The legal and social debate is not simply between those who favor the introduction of same-sex marriage versus those opposed: diverse rationales and defenses have emerged even from within each camp. Opponents of same-sex marriage include, for example, "family-values" conservatives who fear same-sex marriage has the potential to corrupt society, *and* some lesbian feminists who decry marriage as a tool of heteronormative, patriarchal assimilation. Unstable alliances are strewn on both sides of the debate, situating same-sex marriage as an urgent matter whose consequences are unpredictable. In keeping with the themes of this book as a whole, my interest lies in the political, regulatory aspects of the call to legalize gay and lesbian marriage—and particularly in the discursive tensions and contests operating in differing conceptions of how marriage is or should be constituted.

Some jurisdictions have enacted new legislation recognizing same-sex relationships (not always as "marriage" but generally as some form of conjugal relationship); some have tried to insulate or "protect" marriage as an exclusively heterosexual fixture. These responses are not mutually exclusive: in some places, both have occurred. In such a volatile social and legal domain, canvassing all the relevant rules and debates across many and various jurisdictions would require several books and would, in any case, risk rapid obsolescence. In this chapter, therefore, my aim is more modest. I want to identify some of the issues underlying debates about same-sex marriage and consider these in relation to the trajectory of conjugality presented so far. To this end, this chapter will explore the regulatory consequences of excluding/including gay and lesbian couples from the arena of conjugality, focusing on the theoretical motifs used throughout this book: government, corporeality, and performativity.

In the vast and expanding literature on what is generally referred to as "same-sex marriage," there are two main threads of debate. Against the inevitably homophobic "defense" of marriage from any non-heterosexual incursion, some argue for certified marriage to be extended to gay and lesbian couples, contending that same-sex couples should be able to enter certified marriage as "wife and wife" or "husband and husband." This position tends to be represented, somewhat misleadingly, as the dominant homosexual view. Others argue that marriage is an inappropriate vehicle for the regulation of gay and lesbian relationships and that alternatives (including "domestic partnerships" or "civil unions" legislation) should be explored. In some ways, these debates echo the different feminist critiques of marriage outlined in Chapter 2: some see marriage as heterosexist but reformable, others see marriage as an institution whose primary purpose is to proliferate heterosexist norms. My view here, as in Chapter 2, is that framing the debate in this way limits our understanding. A more complex and complete picture emerges when we consider the issue as a problem of government.

RELATIONS OF GOVERNMENT

By now, it is well established that marriage does not merely offer a generalized frame for the particular relationship of spouses to each other. As Nancy Cott (2000) and others have so clearly demonstrated, marriage involves a relationship not just between husband-and-wife pairs, but also between governments and populations, states and subjects. Thus, where marriage is exclusive to heterosexual couples, it does more than simply discriminate against homosexual couples in otherwise identical circumstances. Where marriage is defined through its very exclusion of certain kinds of couples, such discrimination *is* marriage—marking certain kinds of union as lawful and preferred is the very work marriage does.

This is nowhere more evident than in heteroconservative "defenses" of marriage. In the United States and Australia, for example, governments have moved legislation aiming to "protect" marriage from homosexual invasion. In the United States, the Bill Clinton administration enacted the *Defense of Marriage Act* in 1996. Here, marriage is governed on a state by state basis, and each state is bound to recognize as lawful any valid marriage entered into in another state. As Hawaii teetered toward allowing gay and lesbian couples to marry (on the grounds that the exclusion of gay and lesbian couples amounts to sex discrimination), the federal government moved to prevent gay and lesbian marriages contracted in Hawaii from being valid anywhere else. The *Defense of Marriage Act* also specified that "marriage" in any federal law would mean "a person of the opposite-sex who is a husband or wife" (s. 3 [a]; as cited by Feldblum 2001, 61). In Australia, the John Howard government amended the Australian *Marriage Act* (1961) to reassert the axiomatic (but nowhere explicit) requirement that marriage be the union of "one man and one woman."

Attempts to fortify marriage in this way speak to the kinds of homophobic panic epitomized by commentators like Robert Knight and James Q. Wilson, who argue that marriage is and must remain exclusively heterosexual in the service of its social function. This function is no less than to sustain society, "the family," and decency itself, a task of mythical proportions (in both senses of the word). Moreover, the heterosexual imperative of marriage is defended as natural and proper—as necessarily conducive to a productive and stable polity. Once again, however, the precise role of marriage as a bastion of civilization is assumed rather than explained. Knight asserts that "[s]elf-governing people require a robust culture founded on marriage and family, which nurture the qualities that permit self-rule: deferred gratification, self-sacrifice, respect for kinship and law, and property rights. These qualities are founded upon sexual restraint" (1997, 117). Exactly what Knight means by "self-government" and "self-rule" is not clear. (The possibility that he means to invoke liberal democratic rule and its characteristic demand for self-regulatory subjects in the governmental sense seems unlikely.) The idea that marriage is a (pre-political) *foundation* of society, however, is a motif recurring not just in Knight's work but across a range of competing views (Eskridge 1996, 132; Calhoun 2000). Bonding between intimates might be a defining feature of humanness, however, it should not to be confused with marriage itself, which can never be "pre-political" (or even "natural"), given that it demands and constructs a relationship between a governing authority (whether church, state, or another body) and couple. The "nature" of marriage, if such a nature exists, is inevitably social and political as well as personal.

The substance of heteroconservative defenses of marriage is to reiterate marriage as the domain of exclusively heterosexual decency. It seems to be irrefutable that marriage has, in fact, worked historically to accomplish homosexual stigmatization and subordination. William Eskridge (1996) argues a more complex case. In *The Case for Same-Sex Marriage* he presents a "hidden history" of same-sex unions. His aim is to familiarize homosexuality in several senses: first, to allay the shock of the new; and second, to demonstrate the historical capacity of same-sex attracted people to form socially acceptable partnerships and families. While the first is an arguably noble rationale, and the second offers useful parallels, Eskridge's contention that the "one man, one woman" rule has been routinely and successfully breached in the past (or in other cultures) misses the point. After all, it is precisely at the site of the kinds of sex/gender arrangements surveyed by Eskridge that marriage's "normal" sex/gender requirements have been policed and reinscribed (Warner 1999; Halley 2001, 100). In each of his examples of historically or cross-culturally valued same-sex relationships, the relationship in question is heavily gendered. In the Native American *berdache* tradition, for example, it seems that a man might (occasionally and exceptionally) be a "wife," but must assume the typical social place of a woman. For the purposes of marriage regulation, in fact, he *is* a woman, or is treated, at the very least, *as if* he were a woman. The very limited parallel this offers to contemporary gay and lesbian couples is obvious. Will gay and lesbian couples rush to marry where one spouse must "be the wife"? Nowhere in Eskridge's illustrations are there cases of two similarly positioned men or two similarly positioned women marrying just as men and women marry. Rather, a woman "passes" as a husband, a man "passes" as a wife, or a relationship is treated as *something like* a marriage.[2]

"Moral Consummation": Marriage as a Desexualizing Zone

Eskridge is one of the more prominent advocates of same-sex marriage (as certified marriage), as is Andrew Sullivan (1996, 1997), a columnist and former editor of the conservative magazine *New Republic*. Both men see marriage itself as an essentially benign (or better-than-benign) institution in which gay men and women might find forms of social justice and personal respect otherwise denied. Cheshire Calhoun's view is pertinent here. She maintains that "the greatest defect in arguments that defend same-sex marriage by appealing to a moral conception of marriage is that they ignore the connection between marriage bars and the system of heterosexual domination" (2000, 115). This omission allows Sullivan to claim that broadening marriage's scope would not demolish or downgrade the heterosexual marriage stakes. Instead, he argues that heterosexual marriage would remain largely unaffected should same-sex marriage become available. This argument has been echoed by many others: the legalization of same-sex marriage would not succeed as a queer invasion of the heterosexual fortress; the structure of marriage would stand impervious because the infiltration would be small and readily assimilated. Such views reflect an understandable desire for access to the zone of desexualization marriage has historically offered.

It might seem counter-intuitive to describe marriage as a *desexualized* zone, for (as we saw in Chapters 3 and 4) it is precisely concerned with sex acts and their meanings. But observe how marriage is described by commentators on same-sex marriage. Evan Wolfson (another key voice in the American debate) describes marriage as a "relationship of *emotional and financial* commitment and interdependence" (1994, 579; my emphasis). Similarly, Sullivan characterizes marriage as "an *emotional, financial, and psychological* bond between two people" (1996, 179; my emphasis). The conspicuously absent term in both definitions is "sexual." Sullivan argues that that "every right and responsibility that heterosexuals enjoy as public citizens [should] be extended to those who grow up and find themselves *emotionally different*" (171; my emphasis). The difference between gay and straight people is characterized here as "emotional." More worryingly, Sullivan describes those gay and lesbian people supporting a different and more radical project than his own as engaged in an "*orgy* of smashing" (90; my emphasis). In describing queer voices in this way, Sullivan seems to replicate the kinds of sexualizing tactics (Calhoun 2000, 83) more often used by his heteroconservative opponents, even as he rejects the effects of such sexualization for himself. On the other side of the debate, heteroconservatives also tend to downplay the place sex occupies in marriage. Knight defines marriage as a "*social, legal and spiritual* bonding*," (1997, 115; my emphasis). Marriage, for Knight, is founded on "sexual restraint," not sexual compatibility or pleasure (117). Wilson contrasts what he calls the "moral consummation" of heterosex (as marital sex) versus the "pure utility or pleasure alone" of homosex (1997, 140). In all of these men's accounts, the possibility that marriage might be a fundamentally sexual relationship is disavowed or downplayed. Instead, the sexual relationship of spouses seems to be displaced as it is elevated.

In this sense, then, marriage is a zone of desexualization. For those subjects routinely overdetermined by their sexuality—including, historically, girls and young women, black people, people of color, bisexual, transsexual, and gay and lesbian people—marriage might promise a very attractive kind of refuge. Indeed, as Calhoun observes, it is precisely this desexualized zone that facilitates the safe public expression of (ostensibly private) heterosexuality (2000, 83). Some arguments for same-sex marriage, then, are best understood as rejecting the subordinating sexualization of gay and lesbian people. However, because this sexualization of gay and lesbian people is (in part) an effect of marriage itself, framing the right to marry as an exercise in equal treatment invites a kind of discursive crisis over marriage.

LOVING and the Right to Marry

Rather than entering into this discursive crisis, many advocates of same-sex marriage characterize their struggle as the demand for a withheld right. Many have seized the repeal of American anti-miscegenation laws as an analogous precedent for lifting the ban on same-sex marriage. Underscoring the importance of judicial rather than legislative precedents in such debates, the 1967 case of *Loving v. Virginia* is cited again and again.[3] As we saw in Chapter 5, this decision overturned the state of Virginia's anti-miscegenation law and ruled that Mr. and Mrs. Lovings' interracial marriage be recognized as lawful. The decision established, in the United States, something like a constitutional guarantee for marriage. Claiming the "right to marry," then, is a characteristically American strategy (Richards 2001, 27). I have already suggested why the "race analogy" might be troublesome, but several aspects of the comparison warrant review.

First, it should be remembered that while white feminists have in the past analogized sexism and racism (including, sometimes, marriage to slavery), such analogies are nowadays considered troublesome, not least because of their tendency to posit the experience of white women as universal. As Shane Phelan observes: "Historically, white feminists in the US have articulated their oppression along lines borrowed from movements of racial liberation. In so doing, they have sometimes failed to explore the particulars of white women's oppression as such, instead linking prematurely to frameworks developed in other struggles" (1997, 88).

While rejecting any straightforward comparison of either feminist or lesbian experience to the experience of racism, Phelan develops Gloria Anzaldúa's understanding of *mestiza* history and consciousness. Drawing on the strength and courage of cultures surviving colonization and its heavily gendered consequences, Phelan suggests that the "distinctive feature of the [American] Southwest is the survival of indigenous people as distinct peoples, and simultaneously as mixtures, as living history of rapes and slaughters and loves and memories" (82). For Phelan, then, the possibility of a partial analogy between homophobia, sexism, and racism speaks to both separate and interrelated oppressions.

In this limited and careful way, it is possible to identify some of the ways that different orders of oppression share tactics. Foucault's observation that homosexual people are subject to subordinating sexual overdetermination is germane here. In the same way that the very being of "the homosexual" is entirely saturated with the "truth" of sexuality, so sexualization has been deployed to construct black and other people of color as excessively, indecently, improperly desiring/desirable. The double (or even triple) sexualization of black lesbians along axes of sexism, racism, and homophobia invites the possibility of solidarity across these categories. However, even though both racism and homophobia mobilize sexualizing tactics, the demand for gay and lesbian access to marriage is not analogous to the repeal of anti-miscegenation laws.

As noted in Chapter 5, establishing the right to marry white people was never high on the civil rights agenda. Kevin Mumford explains that "the relationship of racism to miscegenation prohibitions differs categorically from the relationship of homophobia to the various manifestations of the defense of marriage movement" (2005, 526–27). Moreover, as the Australian case of Gladys and Mick Daly shows, the regulation of "mixed-race" marriage is often more complex than its typical representation as the triumph of love over adversity suggests. In Australia, permission for the marriage of (Indigenous) Gladys to (non-Indigenous) Mick was premised on the contention that it was desirable for Gladys's Aboriginality to be "bred out." The marriage of this Indigenous woman to a white man was popularly celebrated as a fast lane to assimilation, where assimilation meant, in fact, the erasure and annihilation of Indigenous peoples and cultures. Whether in the United States or elsewhere, then, "we do not need this [ethnic] analogy to argue for [gay and lesbian] civil rights. If we do not need the ethnic paradigm for civil rights, and given its dangers of cultural nationalism and essentialism, then we can and should dispense with it" (Phelan 1997, 82).

For all these reasons, analogizing same-sex marriage prohibition to the historical ban of certain interracial marriages should be avoided.

A Rose by Any Other Name . . .

In my view, a more fundamental problem in the same-sex marriage debates involves not the granting of rights but a more literal war of words. The most interesting and difficult heteronormative objection to same-sex marriage is definitional. According to Knight,

> to describe . . . [same-sex] relationships as "marriage" destroys the definition of marriage altogether. When the meaning of a word becomes more inclusive, the exclusivity that it previously defined is lost.

> [I]f "marriage" . . . ceases to be the term used solely for the social, legal and spiritual bonding of a man and a woman, the term "marriage" becomes useless. (Knight 1997, 114–15)

This definitional defense of heterosexual marriage is difficult to counter because its silences are so often excused from analysis. However, this is not the first time that efforts have been made to maintain the discursive bounds of marriage by allowing other kinds of marriage-like relationship only so long as these are called by another name. O. R. McGregor describes a pamphlet issued by the (British) Mothers' Union in the 1950s. The mothers argued that "continued use of the word 'marriage' to describe second marriages after divorce is an illogical abuse of language. If the second union could be called by some such term as legal concubinage much of the difficulty would disappear" (1957, 109–10).[4] Heteroconservative anxiety around marriage and its "insufficiently" protected borders exposes itself as plainly, materially—even *corporeally*—discursive. As such, it begs a number of difficult questions, to which I will return in due course.

COMING BACK TO THE BODY

A corollary to the sexualizing/desexualizing defense of marriage is its characterization, by those who would maintain marriage's heterosexual exclusivity, as not only morally productive, but also fundamentally procreative. Wilson, for example, makes the risible claim that "without [marriage], the newborn infant is unlikely to survive or, if he survives, to prosper" (1997, 140). Of course the children of unmarried parents *do* survive, and prosper or languish depending on (or even despite) a range of personal and social factors.

Even if marriage were to be understood as normally or desirably procreative, this would not in itself exclude gay and lesbian couples. Children born to a marriage are ordinarily and automatically assumed to be children of the wife and husband. That this is not always a genetically accurate reflection of the child's parentage seems not to have mattered to the coherence of marriage as an "institution." Why then should the genetic parentage of children born to gay or lesbian couples matter any more or less? Indeed, to claim, as many do, that homosex is inevitably non-procreative is misguided. The production of sperm for donation, or the process of insemination, for example, is not necessarily solitary, medicalized activities. If a range of sex acts (apart from the *vera copula* of husband and wife) can be understood as loving and productive, the objection that gay and lesbian marriage is problematically non-reproductive cannot be sustained.

Most telling of all, many children of gay fathers or lesbian mothers are, in fact, the "legitimate" offspring of a valid marriage. Where wives or husbands leave a valid marriage and subsequently enter into lesbian or gay relationships, can their (existing) children be characterized as any less "naturally" conceived than any other child? That the children of lesbian mothers or gay fathers can be left in legal limbo relative to other children whose parents form new conjugal relationships speaks to the fiction of marriage's supposedly procreative ends. After all, do straight fathers and mothers make acceptable parents only so long as their children are conceived in *vera copula* sex?

We know, in any case, that in the English tradition, marriage does not require its parties to produce offspring. There is no barrier to the marriage of infertile people, just as there is no requirement for husband and wife to intend or want to become parents. It might be argued that the association of marriage and reproduction is so axiomatic that it need not be stated explicitly. If this were the case, we ought to expect cases in which a child has been born of a marriage in the absence of consummation to be denied annulment. However, as we saw in Chapters 3 and 4, this is not the case. Marriages have been annulled on the grounds that they were never consummated, despite those marriages having produced offspring. Similarly, we might expect contraceptive practices to confound the validation of a wedding. But again, as we saw in the earlier discussion of consummation, this is not the case. As one judge said, "[T]he institution of marriage generally is not necessary for the procreation of children; nor does it appear to be a principal end of marriage . . . [T]he sterility of the husband or the barrenness of the wife [is] irrelevant" (*Baxter v. Baxter* 1948, 10–11). Thus, consummation does not have to be procreative to count as such, and procreation can occur in the absence of consummation. The *vera copula* sex act, and not its consequences, characterizes marriage.

Evidently, while sexual-genital difference has been a defining condition of marriage, this difference need not necessarily serve procreative ends. The silence is deafening: marriage demands and polices naturalized sex/gender differentiation as a necessary precondition of *heterosexuality itself.* In this way, marriage does not simply reflect or organize heterosexual relations, but works to define and construct them as such. Marriage's heterosexism is mythologized as an invisible force field repelling all that is queer, but it is this mythologizing rather than any property intrinsic to marriage that produces these magnetic effects. This is revealed in the kinds of definitional "circular fiat" noted by Sullivan (1996, 179), in which heteroconservative opponents of same-sex marriage dismiss it as self-evidently oxymoronic. Coolidge and Duncan, for example, argue that if we tamper with the "core" concept of marriage—its heterosexual limits—the institution itself will fall apart (Coolidge and Duncan 2001). What does this suggest? It suggests that marriage (as is—as a certified, heterosexual, politically preferred conjugality) is a prop for itself; regulatory structures that claim to bolster or support marriage actually construct it. Marriage is, in this important sense, entirely imaginary: it is an idea, a concept, a heterosexual phantasm.

The problematics of homosex as non-procreative, then, amount to a conjugal red herring. It is apparent, however, that in marriage's demand for the naturalized sexual-genital differentiation of spouses, homosexual people are shunned and sexualized as improper subjects of marriage. Perhaps, then, the general reluctance of states to admit homosexual couples to marriage is rooted in patriarchal as much as heterosexist imperatives. While Sullivan and many other lobbyists for same-sex marriage do not consider feminist critiques of marriage, lesbian thinkers generally do. In fact, lesbian scholars on same-sex marriage have produced much more ambivalent work concerning its desirability.

Most arguments for same-sex marriage characterize marriage as an intrinsic and almost self-evident social good. For Sullivan, Wolfson, and Eskridge, for example, marriage is a good place that would not be challenged or changed by the entry of gay and lesbian couples. Some thinkers have noticed and criticized this assimilatory tone. Ruthann Robson argues that "lesbian survival is not furthered by embracing the law's rule of marriage. Our legal energy is better directed at abolishing marriage as a state institution and spouse as a legal category" (1992, 127). Paula Ettelbrick (1997) argues a similar case. While acknowledging that the benefits attached to marriage are unfairly denied people in non-matrimonial relationships, she questions the wisdom of addressing this disparity by simply extending marriage's scope. For Robson, Ettelbrick, and others,[5] marriage is essentially and irredeemably heteronormative. Drawing from this understanding of marriage's institutional nature, they argue that marriage resistance, as opposed to the heteronormative assimilation of same-sex marriage, is the appropriate political strategy for gay men and (especially) lesbians.

Others, however, have rejected the assumption that gay and lesbian entry to state-sanctioned marriage would not change the conjugal landscape. Nan Hunter suggests that, when viewed in a "gender systems" context, "same-sex marriage would move beyond the formalistic equality in marriage law that has been achieved to date, and would radically denaturalise the social construction of male/female differentness, once expressed as authority/dependence relationships, that courts have deemed essential to the definition of marriage" (1995, 109). For Hunter and like-minded thinkers, same-sex marriage is conceptualized as a queer political strategy with the potential to instigate change beyond the immediate situation of particular couples. In some ways, celebrating same-sex marriage's queer potential is counter-productive for same-sex marriage lobbyists. The subversion of heterosexual marriage is precisely what conservatives like Robert Knight fear most, and positions the debate almost inevitably as (minority) attack versus (majority) defense. This does not mean, of course, that it is not worthwhile.

The same-sex marriage debates iterate—though with a differently charged emphasis—many of the same difficulties that have, to some extent, beset feminist theorizations of (heterosexual) marriage. As we saw in Chapter 2, feminist analyses of marriage have tended to construct marriage as either essentially benign or incurably patriarchal. Where marriage is understood as institutionally "neutral," feminists suggest that it can (and should) be reformed; this is the "anti-sexist" approach. Where feminists have theorized marriage as an archetypal institution of patriarchy, however, it is understood as irredeemably oppressive to women. Some feminists thus argue that reforming marriage is a doomed enterprise, and suggest that women would be better served by identifying and promoting strategies of marriage resistance—including, perhaps, de facto relationships and lesbianism. If marriage is fundamentally heterosexist, gay and lesbian couples seeking the right to marry may be aligning themselves with and reinforcing a heteronormative system. But what if marriage were no longer premised on the exclusion of gay and lesbian couples? *Would* marriage come to be a more gender-egalitarian place, or would it arrive at a more literal utopia—a *no-place*—where the meaning of marriage as an exclusively heterosexual regulation unravels as an absurd oxymoron? Would same-sex marriage begin to "normalise the queer," sounding, as Judith Butler warns, "its sad finish" (1994, 21)?

Lesbian perspectives on the shape of the same-sex marriage debate are often different from gay men's views. First, gay men's positioning outside of marriage tends not to bear the same meanings that it does for (some) lesbians. This, in turn, suggests that marriage continues to exert sex/gendered effects. That is, it suggests that men and women are differently figured as spouses. This seems patently true; how else can we explain the expectation that a groom's entry into marriage is (still) to be mourned (albeit tragicomically), while for women, marriage continues to be figured as an occasion for congratulation and the scene of Dreams Come True (Geller 2001)? The differences between lesbian and gay contributions to the same-sex marriage debate also invite an inference that marriage resistance might present an occasion for solidarity between lesbians and heterosexual feminists. However, as Calhoun (2000) argues, this is a dangerously slippery assumption.

Where lesbian and feminist interests intersect, they are too often collapsed as "lesbian feminist." It may be tempting to suggest that when the "lesbian" orientation of "lesbian feminist" speaks, marriage is reformable and open to subversion, and that queer imports might serve contingent feminist ends. It may be similarly tempting to suggest that when the "feminist" orientation of "lesbian feminist" speaks, marriage remains a site of blackballed resistance. We already know, however, that feminist tactics of marriage critique and resistance are by no means uniform. Why should it be assumed, then, that lesbian accounts of marriage and same-sex marriage should be any more or less consistent? That the axes of debate exert similarly polarizing forces does not mean that the axes of debate are themselves identical. Given that marriage is a governmental phantasm put to various regulatory purposes (including racism, remember), we should not be surprised that responses to its various regulatory effects differ.

Nonetheless, the same-sex marriage debate produces strange political bedfellows. Where same-sex marriage is thought to offer opportunities for subversion of the gender order, thinkers like E. J.

Graff find themselves "on the same side" as gay conservatives like Sullivan: both argue for the desirability of same-sex marriage, but for entirely different reasons. Attempting to distance themselves from anti-feminist and politically conservative arguments, some feminists have argued that the rationale motivating the struggle for same-sex marriage will determine its effects. Hunter, echoing Nancy Polikoff (1993), asserts that the transformative potential of same-sex marriage depends on the rationales and strategies employed in its campaign. For Hunter, "[t]he social meaning of the legalization of lesbian and gay marriage . . . would be enormously different if legalization resulted from political efforts framed as ending gendered roles between spouses, rather than if it were the outcome of a campaign valorizing the institution of marriage, even if the ultimate 'holding' is the same" (1995, 121).

The strange cogency of this formulation suggests that marriage reflects rather than constructs acceptable forms of conjugality. Such an understanding is inconsistent with Hunter's construction of marriage as "a complete creation of the law" (1995, 110). It suggests that marriage rights will accrue to gay and lesbian couples as a consequence of other social struggles, and would seem to obviate the need for any kind of concerted campaign. It is not clear, in any case, how ending the gendered roles of husband and wife would constitute a queer (as distinct from a feminist) victory. As Calhoun warns, "it is a mistake for feminists to assume that work to end gender subordination will have as much payoff for lesbians as it would for heterosexual women" (2000: 29).

Where same-sex marriage is decried as a relic of heterosexuality, activists like Paula Ettelbrick (who rejects the very terms of the debate) find themselves "allied" with homophobic "family values" conservatives like Wilson and Knight. Both argue against the desirability of same-sex marriage, again, for entirely different reasons. But both Graff and Ettelbrick present arguments relying on or resonant with both feminist and lesbian resistance. I agree with Calhoun that it is a mistake always to collapse lesbian and feminist interests. However, noting the ways in which they diverge relative to marriage does not entirely solve the strange and paradoxical parallels emerging in lesbian, feminist, and lesbian-feminist analyses of same-sex marriage.

Is it possible to unpack and resolve these paradoxical alliances? If it is, there is considerable groundwork to be done. After all, if the question for feminists concerns the potential gender-effects same-sex marriage might produce, perhaps we need to work out why we would expect there to be any such gender effects in the first place. Just as feminist struggles might have fewer payoffs for lesbians, so queer struggles are not necessarily feminist. Assuming that gender effects would follow from the admission of gay and lesbian couples to marriage loads "sex"—or at least the corporeal associations of sex (such as genitalia and hormonal arrangements)—with foundational powers it does not have. Sex does not produce or reflect gender (Butler 1990, 1993). Recall that the historical regulation of marriage has shown remarkably little interest in gender norms as such. An "effeminate" man may marry a "butch" woman; the bride may wear a tuxedo, the groom may wear a gown without invalidating their wedding. Rather, marriage has historically produced dimorphously sexed husbands and wives as a defining precondition of heterosexuality. If it were no longer to do so, this would not mean the collapse of gendered or heterosexist systems, but it might obviate or displace the work marriage has historically performed. Perhaps the links between sexual dimorphism and heterosexism would be weakened given the historical centrality of marriage to heterosexism, but it is more likely that the social apparatus regulating sexual hierarchies would simply shift. After all, marriage is not the only scene of heterosexism.

Yet I would insist, along with most if not all feminists, that marriage *is* gendered. "Spouse" may be a gender-neutral term, but it circumscribes an exclusively and exhaustively gendered universe in which (typically and historically) only women are wives and only men are husbands. If sex does not necessarily produce gender, but marriage is gendered, what animates the different positioning of husbands and wives? In feminist willingness to assume that same-sex marriage might produce gendered effects, perhaps we are attending to the ways that marriage's demand for sexual dimorphism created historical space for the corporeal, material and symbolic scene of women's coverture. As Carole Pateman (1988) and Moira Gatens (1996) have shown, historically marriage has been a vehicle for women's incorporation into the body politic. Wives were historically incorporated into the legal-political identity of their husbands, not the other way around. When a man marries, his identity and that which names it remain undisturbed. (When Sam Stuart marries Wendy Wong, for example, he does not become "Mr. Wendy

Wong.") In marriage, the *tactics* of sexism and heterosexism overlap. Both privilege *vera copula* as a (hetero-)sexual performative. And performatives, of course, produce gender.

PERFORMATIVES REVISITED

I have argued throughout this book that marriage is the scene of a variety of performatives, from the performative utterances of wedding vows to the normative and iterative performativity of cohabitative sex as an indicator of "togetherness." The performatives of marriage have been historically heterosexual and homophobic. In its regulatory boundary-drawing, marriage accomplishes the heavily sexualized subordination of those whom it excludes. I suggested, too, that as it sexualizes Others, marriage clears a desexualized or neutralized zone of privileged, "private," sex. Marital sex is figured as lawful, constructive, (re-)productive, mature, and decent, and not simply as an avenue of corporeal pleasure.

Marriage has sustained gendered relations of (men's) individuality and (women's) dependence whose legal ancestor is coverture. Coverture's archetype expression is union of the flesh; a literal incorporation.[6] "Union" or *copula vera* is constructed as precisely *not* a penis/anus, clitoris/tongue, hand/penis, or any other sexual conjunction. It demands the conjunction of those corporeal representations of (male/female) "sex," and it does so not just axiomatically but specifically and explicitly. The work this does is to redraw and reiterate the line dividing man/woman, simultaneously maintaining its coherence and naturalizing dimorphous sex differentiation as a phantasmic precondition of heterosexuality and as a naturalized locus of gender.

Governmental and performative elements are always interrelated in these historical operations, because performative effects are conventional: they must be sustained through discursive connections between act and effect. Such connections are not entirely arbitrary. When a magician says "Abracadabra," we look to the wand, we suspend our disbelief. Any number of events might occur as the rabbit is pulled from the hat—a dog might bark, war might break out—but we do not understand these other events as "magic." The difficulty in analyzing marriage's performatives is to work out which effects are brought into being performatively and which are merely contingent, and to determine the discursive connections between performatives and their effects. The connections, of course, *are* discursive: being similarly regulatory and similarly lacking any real foundation, marriage is produced in much the same way that gender is.

Identifying the discursive connections between marriage performatives and their gendered effects is a much simpler task when performatives are regulated through conventions whose basis is rule-of-law rather than norms. The sexual performatives of consummation and adultery are easily identified when what we understand by "marriage" is a cluster of rules involving legal pronouncements, but more difficult when marriages "limp" (or sprint) according to a range of largely self-regulated norms. In this context, it is useful to distinguish the "legal recognition of gay and lesbian relationships" from "same-sex marriage." The legal recognition and regulation of same-sex relationships is (outside the United States, at least) widespread and largely unremarkable. Thus, while the Australian federal government might have moved to prevent the extension of certified marriage to gay and lesbian couples, every Australian state recognizes the legitimacy of same-sex partnerships by one means or another. Some states have extended the reach of existing provisions relating to cohabitation, while others have enacted new, purpose-built laws. While some jurisdictions have been quicker and more creative than others, the reforms and innovations enacted have not been terribly controversial.

The Australian Capital Territory (ACT) was one of the first Australian jurisdictions to "recognize" gay and lesbian relationships through its *Domestic Partnerships Act* (1994). The legislative council there surprised itself with its own restraint. Politicians congratulated each other on not dragging the level of debate down to the issue of "same-sex marriage" (Brook 2000). The legislation involved presumptive recognition of a range of relationships—between adult children and their parents, for example—as well as between heterosexual and homosexual cohabitants. The bill attracted little public-political debate precisely in that it was not "about" sex. While homosexual performatives remain "unspeakable" in this context—that is, homosexual relationships are never scrutinized or compared to any kind of standard—they are also *unmarked*. In this sense, such legislation offers a side door to the desexualized zone that the sexual performatives of marriage have historically offered hetereosexuals, without replicating its sex/gender roles.

The prospect of same-sex marriage *as marriage* has also been welcomed in some places, but has attracted a larger share of controversy. I suspect that the degree of controversy attached to the regulation and recognition of same-sex relationships rises with the legal importance of sexual performatives: wherever certified marriage continues to mobilize sexual performatives as part of its legal constitution as marriage, gay and lesbian entry will be denied. Why? Where sexual performatives exist in the service of a heteronormative order whose chief business is to subordinate Others using sexualizing tactics, the notion of a homosexual performative is a contradiction in terms. It is, in a sense, an 'undoing' performative. In a way, those frightened heteroconservatives are right: in a world in which their views still dominate, same-sex marriage *is* oxymoronic; same-sex marriage is oxymoronic wherever marriage continues to operate as a heterosexist phantasm. Thus, a model of marriage premised on homosexual exclusion cannot offer gay and lesbian spouses the same social space offered to heterosexual husbands and wives. And thus, homosexual access to the arena of conjugality will not bring about a greater degree of equality and fairness for gay and lesbian people, but will perhaps reflect it.

Whether same-sex marriage is or is not available, alternatives such as "civil unions" and "domestic partnerships" (if not the "legal concubinage" preferred by the Mothers' Union) might be offered as opt-in models. Alternatively, presumptive indicia of marriage akin to those used to determine heterosexual cohabitation might be extended and applied to same-sex couples. Such frameworks are the regulatory future of marriage, not just for gay and lesbian couples, but for all intimate relationships, sexual or otherwise. In most places, the exemption of marital sex from the subordinating marks of sexualization is no longer accomplished through marriage-performatives. In most jurisdictions, consummation is no longer a legally relevant concept, and in many jurisdictions the only route to exit a marriage is no-fault. The recent Australian decision regarding the validity of *Kevin* (a female-to-male transsexual) and Jennifer's marriage confirms that the legal force of *copula vera* performatives is diminishing. In these jurisdictions, the (homo-)sexual performative's capacity to effect a desexualized zone has already been foreclosed—not by legislative defenses of marriage, but by the erosion of legal-sexual performatives. Instead, the governmental regulation of relationships constructs spouses whose conduct is largely self-regulated against a range of norms.

Normative forms of conjugality signal the legal demise of rule-based sexual performatives like wedding vows and consummation. That is not to say that such performatives might not retain social and personal significance. The pageantry, smoke and mirrors, sentiment, and emotion of weddings may still be meaningful and popular, but witnesses will no longer be required to suspend disbelief in the interests of performative legal magic. In the new conjugal order, sex (in its myriad configurations) as an indicator of "togetherness" lives; *copula vera* as the circuit connecting husband and wife in "union" is dead or dying.

QUEER CONJUGALITY?

We have seen that factions in the same-sex marriage debates cannot be neatly divided into those "for" versus those "against" without collapsing their entirely different animating rationales. To me, this suggests that the terrain being fought over is itself thoroughly unstable. However, this instability seems to go largely unacknowledged, with each participant attempting to name and reclaim a particular conception of "marriage" as its only true definition. Each voice, it seems, seeks to institutionalize a particular version of marriage to the exclusion of competing conceptions. This (entirely, obviously) discursive anxiety is nowhere more obvious than in the heteroconservative claim that same-sex marriage is "oxymoronic." My first observation, then, is that attempts to institutionalize or reinstitutionalize competing understandings and definitions of marriage underscore the unstable terrain of marriage-discourse.

I worry, with Janet Halley (2001), that gay and lesbian couples might be struggling for "the right to marry" without being very sure of what marriage is and does. While it might be foolish to set one's heart on a pig in a poke, gay and lesbian longing for marriage is understandable. Marriage *desexualizes*, and for those weary of being always and excessively characterized by a defining and all-consuming sexuality, it seems to promise relief. That it does not—indeed, cannot—deliver that promise speaks to the nature of marriage as a boundary-marking project. If marriage were no longer to imagine the line between "man" and "woman" that produces heterosexist and sexist effects, it would also no longer desexualize. In other words, that which gay and lesbian couples most want from marriage is precisely that which marriage can never bestow.

None of this is to suggest that marriage might not be meaningful (or subversive) absent its historically sexualizing and desexualizing projects. After all, in many jurisdictions, cohabitation and certified marriage are now almost identical, but weddings remain popular. The performative promises of (valid) weddings still bear legal effects, but weddings are now imbricated in a new range of performatives whose impact is best calculated in an economics of consumption and representation. Moreover, those barred from contracting (or preferring not to enter) a valid wedding sometimes stage alternative ceremonies. It is entirely feasible to suggest that (straight/queer) couples who imitate the ceremony and celebration of weddings without modeling their relationships on certified marriage are engaged in subversive acts. However, in jurisdictions where cohabitation is determined presumptively and limited to heterosexual couples, the consequences of such a ceremony, no matter how it might be shaped, are likely to be different for straight couples. This is a reminder, then, that the state determines what status and obligations arise from marriage, and the state determines whether a marriage (or even a "marriage") exists or not. Even where marriage is almost entirely self-regulated against a range of norms, it remains so at the state's discretion.

Models of conjugality that desist from regulating sex are, in my view, significantly more progressive and attractive than those that do not. Amended models of marriage that do away with sexual-legal performatives are preferable, as are the kinds of regulation constructing "civil unions" in Aotearoa New Zealand and "domestic relationships" in the Australian Capital Territory. But they should not be welcomed as "stepping stones" to (certified, sexually performative) marriage. Placing marriage at the top of the conjugal tree consolidates a hierarchy of relationships that no longer reflects social values and is better undone. Prizing marriage as such plays into heterosexism's exclusionary tactics, devaluing all that is not-marriage as it fuels the paranoid defense of marriage as the "natural" domain of majority-heterosexuality besieged by minority attack. Elaborating a different political tactics is the final task of this book.

CHAPTER 9

CONCLUSION:
SEX, MARRIAGE, AND CONJUGALITY

Marriage no longer makes sense. By this, I do not mean that marriage is no longer a meaningful arrangement, but rather that its discursive coherence as a regulatory system is unraveling. As a mechanism of status relying on patriarchal and heterosexist regulatory orders, it is no longer viable. Theoretically and experientially, the old forms are being rejected. Where cohabitation counts, for certain purposes, as "marriage," where covenant marriage, civil unions, and domestic partnerships compete as alternative forms of conjugality, and where certified marriage is defined in increasingly diverse and/or self-regulated ways, the world of intimate relationships can no longer be easily divided into that which is marriage and that which is not. The field of analysis has opened up. Not marriage but *conjugality* is the appropriate regulatory (and thus analytical) field.

Conjugality is a territory: an unstable, sometimes dangerous place whose boundaries bleed, expand, and contract. Certified, "traditional" marriage is a dot on its map, and it, too, refuses to stand still. Cohabitation, civil unions, and any number of other regulatory schema are no longer merely satellite towns, but themselves play an important part in shaping conjugality. At one time the territory's borders were closed to gay and lesbian couples, but access is now available to some if not all of conjugality's destinations. In the twenty-first century, to speak of marriage is, in fact, to speak of marriage *more or less.* The territory itself has shifted: what was once a kingdom ruled by certified marriage and its scepter of adversarial law is now a more fundamentally liberal province in which self-regulation and government, through a proliferation of norms and choices, characterizes conjugality.

My first conclusion, then, is that the intellectual value of understanding marriage as a stable social institution has expired. Those who would govern intimate relationships should consider, instead, a non-hierarchical model in which certified marriage and other options exist as a cluster of relationships. It is time to stop defining and redefining marriage, and to begin governing, celebrating, and criticizing conjugality. The question no longer concerns what (mere) marriage is and does, but how each element within a range of conjugal relationships is constituted and governed. I have suggested throughout this book that the theoretical tools most appropriate for this task include the concepts of corporeality, government, and performativity. Let us consider, then, in this brief concluding chapter, how some of the insights afforded by those tools might be drawn together.

I have argued that any form of conjugality should be understood as a relationship not merely between spouses each to the other, but also as a relationship between spouses and the state. Marriage is governmentally established and defined. It is subject to a range of definitional anxieties because it is, in a very real sense, just a word. Such anxieties betray their own discursive foundations. Sex/gender conservatives like David Orgon Coolidge and William C. Duncan, for example, worry that same-sex marriage might be "a logical 'wedge' by which the legal concept of marriage can be deconstructed" (2001, 641). But same-sex marriage does not need to be lawful to accomplish this. As Coolidge and Duncan acknowledge, marriage is a "concept," an "idea"—and ideas and concepts can be deconstructed using theory alone. What these authors' anxieties reveal (and in some ways, they stand in the equivalent of a social gale with their skirts blowing high over their heads) is that marriage is *merely* an idea; it is a social-legal phantasm.

In this sense, its construction is neither always legally formative nor merely reflective. Conjugality is dynamic; it is a scene of permanent governmental provocation. As we saw in Chapter 6, the templates of regulation offered for exiting marriage through divorce, for example, sometimes see spouses refracting their experience through those templates in especially distorting ways. Similarly, while the highly self-regulatory form of marriage available in places where the only route to divorce is no-fault separation offers a high degree of flexibility for spouses, it does not mean that such marriages are entirely determined by their subjects. In these circumstances, marriage may be "what we make it," but the construction paper from which couples build their own institution is both uniform and subject to limited distribution. States continue to determine both the limits of marriage and the availability of other means of relationship recognition and regulation.

To suggest that conjugality is a legal phantasm is not to suggest that it does not have real, material effects. As we saw in Chapters 4 and 5, marriage has routinely connected its subjects to "good" citizenship. Elizabeth Povinelli alludes to this connection when she identifies "a liberal humanist claim that what makes us most human is our capacity to base our most intimate relations, our most robust governmental institutions, and our economic relations on mutual and free recognition of the worth and value of another person, rather than basing these connections on, for example, social status or the bare facts of the body" (2006, 5).

Povinelli's observation is astute, but marriage does exercise an especially corporeal hold, and in this respect it certainly addresses "the bare facts of the body." As we saw in Chapter 3, definitional anxieties over conjugality relate not only to the failure of "marriage" to maintain discursive coherence over time and space, but also to its constituent "men" and "women." In this respect, marriage does not merely manage the (pre-existing) corporeal differentiation of men and women, but creates it. In its historical demand for one man and one woman, marriage draws a line between them. That conjugality can now contemplate (in some jurisdictions, at least) the possibility of a penis-less man speaks at once to feminist challenges to the certainty and stability of "sex," even as it reinscribes the feminine as that which must be marked and produced (as 'lack') on the body.

Marriage's corporeal hold sexes subjects in a dual sense. As noted earlier, it brings sex into being as male/female differentiation, but it does so in the interests of privileging and preferring heterosexuality. In the field of conjugal regulation, heterosexuality has historically stood as an unmarked category. In its exclusively heterosexual form, then, marriage can be understood as one of a number of mechanisms for sexualizing queer subjects. Such sexualization is a subordinating tactic, a way to characterize sexual Others in ways that perpetuate their "deviance." As Foucault (and others since) have argued, sexual orientation is thus morally synecdochical: It saturates or contaminates the entire person, producing subjects overdetermined by their sexuality. As Cheshire Calhoun (2002) explains, when gay and lesbian individuals are reduced to an exaggerated and heavily sexualized subjectivity, they are produced as frighteningly, excessively sexual. As we saw in Chapter 5, racism has at times relied on a similar sexualization. One of marriage's key corporeal effects, then, is to sexualize "Others," rendering them less than properly human, as it desexualizes or neutralizes heterosexuality.

Marriage can thus be conceived as a zone in which governmental interest in (heterosexual) sex acts is processed. The arena of lawful conjugality facilitates heterosexual exemption from the subordinating marks of sexualization. In this very concrete, very corporeal place, heterosexuality can enjoy its status as the locus of unmarked and unremarkable (but legally circumscribed) desire. Marriage naturalizes, neutralizes, and normalizes gender-dimorphous heterosexuality. This unmarked and unremarkable status is often conflated, rightly or wrongly, with "the private." As Calhoun asserts, "heterosexuals may claim that their heterosexual lives of dating, flirting, marriage, and procreating are their 'private' business—not open for debate—while simultaneously enacting those 'private' lives in public space. The liberty to conduct one's private life in this public non-politicized space is precisely what gay men and lesbians do not have" (2000, 94). Marriage thus "privatizes" desire in the sense that it exempts heterosexuality from a subordinating sexualization, but it is neither private nor (as Calhoun suggests) "pre-political." Rather, marriage is *thoroughly* political, thoroughly governmental. It is endlessly constituted and reconstituted, (mythically) civilizing as it desexualizes.

This "civilizing" desexualization has been historically and routinely accomplished by making certain sex acts performative. In the government of marriage, sex acts such as consummation, condonation, and adultery have borne important legal meanings. Sex, in these circumstances, is not just sex. Consummation seals the performative utterances of weddings by corporeally enacting marriage as a unification, as producing "one flesh." Condoning sex reiterates and repairs union, reestablishing marriage where grounds for its dissolution have arisen. Lawful, legally inscribed sex acts produce subjects whose desire is hitched, so to speak, to governmental rationales. Some jurisdictions, however, no longer entertain the performative magic of (hetero-)sex. It is no longer always necessary to consummate a marriage in order to ensure its validity. The range of performative sex acts framing the coherence of fault-based divorce has also diminished as no-fault provisions have taken hold. Relinquishing the performative éclat of heterosex yields a number of paradoxical effects.

Staving off the potential resexualization of non-marital (hetero-)sex, the regulation of cohabitation has seen sex acts become mundanely, normatively performative. More than this, where certified marriage no longer allows transformative sex acts to do the work of "desexualizing" heterosex, even certified marriage becomes almost entirely normative. Where marriage is constituted through the measurement of behavior against normative indicia, sex acts no longer work as a switch connecting the spousal circuit of marriage "on" or "off," but rather congeal—over time, repetitively—as "marriage." It is in the construction of marriage as togetherness (or *consortium vitae*) that the discursive instability of marriage is thus most obviously revealed. As we saw in Chapter 7, cohabitation does not simulate marriage so much as marriage simulates cohabitation.

The movement of marriage from rule-based corporeal union to normatively defined togetherness has had other effects, too. Recent research points to the uncoupling of weddings and marriage. While I would maintain that their separation is incomplete, it does seem that the *signs* of performative "magic"—the sparkle and smoke, costumes and cake—now characterize weddings more than their transformative links to marriage. This is especially evident where cohabitation as a prelude to certified marriage is popular. (In Australia, this is the vast majority: over three-quarters of Australian couples registering a marriage in 2005 had lived together prior to their marriage [Australian Bureau of Statistics 2007].) After all, where marriage simulates cohabitation, there is often no material difference between a couple's cohabitative versus married life. Weddings might have become a site of parody and pageantry (Freeman 2002), but their articulation to conjugality remains important. A valid wedding registers a lawful marriage and secures a couple's access (in theory, at least) to that "private," desexualized, and privileged zone of conjugality.

Increasingly, however, alternatives to certified marriage are offering something similar. In Aotearoa New Zealand, for example, civil unions are offered as a registered alternative to (certified) marriage. The most substantial difference between a marriage and a civil union in New Zealand is that while heterosexual couples are permitted to choose either form, gay and lesbian couples are limited to civil unions. The distinction between the two simultaneously underlines certified marriage's historically desexualizing work, even as it establishes an arguably equivalent zone for sexual Others. The irony, of course, is that this access to a somewhat desexualized arena has occurred precisely as sexual performatives have been retired from the conjugal stage, thus forestalling the subversive prospect of specifically lawful (homo-)sexual performatives.

Perhaps figuring conjugal sex as normative has served to raise questions about the efficacy and appropriateness of imbuing sex acts with more spectacularly performative effects. In any case, there are ironies and paradoxes in allowing gay and lesbian couples access to lawful conjugality just as its sexual performatives are being erased (thus reproducing the "unspeakable" nature of homosexuality in both speech and sex acts). In the end, it would seem that each of the forms of conjugality discussed here—from certified (heterosexual) marriage to same-sex marriage, from cohabitation to civil unions— are coming increasingly to resemble each other. This seems to suggest that the historical moment at which a critical mass accepts the existence and value of gay and lesbian relationships is likely to be precisely the moment marriage loses its heteronormative purchase.

Granting gay and lesbian couples access to certified marriage might seem like opening the door to institutional equality. Homosexual yearning for a place in which same-sex conjugality can exist within the same public/private parameters of desexualized conjugality is for some an attractive prospect. But access to certified marriage will not cause the door to equality to open; it will be the *result* of its opening. Since marriage has been built into a wall whose very purpose has been to divide hetero- and homosexual subjects, as soon as gay and lesbian couples have access to the status operations certified marriage produces, such status will cease to mark the differentiations it presently sustains. This is, I am glad to say, already happening.

I suspect it will be a matter of time before governments rationalize the proliferation of legislative tiers of conjugality and move to universalize their regulation—perhaps as "marriage," perhaps as some other conjugal relationship. It is not difficult to imagine an arena of conjugality in which heterosexual, homosexual, and asexual relationships are treated indistinguishably. Why should the state care whether parties in some kind of interdependent relationship engage in bondage and fisting, *copula vera*, or milk and cookies? Conjugality might still typically or normally imply a sexual relationship between spouses, but with the abolition of sexual performatives and their desexualizing functions, a sexual relationship would no longer be a necessary or fundamental component of conjugality. Likewise, there would be no need to police determinations of sex/gender corporeality. Conceiving of conjugality in this way would not herald the imminent abolition of marriage. Those who wish to call their relationships "marriage" and seek religious endorsement for them could do so, but this need not entail preferential treatment by the state. Religious marriage would simply be constituted as a subset of the more broadly defined arena of conjugality. For many people, the veils and tuxedoes, churches and confetti, and other symbolic accoutrements of wedding will continue to form an important element of conjugality. Whatever we call it, marriage is likely to remain popular, and it will, for some time at least, remain (partially and perhaps unpredictably) tethered to its heterosexist and patriarchal past.

Conjugal bodies politic offer simultaneous threats and promises. The promise is that the abstract individual of liberal political theory and jurisprudence may be destabilized or even replaced by a configuration of subjects engaged in corporeal relations with each other and bearing certain responsibilities for each other. The threat is that it is the regulation of sex, especially, that has been deployed to inscribe political subjects as other than individual, constructing and reiterating sex/gender differences that have historically privileged men, whiteness, and heterosexuality. We need to recognize the political weight attaching to the uttered and sexual performatives of marriage: subjects who promise in particular, sexually loaded ways are celebrated and valorized; subjects who take on the discursive transformation of certified marriage have been (and in some places still are) *politically preferred*. In that the transformative effects of marriage's performatives have subjugated women in the past, they have been rightly challenged and to some extent destabilized. However, they might yet carry some potential for theorizing political subjectivities—even *liberal* political subjectivities—as other-than-individual, embodied actors.

I said at the very beginning of this book that I would not discuss the experience of marriage so much as how relationships are governed. I think, in the end, that the two can only ever be conceptually distinct. The way marriage and marriage-like relationships are governed colors our experience of conjugality. Though I have not discussed the emotional investments we bring to sexually affective relationships, I am convinced that respecting people's search for conjugal happiness means not dismissing marriage but critically interrogating it. In the absence of definitive answers concerning the absolute merits or dangers of conjugality, the temptation is to suggest that in the perpetual demolition, renovation, and reconstruction of marriage, there is room for a number of feminist-building sites. In my more hopeful moods, I see "the master's tools" being used in the service of subversively feminist architects. On darker days, all I can see is that each of us, married or not, is dirtied as marriage's "institutional" brick dust settles around us.

A couple of months ago, I asked my seven-year-old niece what she would like as a gift for her birthday. I was half hoping that she would ask for a bride doll so that I could I finish this book with an end arriving at the beginning, and point to the continuities underlying my discussion of conjugality as a dynamic and flexible field. But my niece has been enjoying a series of wildlife documentaries, and she asked for a book about birds.

LIST OF CASES

American Law Reports (1953) Annotation: Condonation of cruel treatment as defense to action for divorce. 32 ALR 2d, 107–76.

Atkins v. Atkins (1942) 2 All ER 637 (Ch.D).

Attorney-General v. Otahuhu Family Court (1995) NZLR 603.

B. (L.) v. B. (R.) (1965) 3 All ER 263.

Baxter v. Baxter (1948) Times LR 8–11.

Bellinger (FC) (Appellant) v. Bellinger (2003) UKHL 21, on appeal from EWCA Civ 1140.

Boyd v. Boyd (1955) P. 126.

Buckland v. Buckland (orse Camilleri) (1965) P. 296.

C and D: see *Re the Marriage of C and D (falsely called C)* (1979) 35 FLR 340.

Clark v. Clark (1958) C.A. The Times. June 25, 1958; C.L. 335.

Clarke v. Clarke (1943) 2 All E.R. 540.

Cooper v. Cooper (1955) P. 99, p. 115.

Corbett v. Corbett (1970) 2 All ER 33.

Evans v. Evans (1965) 2 All ER 789.

G. v. G. (1952) Supreme Court of Victoria. Victoria Law Reports, pp. 402–10.

Gray v. Department of Social Security (1992) Social Security Reporter, 70, 1009.

Heffernan v. Heffernan (1953) V.L.R 321.

Henderson v. Henderson (1944) A.C. 49, 32–33; 60 T.L.R.

Hucker v. Department of Social Security (1992) Social Security Reporter 66, 935.

Huffine v. Huffine (1947) CP Ohio Ops 56, 48 Ohio L Abs 430, 74 NE2d 764.

Jodla v. Jodla (1960) 1 W.L.R. 236. (Weekly Law Reports, pp. 236–39.)
Kantaras (1998). See *Re Marriage and Michael J. Kantaras.*
Kevin (2001). See *Re Kevin.*
King v. King (1953) AC 124; (1952) 2 TLR 429; (1952) 2 All ER 584 HL.
L. v. L. (1949) 1 All ER 141.
Lang v. Lang (1955) AC 402 (HL).
Le Brocq v. Le Brocq (1964) 3 All ER 464 (CA).
Lee v. Lee (1928) 3 S.W. 2d 672.
Locke v. Locke (1956), 95 C.L.R. 165. High Court of Australia.
Loving v. Virginia (1967) 388 US 1.
M v M (A) (1984) 42 RFL 2d 55.
MacLennan v. MacLennan (1958) S.C. 105. Court of Session (Scotland).
McKim (1972). See *Re Marriage of McKim.*
McKinnon v. McKinnon (1942) S.A.S.R. 107. Supreme Court of South Australia.
Mehta v. Mehta (1945) 2 All ER 690.
Otahuhu (1995). See *Attorney-General v. Otahuhu* (1995).
P. v. P. (1964) 3 All ER 919.
P. (D.) v. P. (J.) (1965) 2 All ER 456.
Parojcic v. Parojcic (1959) 1 All ER 1.
R. v. Harris (1971) 55 CAR 290.
Re Kevin (validity of marriage of transsexual) (2001) Fam CA 1074.
Re Marriage and Michael J. Kantaras v. Linda Kantaras (Case number: 98-5375 CA 511998 DR 005375xxxxWS).
Re Marriage of McKim (1972) 6 Cal. 3d 673.
Re the Marriage of C and D (falsely called C) (1979) 35 FLR 340.
Rumbelow v. Rumbelow and Hadden (1965) 2 All E.R. 767 (C.A.).
S. v. S. (orse C.) (1956) P.1.
S.Y. v. S.Y. (orse. W.) (1963) P. 37 (C.A.).
Sapsford v. Sapsford and Furtado (1954) P. 394–402.
Silver v. Silver (1955) 2 All ER 614.
S.T. (formerly J. v J.) (1998) 1 All ER 431.
Szechter (orse Karsov) v. Szechter (1971) P. 286.
Thompson v. Thompson (1938) P. 162.
Todd (No. 2) (1976) F.L.C. 90-008.
Tozer v. Department of Social Security (1982) Social Security Appeals Tribunal. *Social Security Reporter* 10, 99.
W. v. W. (1967) 3 All ER 178.
White v. White (1948) 2 All E.R. 151.
Wieland v. Department of Social Security (1993) Social Security Reporter, 76, 1108.
Willan v. Willan (1958) Court of Appeal, W. (D) No. 369.
Williams v. Williams (1964) AC 698 (HL).
Winnan v. Winnan (1949) P. 174; 65 T.L.R.22; (1948) 2 All E.R. 862.
Wright v. Wright (1950) 153 Neb 18, 43 NW2d 424.

REFERENCES

Alibhai-Brown, Yasmin, and Anne Montague. 1992. *The colour of love: mixed race relationships.* London: Virago.

Allen, Anita L. 2000. Interracial marriage: Folk ethics in contemporary philosophy. In *Women of color and philosophy: A critical reader,* ed. Naomi Zack, 182–206. Malden, MA: Blackwell.

Alsop, Rachel, Annette Fitzsimons, and Kathleen Lennon. 2002. *Theorizing gender.* Cambridge, UK: Polity.

Amadiume, Ifi. 1987. *Male daughters, female husbands: Gender and sex in an African society.* London: Zed.

American Law Reports. 1953. *See* List of Cases.

Andreasen, Kirstin. 2004. Did *Loving v. Virginia* need its slippery slope? *Journal of Contemporary Legal Issues* 14 (1): 89–95.

Aries, Philippe, and Georges Duby. 1987–1991. *A History of private life.* 5 vols. Cambridge, MA: The Belknap Press of Harvard Univ. Press.

Arlington County Public Affairs Division. 2006. News release, January 31, 2006. http://www.arlingtonva.us/NewsReleases/Scripts/ViewDetail .asp?Index=1958.

Astell, Mary. 1706. Reflections upon marriage. In *The first english feminist: Reflections upon marriage and other writings by Mary Astell,* ed. Bridget Hill, 67–132. Aldershot, EN: Gower/Maurice Temple Smith, 1986.

Attwood, Bain, and John Arnold, eds. 1992. Introduction. *Power, knowledge and Aborigines. Special issue of Journal of Australian Studies* 35: i–xvi.

Atwood, Margaret. 1978. *The edible woman.* Toronto: McClelland and Stewart-Bantam.

Austin, J. L. 1962. *How to do things with words*. London: Oxford Univ. Press.

Australia, HR. See Australia, House of Representatives.

Australia. HREOC. See Australia, Human Rights and Equal Opportunity Commission.

Australia, House of Representatives. 1959. Matrimonial Causes Bill, second reading debate. (Hansard.)

Australia, House of Representatives. 1975. Family Law Bill, second reading debate. (Hansard.)

Australia. Human Rights and Equal Opportunity Commission. 1997. *Bringing them home: the report of the national enquiry into the separation of Aboriginal and Torres Strait Islander children from their families.* Sydney: Human Rights and Equal Opportunity Commission.

Australia. Law Reform Commission. 1986. *The recognition of Aboriginal customary laws*. Report No 31 Volume 1. Canberra: Australian Government Publishing Service.

Australian Archives. 1959. Refusal of permission for marriage of M. Daly and G. Namagu, Northern Territory. File no: A452: 1959/3783. Mitchell, ACT: Australian Archives.

Australian Bureau of Statistics. 2007. *Marriages, Australia, 2005*. 3306.0.55.001.

Australian Bureau of Statistics. 1967–1974. Annual publications on marriage and divorce. http://www.abs.gov.au/.

Bailey, Rebecca J. 1979. Family law—Decree of nullity of marriage of true hermaphrodite who has undergone sex-change surgery. *Australian Law Journal* 53 (9): 659–60.

Bailey-Harris, Rebecca. 1996. Law and the unmarried couple—oppression or liberation? *Child and Family Law Quarterly* 8 (2): 137–47.

Baird, Robert M., and Stuart E. Rosenbaum, eds. 1997. *Same-sex marriage: The moral and legal debate*. Amherst, NY: Prometheus.

Baldini, Gwen. 1995. A whole world of difference. In *City women, country women: Crossing the boundaries*, ed. Jocelynne A. Scutt, 117–31. Melbourne: Artemis.

Banner, Lois W. 2000. Review essay (Chancer, LeMoncheck, Ussher). *Signs* 26 (1): 258–61.

Barber, E. H. E. 1969. Divorce—the changing law. In *Divorce, society and the law*, ed. H. A. Finlay, 69–86. Melbourne: Butterworths.

Barrett, Michele, and Mary McIntosh. 1982. *The anti-social family*. London: Verso.

Barwick, Garfield. 1961. Some aspects of the new Matrimonial Causes Act. *Sydney Law Review* 3 (3): 409–38.

Basch, Norma. 1999. *Framing American divorce: From the revolutionary generation to the Victorians.* Berkeley: Univ. of California Press.

Baudrillard, Jean. 1988 Simulacra and simulations. In *Jean Baudrillard: Selected writings,* ed. Mark Poster, 166–84. Cambridge, UK: Polity.

BBC News Online. 1999. Jagger marriage annulled. http://news.bbc.co.uk/2/low/uk_news/419374.stm.

Bell, Diane. 1980. Desert politics: Choices in the marriage market. *Women and colonization: Anthropological perspectives,* eds. M. Etienne and E. Leacock, 239–69. New York: Praeger.

———. 1981. Women's business is hard work: Central Australian Aboriginal women's love rituals. *Signs: Journal of Women in Culture and Society* 7 (2): 314–37.

———. 1988. Choose your mission wisely. In *Aboriginal Australians and Christian missions: Ethnographic and historical studies,* eds. Tony Swain and Deborah Bird Rose, 338–52. Bedford Park: Australian Association for the Study of Religions.

Bell, Vikki. 1993. *Interrogating incest: Feminism, Foucault, and the law.* London: Routledge.

Bergen, Raquel Kennedy. 2004. Studying wife rape: Reflection on the past, present and future. *Violence Against Women* 10 (12): 1407–16.

Bernard, Jessie. 1972. *The future of marriage.* London: Souvenir.

Berndt, Ronald. 1961. Tribal marriage in a changing social order. *University of Western Australia Law Review* 5 (3): 326–46.

Berns, S. 2000. Folktales of legality: Family law in the procedural republic; The narrative structure of family law. *Law and Critique* 11 (1): 1–24.

Biondi, Jane. 1999. Who pays for guilt? Recent fault-based divorce reform proposals, cultural stereotypes and economic consequences. *Boston College Law Review* 40 (2): 611–32.

Bird, Carmel, ed. 1998. *The stolen children: Their stories.* Sydney: Random House.

Bissett-Johnson, Alastair, and David C. Day. 1986. *The new divorce law: A commentary on the Divorce Act, 1985.* Toronto: Carswell.

Bittman, Michael, and Jocelyn Pixley. 1997. *The double life of the family.* St. Leonards, NSW: Allen and Unwin.

Blackwood, Evelyn, ed. 1986. *The many faces of homosexuality: Anthropological approaches to homosexual behavior.* New York: Harrington Park.

Blackstone, William. 1773. Commentaries on the laws of England: A reprint of the first edition with supplement. Book 3. London: Dawsons of Pall Mall, 1966.

Bockus, Frank. 1993. *Couple therapy.* Northvale: Jason Aronson.

Boden, Sharon. 2003. *Consumerism, romance and the wedding experience.* New York: Palgrave Macmillan.

The Bodyguard. 1992. Motion picture. Directed by Mick Jackson. Written by Lawrence Kasdan. Starring Kevin Costner, Whitney Houston and Gary Kemp. Warner Brothers.

Boswell, John. 1980. *Christianity, social tolerance, and homosexuality: Gay people in western Europe from the beginning of the Christian era to the fourteenth century.* Chicago: Univ. of Chicago Press.

———. 1994. *Same-sex unions in premodern Europe.* New York: Villard.

Boyd, Susan B. 2003. *Child custody, law and women's work.* Ontario: Oxford Univ. Press.

Bradford, Laura. 1997. The counterrevolution: A critique of recent proposals to reform no-fault divorce laws. *Stanford Law Review* 49 (3): 607–36.

Bratt, Carolyn S. 1984. Incest statutes and the fundamental right of marriage: Is Oedipus free to marry? *Family Law Quarterly* 18 (3): 257–309.

Brehm, Sharon S. 1992. *Intimate Relationships.* 2nd ed. New York: McGraw-Hill.

Brinig, Margaret F. 1998. The Supreme Court's impact on marriage, 1967–90. *Howard Law Journal* 41 (2): 271–87.

Brinig, Margaret F., and Steven M. Crafton. 1994. Marriage and opportunism. *Journal of Legal Studies* 23 (2): 869–94.

Brock, Peggy. 1995. Aboriginal families and the law in the era of segregation and assimilation, 1890s–1950s. In *Sex, power and justice: Historical perspectives on law in Australia,* ed. Diane Kirkby, 133–49. Melbourne: Oxford Univ. Press.

Brook, Heather. 1997. The troubled courtship of Gladys and Mick. *Australian Journal of Political Science* 32 (3): 419–36.

———. 2000. How to do things with sex. In *Law and sexuality: The global arena,* eds. Carl Stychin and Didi Herman, 132–50. Minneapolis: Univ. of Minnesota Press.

———. 2002. Stalemate: Rethinking the politics of marriage. *Feminist Theory* 3 (1): 45–56.

———. 2004. Just married? Adversarial divorce and the conjugal body politic. *Feminism & Psychology.* 14 (1): 81–99.

Brown, Kathleen M. 1996. *Good wives, nasty wenches, and anxious patriarchs: Gender, race, and power in colonial Virginia.* Chapel Hill: Univ. of North Carolina Press.

Browning, Sandra Lee, and R. Robin Miller, eds. 1999. *Til death do us part: A multicultural anthology on marriage (Contemporary Studies in Sociology).* Stanford, CT: JAI.

Burbury, Stanley. 1963. Family Law: Some extra-judicial reflections upon two years judicial experience of the Commonwealth Matrimonial Causes Act 1959. *Australian Law Journal* 36 (10): 283–307.

Butler, Judith. 1990. *Gender trouble: feminism and the subversion of identity.* New York: Routledge.

———. 1991. Imitation and gender insubordination. In *Inside/out: Lesbian theories, gay theories,* ed. Diana Fuss, 13–31. New York: Routledge.

———. 1992. The body you want: Liz Kotz interviews Judith Butler. *Artforum* 31 (3): 82–89.

———. 1993. *Bodies that matter: On the discursive limits of "sex.";* New York: Routledge.

———. 1994. Against proper objects. *differences* 6 (2–3): 1–26.

———. 1996. Sexual inversions. In *Feminist interpretations of Michel Foucault,* ed. Susan J. Hekman, 59–75. University Park, PA: Pennsylvania Univ. Press.

———. 1997. *Excitable speech: A politics of the performative.* New York and London: Routledge.

———. 2000. *Antigone's claim: kinship between life and death.* New York: Columbia Univ. Press.

Caldwell, Katherine L. 1998. Not Ozzie and Harriet: postwar divorce and the American liberal welfare state. *Law and Social Inquiry* 23 (1): 1–53.

Calhoun, Cheshire. 2000. *Feminism, the family, and the politics of the closet: Lesbian and gay displacement.* Oxford: Oxford Univ. Press.

Califia, Pat. 1997. *Sex changes: The politics of transgenderism.* San Francisco: Cleis.

Callahan, Parnell J. T. 1967. *The law of separation and divorce.* Dobbs Ferry, NY: Oceana.

Callender, Charles, and Lee M. Kochems. 1983. The North American Berdache. *Current Anthropology* 24 (4): 443–56.

Camfoo, Tex. 2000. *Love against the law: The autobiographies of Tex and Nelly Camfoo.* ed. Gillian Cowlishaw. Canberra: Aboriginal Studies.

Carcach, Carlos, and Marianne James. 1998. *Homicide between intimate partners in Australia.* Canberra: Australian Institute of Criminology. http://www.aic.gov.au/publications/tandi/tandi90.html.

Card, Claudia. 1996. Against marriage and divorce. *Hypatia* 11 (3): 1–23.

Carmichael, Gordon A. 1988. *With this ring: First marriage patterns, trends and prospects.* Canberra: Australian Institute of Family Studies.

Carney, Terry. 2006. *Social security law and policy.* Leichhardt, NSW: Federation.

Carter, Stephen L. 1998. "Defending" marriage: A modest proposal. *Howard Law Journal* 41 (2): 215–28.

Chambers, David. 1996. What if? The legal consequences of marriage and the legal needs of lesbian and gay couples. *Michigan Law Review* 95: 447.

Chapman, F. A. R. 1968. *Law and marriage.* New York: McGraw Hill.

Chapman, Robert B. 2000. Coverture and cooperation: The firm, the market, and the substantive consolidation of married debtors. *Bankruptcy Developments Journal* 17 (1): 105–220.

Charsley, Simon R. 1993. The rise of the British wedding cake. *Natural History* 102 (12): 58–68.

Chester, Robert, and Jane Streather. 1972. Cruelty in English divorce: Some empirical findings. *Journal of Marriage and the Family* 34 (4): 706–12.

Chisholm, R., and O. Jessep. 1981. Fault and financial adjustment under the Family Law Act. *University of New South Wales Law Journal* 4 (2): 43–71.

Cho, George. 1991. The De Facto Relationships Act 1984 (NSW): Blurring the distinction between de jure marriages and de facto relationships. *Australian Journal of Family Law* 5 (1): 19–36.

Clark, Homer H., Jr. 1968. *Law of domestic relations in the United States.* Hornbook Series. St. Paul, MN: West.

Clive, Eric M. 1992. *The law of husband and wife in Scotland.* 3rd ed. Edinburgh: W. Green/Sweet and Maxwell.

Clute, Sylvia. 1991. Divorce denied: Have mental cruelty, constructive desertion and reasonable apprehension of bodily harm been abolished in Virginia? *University of Richmond Law Review* 25 (2): 273–90.

Colker, Ruth. 1991. Marriage. *Yale Journal of Law and Feminism* 3 (2): 321–26.

Collier, Richard. 1995. *Masculinity, law and the family.* London: Routledge.

Collins, Randall. 1985. *Sociology of marriage and the family: Gender, love and property.* Chicago: Nelson Hall.

Collins, Patricia H. 1990. *Black feminist thought.* London: Unwin Hyman.

Constable, Nicole. 2003. *Romance on a global stage: Pen pals, virtual ethnography, and "mail order" marriages.* Berkeley and Los Angeles: Univ. of California Press.

Coolidge, David Orgon. 1998. Playing the *Loving* card: Same-sex marriage and the politics of analogy. *BYU Journal of Public Law* 12 (2): 201–38.

Coolidge, David Orgon, and William C. Duncan 2001. Reaffirming marriage: A presidential priority. *Harvard Journal of Law and Public Policy* 24 (2): 623–51.

Coombs, Mary. 1998. Sexual dis-orientation: transgendered people and same-sex marriage. *UCLA Women's Law Journal* 8 (2): 219–66.

Coontz, Stephanie. 1992. *The way we never were: American families and the nostalgia trap.* New York: Basic Books.

Coontz, Stephanie. 2005. *Marriage, a history: From obedience to intimacy, or how love conquered marriage.* New York: Viking.

Cott, Nancy. 2000. *Public vows: A history of marriage and the nation.* Cambridge, MA: Harvard Univ. Press.

Courtney, Susan. 2005. *Hollywood fantasies of miscegenation*. Princeton: Princeton Univ. Press.

Cowlishaw, Gillian. 1999. *Rednecks, eggheads and blackfellas: A study of racial power and intimacy in Australia*. Ann Arbor: Univ. of Michigan Press.

Cretney, S. M., and J. M. Masson. 1997. *Principles of family law*. 6th ed. London: Sweet and Maxwell.

Cronan, Sheila. 1973. Marriage. In *Radical Feminism*, ed. Anne Koedt et al., 213–21. New York: Quadrangle.

Currah, Paisley. 2003. The transgender rights imaginary. *The Georgetown Journal of Gender and the Law* 4 (2): 705–20.

Currie, Dawn H. 1993. "Here comes the bride": The making of a "modern traditional" wedding in western culture. *Journal of Comparative Family Studies* 24 (3): 403–22.

Cuthbert, Denise. 2000. Mothering the "Other": Feminism, colonialism and the experiences of non-Aboriginal adoptive mothers of Aboriginal children. *Balayi: Culture, Law and Colonialism* 1 (1): 31–51.

Da Costa, D. Mendes. 1970. The Divorce Act 1968 and grounds based on matrimonial fault. *Osgoode Hall Law Journal* 7 (2):111–54.

Daileader, Celia. 2005. *Racism, misogyny, and the 'Othello' myth: Interracial couples from Shakespeare to Spike Lee*. Cambridge: Cambridge Univ. Press.

Daniels, Jessie. 1997. *White lies: Race, class, gender and sexuality in white supremacist discourse*. New York: Routledge.

Davidoff, Leonore. 1974. Mastered for life: Servant and wife in Victorian and Edwardian England. *Journal of Social History* 7 (4): 406–28.

Davis, Angela Y. 1981. Rape, racism and the myth of the black rapist. In *Women, Race & Class*, 172–201. New York: Vintage.

———. 1998. *The Angela Y. Davis reader*. ed. Joy James. Malden, MA: Blackwell.

Day, Lincoln H. 1964. Patterns of divorce in Australia and the United States. *American Sociological Review* 29 (4): 509–22.

Dean, Mitchell. 1999. *Governmentality: Power and rule in modern society*. London: Sage.

Deech, Ruth. 1980. The case against legal recognition of cohabitation. *International and Comparative Law Quarterly* 29 (2 and 3): 480–97.

Delphy, Christine, and Diana Leonard. 1992. *Familiar exploitation: A new analysis of marriage in contemporary western societies*. Cambridge, UK: Polity.

Deming, Will. 1995. *Paul on marriage and celibacy: The Hellenistic background of 1 Corinthians 7*. Cambridge: Cambridge Univ. Press.

Destro, Robert A. 1997. Law and the politics of marriage: *Loving v. Virginia* after 30 years; Introduction. *Catholic University Law Review* 47 (4): 1207–30.

Dickey, Anthony. 2002. *Family law*. 4th ed. Sydney: Lawbook.

Diduck, Alison, and Katherine O'Donovan, eds. 2006. *Feminist perspectives on family law*. London: Routledge Cavendish.

Dnes, Antony W., and Robert Rowthorn, eds. 2002. Introduction. *The law and economics of marriage and divorce* 1–9. Cambridge: Cambridge Univ. Press.

Douthwaite, Graham. 1979. *Unmarried couples and the law*. Indianapolis: Allen Smith.

Dworkin, Andrea. 1987. *Intercourse*. New York: Free Press.

Dyer, Richard. 1997. *White*. New York: Routledge.

Easteal, Patricia. 1993. *Killing the beloved: Homicide between adult sexual intimates*. Canberra: Australian Institute of Criminology.

Edwards, Coral, and Peter Read, eds. 1989. *The lost children: Thirteen Australians taken from their Aboriginal families tell of the struggle*. Sydney: Doubleday.

Eekelaar, John. 1991. *Regulating divorce*. Oxford: Clarendon.

Eekelaar, John, and Mavis Maclean, eds. 1994. *Family law*. Oxford: Oxford Univ. Press.

Ellinghaus, Katherine. 2001. Regulating Koori marriages: The 1886 Victorian Aborigines Protection Act. *Journal of Australian Studies* 67: 22–29.

Elliott, Dyan. 1993. *Spiritual marriage: Sexual abstinence in medieval wedlock*. Princeton: Princeton Univ. Press.

Ellman, Ira Mark. 1997. The misguided movement to revive fault divorce, and why reformers should look instead to the American Law Institute. *International Journal of Law, Policy and the Family* 11 (2): 216–45.

Engels, Friedrich. 1902. *The origin of the family, private property and the state*. trans. E. Untermann. Chicago: C. H. Kerr.

Eskridge, William N., Jr. 1996. *The case for same-sex marriage: From sexual liberty to civilized commitment*. New York: Free Press.

Ettelbrick, Paula L. 1997. Since when is marriage a path to liberation? In *Same-sex marriage: The moral and legal debate*, eds. Robert M. Baird and Stuart E. Rosenbaum, 164–68. Amherst, NY: Prometheus.

———. 2001. Domestic partnerships, civil unions, or marriage: One size does not fit all. *Albany Law Review* 64 (3): 905–15.

Everett, Craig A., ed. 1997. *Divorce and remarriage: International studies*. New York: Haworth.

Fatal Attraction. 1987 (Motion picture.) Dir. Adrian Lyne. Starring Michael Douglas, Glenn Close, and Anne Archer. Paramount Pictures.

Fehlberg, Belinda, and Bruce Smyth. 2000. Pre-nuptial agreements for Australia: Why not? *Australian Journal of Family Law* 14 (6): 80–116.

Feldblum, Chai R. 2001. The limitations of liberal neutrality arguments in favour of same-sex marriage. In *Legal recognition of same-sex partnerships: A study of national, European and international law*, eds.

Robert Wintemute and Mads Andeæs, 55–74. Oxford and Portland, OR: Hart.

Field, Deborah A. 1998. Irreconcilable differences: Divorce and conceptions of private life in the Khrushchev era. *The Russian Review* 57 (4): 599–613.

Fine, Mark A., and David R. Fine. 1994. An examination and evaluation of recent changes in divorce laws in five western countries: The critical role of values. *Journal of Marriage and the Family* 56 (2): 249–63.

Fine, Michelle. 2004. Witnessing Whiteness. In *Off white: Readings on power, privilege, and resistance*, 2nd edition, eds. Michelle Fine, Linda Powell Pruitt, and April Burns, 245–56, New York: Routledge.

Fineman, Martha Albertson. 1994. Preface to *The public nature of private violence: The discovery of domestic abuse*, eds. M. A. Fineman and R. Mykitiuk, xi–xviii. New York: Routledge.

Fineman, Martha Albertson, and Roxanne Mykitiuk, eds. 1994. *The public nature of private violence: The discovery of domestic abuse*. New York: Routledge.

Finlay, H. A., ed. 1969. *Divorce, society and the law*. Melbourne: Butterworths.

———. 1980. Sexual identity and the law of nullity. *Australian Law Journal* 54 (3): 115–26.

———. 1997. Hapless creatures and beastly propensities: The introduction of divorce into Tasmania in 1860. *Australian Journal of Legal History* 3 (1): 41–72.

Finlay, H. A., and Rebecca J. Bailey-Harris. 1989. *Family law in Australia*. 4th ed. Sydney: Butterworths.

Flory, Heather. 2000. "I promise to love, honor, obey . . . and not divorce you": Covenant marriage and the backlash against no-fault divorce. *Family Law Quarterly* 34 (1): 133–47.

Foreman, Carol, and Stephen O'Ryan. 1985. *Guide to the De Facto Relationships Act New South Wales*. Sydney: Butterworths.

Foster, Michael Smith. 1999. *Annulment: The wedding that was: how the church can declare a marriage null*. New York: Paulist.

Foucault, Michel. 1978. *The history of sexuality: Volume 1: An introduction*. Harmondsworth: Penguin.

———. 1983. The Subject and Power. In *Michel Foucault: Beyond structuralism and hermeneutics*, 2nd ed. eds. Hubert L. Dreyfus and Paul Rabinow, 208–26. Chicago: Univ. of Chicago Press.

———. 1991. Governmentality. In *The Foucault effect: Studies in governmentality*, eds. G. Burchell, C. Gordon and P. Miller, 87–104. London: Harvester Wheatsheaf.

Frankenberg, Ruth. 1993. *White women, race matters: The social construction of whiteness*. Minneapolis: Univ. of Minnesota Press.

Fraser, Nancy. 1983. Foucault's body language. *Salmagundi* 61 (Fall): 55–70.

Frazer, Elizabeth, and Nicola Lacey. 1993. *The politics of community: A feminist critique of the liberal-communitarian debate.* New York: Harvester Wheatsheaf.

Freeman, Dorothy R. 1990. *Couples in conflict: Inside the counselling room.* Milton Keynes: Open Univ. Press.

Freeman, Elizabeth. 2002. *The wedding complex: Forms of belonging in modern American culture.* Durham, NC: Duke Univ. Press.

Freeman, Michael D. A., and Christina Lyon. 1983. *Cohabitation without marriage: An essay in law and social policy.* Aldershot: Gower.

Friedan, Betty. 1963. *The feminine mystique.* London: Victor Gollancz.

Friedman, Lawrence M. 2000. A dead language: Divorce law and practice before no-fault. *Virginia Law Review* 86 (7): 1497–536.

Ganter, Regina. 2005. *Mixed relations: Narratives of Asia/Aboriginal contact in North Australia.* Crawley, WA: Univ. of Western Australia Press.

Gatens, Moira. 1991. *Feminism and philosophy: Perspectives on difference and equality.* Cambridge, UK: Polity.

———. 1996. *Imaginary bodies: Ethics, power and corporeality.* London: Routledge.

Gatens, Moira, and Alison Mackinnon, eds. 1998. *Gender and institutions: Welfare, work and citizenship.* Melbourne: Cambridge Univ. Press.

Geller, Jaclyn. 1999. The contemporary wedding invitation: A social document in crisis. *Salmagundi* 121–22 (Winter): 175–88.

Geller, Jaclyn. 2001. *Here comes the bride: Women, weddings and the marriage mystique.* New York: Four Walls Eight Windows.

Giddens, Anthony. 1992. *The transformation of intimacy.* Cambridge, UK: Polity.

Gilbert, Paul H. 1991. *Human relationships: A philosophical introduction.* Oxford: Blackwell.

Gillis, John R. 1985. *For better, for worse: British marriages, 1600 to the present.* New York: Oxford Univ. Press.

Glendon, Maryanne. 1989. *The Transformation of Family Law.* Chicago: Univ. of Chicago Press.

Goda, Paul J. 1967. The historical evolution of the concepts of void and voidable marriages. *Journal of Family Law* 7: 297–308.

Golder, Hilary, and Diane Kirkby. 1995. Marriage and divorce law before the *Family Law Act* 1975. In *Sex, power and justice: historical perspectives on law in Australia,* ed. Diane Kirkby, 150–67. Oxford: Oxford Univ. Press.

Goldman, Emma. 1972. Marriage and Love. In *Red Emma speaks: Selected writings and speeches.* ed. Alix Kates Shulman. New York: Random House.

Goodale, Jane C. 1971. *Tiwi wives: A study of the women of Melville Island, North Australia.* Seattle: Univ. of Washington Press.

Goode, W. J. 1993. *World changes in divorce patterns.* New Haven, CT: Yale Univ. Press.

Goody, J., ed. 1973. *The character of kinship.* London: Cambridge Univ. Press.

Gordon, Albert I. 1964. *Intermarriage: Interfaith, interracial, interethnic.* Boston: Beacon.

Gordon, Charles. 1986. New immigration legislation: The Immigration Reform and Control Act of 1986, the Marriage Fraud Act, the State Department Efficiency Bill. *Georgetown Immigration Law Journal* 1 (3): 641–65.

Graff, E. J. 1997. Retying the knot. In *Same-sex marriage: Pro and con: A reader,* ed. Andrew Sullivan, 134–38. New York: Vintage.

Grammick, Jeannine, ed. 1989. *Homosexuality in the priesthood and the religious life.* New York: Crossroad.

Graycar, Regina. 1987. Social security and personal income taxation. In *Life without marriage: A woman's guide to the law,* eds. Regina Graycar and Deena Shiff, 101–35. Sydney: Pluto.

Graycar, Regina, and Jenny Morgan. 1990. *The hidden gender of law.* Leichhardt, NSW: Federation.

Green, Judge Joyce Hens, John V. Long, and Roberta L. Murawski. 1986. *Dissolution of marriage.* Family Law Series. Colorado Springs, CO: Shepard's/McGraw-Hill.

Greer, Germaine. 1970. *The Female Eunuch.* London: MacGibbon and Kee.

Grillo, Trina, and Stephanie M. Wildman. 1991. Obscuring the importance of race: The implication of making comparisons between racism and sexism (or other –isms). *Duke Law Journal* 1991 (2): 397–412.

Grimshaw, Jean. 1986. *Feminist philosophers: Women's perspectives on philosophical traditions.* London: Harvester Wheatsheaf.

Grimshaw, Patricia. 2002. Interracial marriages and colonial regimes in Victoria Australia and Aotearoa/New Zealand. *Frontiers* 23 (3): 12–28.

Grossman, Joanna, and Chris Guthrie. 1996. The road less taken: Annulment at the turn of the century. *American Journal of Legal History* 40 (3): 307–30.

Grosz, Elizabeth. 1988. The in(ter)vention of feminist knowledges. In *Crossing Boundaries: Feminisms and the Critique of Knowledges,* eds. Barbara Caine, Elizabeth A. Grosz, and Marie de Lepervanche, 92–104. Sydney: Allen and Unwin.

Grover, Chris, and Keith Soothill. 1999. Bigamy: Neither love nor marriage, but a threat to the nation? *Sociological Review* 47 (2): 332–44.

Gsell, F. X. 1956. *"The bishop with 150 wives": Fifty years as a missionary.* Sydney: Angus and Robertson.

Guess Who's Coming to Dinner? 1967. Motion picture. Dir. Stanley Kramer. Written by William Rose. Starring Spencer Tracy, Katharine Hepburn, Sidney Poitier and Katharine Houghton. Columbia Pictures.

Guttiérrez, Natividad. 1995. Miscegenation as nation-building: Indian and immigrant women in Mexico. In *Unsettling settler societies: Articulations of gender, race, ethnicity and class*, eds. Daiva Stasiulis and Nira Yuval-Davis, 161–87. London: Sage.

Hafner, Julian. 1993. *The end of marriage: Why monogamy isn't working.* London: Century.

Hale, Matthew. 1713. *The history of the common law of England: written by a learned hand.* Littleton, CO: F. B. Rothman., 1987.

Halem, Lynne Carol. 1980. *Divorce reform: Changing legal and social perspectives.* New York: The Free Press.

Halley, Janet. 2001. Recognition, rights, regulation, normalisation: Rhetorics of justification in the same-sex marriage debate. In *Legal recognition of same-sex partnerships: A study of national, European and international law*, eds. Robert Wintemute and Mads Andenæs, 97–113. Oxford and Portland, OR: Hart.

Hambly, David, and J. Neville Turner. 1971. *Cases and materials on Australian family law.* Sydney: The Law Book Company Ltd.

Hamilton, Annette. 1981. A complex strategical situation: Gender and power in Aboriginal Australia. In *Australian women: Feminist perspectives*, eds. Norma Grieve and Patricia Grimshaw, 69–85. Melbourne: Oxford Univ. Press.

Hamilton, Cicely. 1981. *Marriage as a trade.* London: The Women's Press.

Handschu, Barbara, and Mary Kay Kisthardt. 2003. The role of fault. *The National Law Journal* 25 (30): B6.

Hardy, Thomas. 1939. *The mayor of Casterbridge.* London: Macmillan.

Hartog, Hendrik. 2000. *Man and wife in America: A history.* Cambridge, UK: Harvard Univ. Press.

Hasday, Jill Elaine. 2000. Contest and consent: A legal history of marital rape. *California Law Review* 88 (5): 1373–505.

Hasson, E. 2003. Setting a standard or reflecting reality? The "role" of divorce law, and the case of the Family Law Act 1996. *International Journal of Law, Policy and the Family* 17 (3): 338–66.

Hawaii. Commission on Sexual Orientation and the Law. 1996. Report of the Hawaii Commission on Sexual Orientation and the Law. In *Same-sex marriage: The moral and legal debate*, ed. Robert M. Baird and Stuart E. Rosenbaum, 211–26. Amherst, NY: Prometheus.

Hegy, Pierre, and Joseph Martos, eds. 2000. *Catholic divorce: The deception of annulments.* New York: Continuum.

Hekman, Susan J., ed. 1996. *Feminist interpretations of Michel Foucault.* University Park, PA: Pennsylvania State Univ. Press.

Hekman, Susan J. 1999. *The future of differences: Truth and method in feminist theory*. Cambridge, UK: Polity.

Henn, Thomas, and Jocelyne Boujos. 2003. The penthouse, the porsche or the pension: Superannuation and divorce. *Revenue Law Journal* 13: 28–84.

Higginbotham, A. Leon, Jr., and Barbara K. Kopytoft. 2000. Racial purity and interracial sex in the law of colonial and antebellum Virginia. In *Interracialism: Black-white intermarriage in American history, literature, and law*, ed. Werner Sollors, 81–139. New York: Oxford Univ. Press.

Hirsch, Susan F. 1994. Introduction. to section 1, Images of Violence. In *The public nature of private violence: The discovery of domestic abuse*, ed. Martha Fineman and Roxanne Mykitiuk, 3–10. New York: Routledge.

Hodes, Martha, ed. 1999. *Sex, love, race: Crossing boundaries in North American history*. New York: New York Univ. Press.

Hoffman, Corinne. 2005. *The white Masai*. London: Arcadia.

Holmes, Mary. 2000. When is the personal political? The president's penis and other stories. *Sociology* 34 (2): 305–21.

Honoré, Tony. 1978. *Sex law*. London: Duckworth.

hooks, bell. 1982. *Ain't I a woman: Black women and feminism*. London: Pluto.

Hosking, Marion. 2005. *Why doesn't she leave? The story of a women's refuge*. Taree, New South Wales: Manning District Emergency Accommodation.

Howard, Vicki. 2006. *Brides Inc.: American weddings and the business of tradition*. Philadelphia: Univ. of Pennsylvania Press.

Hudson, Liam, and Bernadine Jacot. 1995. *Intimate relationships: The natural history of desire*. New Haven, CT: Yale Univ. Press.

Hughes, Colin A. 1965. The marriage of Mick and Gladys: A discretion without an appeal. In *Decisions: Case studies in Australian administration*, eds. B. B. Schaffer and D.C. Corbett, 302–23. Melbourne: F. W. Chesire.

Hunter, Nan D. 1995. Marriage, law and gender: A feminist inquiry. In *Sex wars: Sexual dissent and political culture*, eds. Lisa Duggan and Nan D. Hunter, 107–22. New York and London: Routledge.

Ingraham, Chrys. 1999. *White weddings: Romancing heterosexuality in popular culture*. New York: Routledge.

Jackson, Stevi. 1996. Heterosexuality as a problem for feminist theory. In *Sexualizing the social: Power and the organisation of sexuality*, eds. Lisa Adkins and Vicki Merchant, 15–34. Basingstoke and London: Macmillan.

Jacob, Herbert. 1988. *Silent revolution: The transformation of divorce law in the United States*. Chicago and London: Univ. of Chicago Press.

Jacobson, Cardell K., Acheampong Yaw Amoateng, and Tim B. Heaton. 2004. Inter-racial marriages in South Africa. *Journal of Comparative Family Studies* 35 (3): 443–58.

James, Nancy. 1995. Domestic violence: A history of arrest policies and a survey of modern laws. *Family Law Quarterly* 28 (3): 509–20.

Japanese Story. 2003. Motion picture. Dir. Sue Brooks. Starring Toni Collette and Gotaro Tsunashima. Samuel Goldwyn Films.

Jebb, Mary Anne, and Anna Haebich. 1992. Across the great divide: Gender relations on Australian frontiers. *Gender Relations in Australia*, eds. Kay Saunders and Raymond Evans, 20–41. Sydney: Harcourt Brace.

Jedda, 1955. Motion picture. Dir. Charles Chauvel. Starring Ngarla Kunoth, Robert Tudawali, Betty Suttor. Charles Chauvel Productions.

Jeffreys, Sheila. 2004. The need to abolish marriage. *Feminism & Psychology* 14 (2): 327–31.

Jones, Jill. 1998. Fanning an old flame: Alienation of affections and criminal conversation revisited. *Pepperdine Law Review* 26 (1): 61–88.

Joske, P. E. 1969. *Matrimonial causes and marriage law and practice of Australia and New Zealand*. 5th ed. Sydney: Butterworths.

Jungle Fever. 1991. Motion picture. Dir. Spike Lee. Starring Wesley Snipes and Annabella Sciorra. Universal Pictures.

Katter, Norman A. 1987. *Conduct, fault and family law*. with a foreword by the Hon. Mr. Justice G.E. Lambert. Sydney: Law Book.

Kay, Herma Hill. 1987. Equality and difference: A perspective on no-fault divorce and its aftermath. *University of Cincinnati Law Review* 56 (1): 1–90.

———. 1991. Private choices and public policy: Confronting the limitations of marriage. *Australian Journal of Family Law* 5 (1): 69–85.

———. 2002. No-fault divorce and child custody: Chilling out the gender wars. *Family Law Quarterly* 36 (1): 27–47.

Kennedy, Randall. 2003. *Interracial intimacies: Sex, marriage, identity and adoption*. New York: Pantheon.

———. 1997. How are we doing with *Loving*: Race, law, and intermarriage. *Boston University Law Review* 77: 815–22.

Knight, Robert H. 1997. How domestic partnerships and "gay marriage" threaten the family. In *Same-sex marriage: The moral and legal debate*, eds. Robert M. Baird and Stuart E. Rosenbaum, 108–21. Amherst, NY: Prometheus.

Koppelman, Andrew. 2001. The miscegenation analogy in Europe, or, Lisa Grant meets Adolf Hitler. *In Legal recognition of same-sex partnerships: A study of national, European and international law*, eds. Robert Wintemute and Mads Andenæs, 623–33. Oxford and Portland, OR: Hart.

———. 1997. The miscegenation precedents. In *Same-sex marriage: Pro and con, a reader*, ed. Andrew Sullivan, 335–42. New York: Vintage.

Krause, Harry D. 1983. *Family law: Cases, comments and questions*. 2nd ed. St. Paul, MN: West.

Landes, Joan B., ed. 1998. *Feminism, the public and the private.* Oxford Readings in Feminism Series. Oxford and New York: Oxford Univ. Press.

Landis, Judson T., and Mary G. Landis, eds. 1952. *Readings in marriage and the family.* New York: Prentice-Hall.

Lecours, André, ed. 2005. New institutionalism: Issues and Questions. In *New institutionalism: Theory and analysis,* 3–26. Toronto: Univ. of Toronto Press.

Lecours, Andre, ed. 2005. *New institutionalism: Theory and analysis.* Toronto: Univ. of Toronto Press.

Levi-Strauss, Claude. 1969. *The elementary structures of kinship.* eds. J. H. Bell, J. R. von Sturmer, and R. Needham. London: Eyre and Spottiswoode.

Lombardo, Paul A. 1988. Miscegenation, eugenics, and racism: Historical footnotes to *Loving v. Virginia. UC Davis Law Review* 21 (2): 421–52.

Lubin, Peter, and Dwight Duncan. 1998. Follow the footnote, or the advocate as historian of same-sex marriage. *Catholic University Law Review* 47 (4): 1271–1325.

MacDougall, D. J. 1966. Proposals to reform the law of condonation. *Australian Law Journal* 39 (9): 295–301.

MacKenzie, Norman. 1962. *Women in Australia: A report to the social science research council of Australia.* Melbourne: F. W. Cheshire.

Mackenzie, Robin. 1992. Transsexuals' legal status and same sex marriage in New Zealand: *M v. M. Otago Law Review* 7 (4): 556–77.

Mackie, Vera. 2001. The trans-sexual citizen: Queering sameness and difference. *Australian Feminist Studies* 16 (35): 185–92.

Mamashela, Mothokoa. 2004. New families, new property, new laws: The practical effects of the Recognition of Customary Marriages Act. *South African Journal on Human Rights* 20 (4): 616–41.

Marcosson, Samuel A. 1992. Harassment on the basis of sexual orientation: A claim of sex discrimination under Title VII. *Georgetown Law Journal* 81 (1): 1–38.

Marcus, Isabel. 1994 Reframing "domestic violence": Terrorism in the home. In *The public nature of private violence: The discovery of domestic abuse,* eds. Martha A. Fineman and Roxanne Mykitiuk, 11–35. New York: Routledge.

Marvell, Thomas B. 1989 Divorce rates and the fault requirement. *Law and Society Review* 23 (4): 543–67.

Marwick, M. G. 1969. The comparative sociology of divorce. In *Divorce, society and the law,* ed. H. A. Finlay, 87–110. Melbourne: Butterworths.

Mathabane, Mark, and Gail Mathabane. 1992. *Love in black and white: The triumph of love over prejudice and taboo.* New York: HarperCollins.

Mattingley, Christobel. 1988. *Survival in our own land: "Aboriginal" experiences in "South Australia" since 1836, told by Nungas and others.* eds.

Christobel Mattingley and Ken Hampton. Adelaide, SA: Aboriginal Literature Development Assistance Association Inc.; Sydney: Hodder and Stoughton.

Maushart, Susan. 2001. *Wifework: What marriage really means for women.* New York: Bloomsbury.

McConvill, James, and Eithne Mills. 2003. *Re Kevin* and the right of transsexual persons to marry in Australia. *International Journal of Law, Policy and the Family* 17 (3): 251–74.

McGrath, Ann. 1987. *Born in the cattle: Aborigines in cattle country.* Sydney: Allen and Unwin.

McGregor, O. R. 1957. *Divorce in England.* London: Heinemann.

McLennan, John F. 1970. *Primitive marriage.* Chicago: Univ. of Chicago Press.

McNamara, Robert, Maria Tempenis, and Beth Walton. 1999. *Crossing the line: Interracial couples in the south.* Westport, CT: Greenwood.

Menefee, Samuel. 1981. *Wives for sale: An ethnographic study of British popular divorce.* New York: St. Martins.

Messerschmidt, James. 1997. *Crime as structured action.* Thousand Oaks, CA: Sage.

Mill, John Stuart. 1832. Early essays on marriage and divorce. In *John Stuart Mill and Harriet Taylor: Essays on Sex Equality,* ed. Alice S. Rossi, 67–85. Chicago: Univ. of Chicago Press, 1970.

Montemurro, Beth. 2006. *Something old, something bold.* New Brunswick, NJ: Rutgers Univ. Press.

Moran, Rachel F. 2001. *Interracial intimacy: The regulation of race and romance.* Chicago: Univ. of Chicago Press.

Moreton-Robinson, Aileen. 2000. *Talkin' up to the white woman.* Brisbane: Univ. of Queensland Press.

Mörner, Magnus. 1967. *Race mixture in the history of Latin America.* Boston: Little, Brown.

Mumford, Kevin. 2005. The miscegenation analogy revisited: Same-sex marriage as a civil rights story. *American Quarterly* 57 (2): 523–31.

Newbeck, Phyl. 2004. *Virginia hasn't always been for lovers: Interracial marriage bans and the case of Richard and Mildred Loving.* Carbondale, IL: Southern Illinois Univ. Press.

New South Wales, Parliament, Legislative Assembly. 1984. De Facto Relationships Bill, second reading debate. (Hansard.)

Nielsen, Linda. 1990. Family rights and the "registered partnership" in Denmark. *International Journal of the Law and the Family* 4 (3): 297–99.

Nolan, Laurence C. 1998. The meaning of *Loving:* Marriage, due process and equal protection (1967–1990) as equality and marriage, from *Loving* to *Zablocki. Howard Law Journal* 41 (2): 245–70.

Northern Territory Administration, Welfare Branch 1958. *Annual Report 1957–58.*

Northern Territory Administration, Welfare Branch 1959. *Annual Report 1958–59.*

Northern Territory News. 1959 Editorial. August 18.

Nussbaum, Martha. 1997. Narratives of hierarchy: *Loving v. Virginia* and the literary imagination. *Quinnipiac Law Review* 17: 337–55.

Oboler, Regina S. 1980. Is the female husband a man? Woman/woman marriage among the Nandi of Kenya. *Ethnology* 19 (1): 69–88.

O'Donnell, William J., and David A. Jones. 1982. *The law of marriage and marital alternatives.* Lexington, MA: Lexington Books.

Okin, Susan Moller. 1989. *Justice, gender and the family.* New York: Basic Books.

Oldham, J. Thomas. 2000. Lessons from *Jerry Hall v. Mick Jagger* regarding U.S. regulation of heterosexual cohabitants or, can't get no satisfaction. *Notre Dame Law Review* 76 (5): 1409–34.

Oliver, Dawn. 1987. *Cohabitation: The legal implications.* Bicester, UK: CCH.

Omi, Michael, and Howard Winant. 1986. *Racial formation in the United States from the 1960s to the 1980s.* New York: Routledge and Kegan Paul.

O'Neill, William L. 1967. *Divorce in the progressive era.* New Haven: Yale Univ. Press.

Osborne, Catherine. 1994. *Eros unveiled: Plato and the god of love.* Oxford: Oxford Univ. Press.

Otlowski, Margaret. 1990. The legal status of a sexually reassigned transsexual: *R v. Harris and McGuiness* and beyond. *Australian Law Journal* 64 (1–2): 67–74.

Otnes, Cele C., and Elizabeth H. Pleck. 2003. *Cinderella dreams: The allure of the lavish wedding.* Berkeley: Univ. of California Press.

Outhwaite, R. B., ed. 1981. *Marriage and society: Studies in the social history of marriage.* London: Europa.

Owen, June Duncan. 2002. *Mixed matches: Interracial marriage in Australia.* Sydney: UNSW.

Parker, Andrew, and Eve Kosofsky Sedgwick, eds. 1995. Introduction: Performativity and performance. In *Performativity and performance.* 1–18. New York and London: Routledge.

Parker, Stephen. 1990. *Informal marriage, cohabitation and the law, 1750–1989.* London: Macmillan.

Parker, Stephen, Patrick Parkinson, and Juliet Behrens. 1994. *Australian family law in context: Commentary and materials.* Sydney: The Law Book.

Parkman, Allen M. 2002. Mutual consent divorce. In *The law and economics of marriage and divorce*, eds. Antony W. Dnes and Robert Rowthorn, 57–69. Cambridge: Cambridge Univ. Press.

Parry, Martin. 1993. *The law relating to cohabitation*. 3rd ed. London: Sweet and Maxwell.

Pascoe, Peggy. 1996. Miscegenation law, court cases, and ideologies of "race" in twentieth-century America. *The Journal of American History* 83 (1): 44–69.

Pascoe, Peggy. 1991. Race, gender, and intercultural relations: The case of interracial marriage. *Frontiers* 12 (1): 5–19.

Passingham, Bernard, and Caroline Harmer. 1985. *Law and practice in matrimonial causes*. 4th ed. London: Butterworths.

Pateman, Carole. 1989. *The disorder of women*. Cambridge, UK: Polity.
———. 1988. *The sexual contract*. Cambridge, UK: Polity.

Pawlowski, Mark. 1996. Cohabitation contracts: Are they legal? *New Law Journal* 146 (6754): 1125–26.

Pearce, T. A. 1969. The broken marriage—is modern divorce the answer? In *Divorce, society and the law*, ed. H. A. Finlay, 53–68. Melbourne: Butterworths.

Perkins, Rollin Morris. 1972. *Cases and materials on criminal law and procedure*. 4th ed. Mineola, N.Y.: Foundation.

Perry, Barbara, and Michael Sutton. 2006. Seeing red over black and white: Popular and media representations of inter-racial relationships as precursors to racial violence. *Canadian Journal of Criminology and Criminal Justice* 48 (6): 887–904.

Phelan, Shane, ed. 1997. Lesbians and Mestizas: Appropriation and equivalence. In *Playing with fire: Queer politics, queer theories*, 75–95. New York: Routledge.

Phillips, Roderick. 1988. *Putting asunder: A history of divorce in western society*. Cambridge: Cambridge Univ. Press.

Pierce, Christine. 1997. Gay marriage. In *Same-sex marriage: The moral and legal debate*, eds. Robert M. Baird and Stuart E. Rosenbaum, 169–79. Amherst, NY: Prometheus.

Pix. 1960. A wedding in black & white: Aboriginal girl, white drover eventually find happiness. January 23: 6–7.

Pleck, Elizabeth H., and Cele C. Otnes. 2006. Response. *Journal of Women's History* 18 (4): 123–27.

Polikoff, Nancy D. 1993. We will get what we ask for: Why legalizing gay and lesbian marriage will not dismantle the legal structure of gender in every marriage. *Virginia Law Review* 79 (7): 1535–50.

Popovic, Neil A. F. 1994. The game of the name. *Ms* 5 (3): 96.

Povinelli, Elizabeth. 2006. *Empire of love: Toward a theory of intimacy, genealogy, and carnality*. Durham, NC: Duke Univ. Press.

Pratt, Robert A. 1998. Crossing the color line: A historical assessment and personal narrative of *Loving v. Virginia*. *Howard Law Journal* 41 (2): 229–44.

Pringle, Rosemary, and Sophie Watson. 1990. Fathers, brothers, mates: The fraternal state in Australia. In *Playing the state: Australian feminist interventions*, ed. Sophie Watson, 229–43. Sydney: Allen and Unwin.

Quale, G. Robina. 1988. *A history of marriage systems.* New York: Greenwood.

Rajkowski, Pamela. 1995. *Linden girl: A story of outlawed lives.* Nedlands, WA: Univ. of Western Australia Press.

Rasmusen, Eric. 2002. An economic approach to adultery law. In *The law and economics of marriage and divorce*, eds. Antony Dnes and Robert Rowthorn, 70–91. Cambridge: Cambridge Univ. Press.

Reekie, Gail. 1998. *Measuring immorality: Social inquiry and the problem of illegitimacy.* Cambridge and Melbourne: Cambridge Univ. Press.

Reynolds, Philip Lyndon. 1994. *Marriage in the western church: The Christianisation of marriage during the Patristic and early medieval periods.* Leiden and New York: E. J. Brill.

Rheinstein, Max. 1972. *Marriage stability, divorce, and the law.* Chicago: Univ. of Chicago Press.

Rich, Adrienne. 1977. *Of woman born: Motherhood as experience and institution.* London: Virago.

———. 1980. Compulsory heterosexuality and lesbian existence. *Signs* 5 (4): 631–60.

Richards, David A. J. 2001. Introduction: Theoretical perspectives. In *Legal recognition of same-sex partnerships: A study of national, European and international law*, eds. Robert Wintemute and Mads Andenæs, 25–30. Oxford and Portland: Hart.

Riddiford, Tracy. (Vida Films). 2005. Personal communication, November 11.

Robinson, Charles Frank, II. 2003. *Dangerous liaisons: Sex and love in the segregated south.* Fayetteville: Univ. of Arkansas Press.

Robson, Ruthann. 1992. *Lesbian (out)law: Survival under the rule of law.* Ithaca, NY: Firebrand.

Roe, Tony. 2007. Just (not) married. *Solicitors Journal* 151 (6): 186–87.

Roen, Katrina. 2002. "Either/or" and "both/neither": Discursive tensions in transgender politics. *Signs* 27 (2): 501–22.

Romano, Renee C. 2003. *Race mixing: Black-white marriage in postwar America.* Cambridge, UK: Harvard Univ. Press.

Root, Maria P. P. 2001. *Love's revolution: Interracial marriage.* Philadelphia: Temple Univ. Press.

Rose, Deborah Bird, and Tony Swain, eds. 1988. Introduction. *Aboriginal Australians and Christian missions: Ethnographic and historical studies*, 1–8. Bedford Park, SA: Australian Association for the Study of Religions.

Rose, Nikolas. 1987. Beyond the public/private division: Law, power and the family. *Journal of Law and Society* 14 (1): 61–76.

———. 1989. *Governing the soul: The shaping of the private self.* London: Routledge.

———. 1996. Governing "advanced" liberal democracies. In *Foucault and political reason: Liberalism, neo-liberalism and rationalities of government*, eds. Andrew Barry, Thomas Osborne, and Nikolas Rose, 37–64. London: UCL.

Rose, Randall L., and Stacy L. Wood. 2005. Paradox and the consumption of authenticity through reality television. *Journal of Consumer Research* 32 (2): 297–311.

Rosenblatt, Paul C., Terri Karis, and Richard R. Powell. 1995. *Multiracial couples: Black and white voices.* Thousand Oaks, CA: Sage.

Ross, Josephine. 2002. The sexualisation of difference: A comparison of mixed-race and same-gender marriage. *Harvard Civil Rights-Civil Liberties Law Review* 37 (2): 255–88.

Rousseau, Jean-Jacques. 1974. *Emile.* trans. Barbara Foxley. London: Dent.

Roy, Kartik C., and Jörn Sideras, eds. 2006. *Institutions, globalisation and empowerment.* Cheltenham, UK: Edward Elgar.

Russell, Bertrand. 1958. *Marriage and morals.* London Allen and Unwin.

Russell, Denise. 1995. *Women, madness and medicine.* Cambridge, UK: Polity.

Ryan, Fergus W. 1998. "When divorce is away, nullity's at play": A new ground for annulment, its dubious past and its uncertain future. *Trinity College Law Review* 1: 15–36.

Saalfield, Catherine. 1993. Lesbian Marriage . . . (K)not! In *Sisters, sexperts, queers: Beyond the lesbian nation*, ed. Arlene Stein, 187–95. New York: Plume.

Saks, Eva. 2000. Representing miscegenation law. In *Interracialism: Black-white intermarriage in American history, literature, and law*, ed. Werner Sollors, 61–80. New York: Oxford Univ. Press.

Sandell, Jillian. 1994. The cultural necessity of queer families. *Bad Subjects* 12. http://bad.eserver.org/.

Sarantakos, Sotirios. 1994. Unmarried cohabitation: Options, limits and possibilities. *Australian Journal of Marriage and Family* 15 (3): 148–60.

Sawer, Marian, ed. 1996. *Removal of the Commonwealth marriage bar: A documentary history.* Canberra: Centre for Research in Public Sector Management, University of Canberra.

Schimmerling, Thomas E. 1997. The no-fault debate: Is blame better? *Trial* 33 (8): 33–37.

Schoenfeld, Elizabeth. 1996. Drumbeats for divorce reform. *Policy Review* (May–June): 8–10.

Scott, Elizabeth. 2002. Marital commitment and the legal regulation of divorce. In *The law and economics of marriage and divorce*, eds. Antony W. Dnes and Robert Rowthorn, 35–56. Cambridge: Cambridge Univ. Press.

Scutt, Jocelynne A. 1990. *Women and the law: Commentary and materials.* Sydney: Law Book.

———. 1995. Judicial bias or legal bias? Battery, women and the law. *Journal of Australian Studies* 43: 130–43.

Scutt, Jocelynne A., and Di Graham. 1984. *For richer, for poorer: Money, marriage and property rights.* Ringwood, VIC: Penguin.

Searle, John R. 1989. How performatives work. *Linguistics and Philosophy* 12 (5): 535–58.

Seculow, Jay Alan, and John Tuskey. 1998. Sex and sodomy and apples and oranges—Does the constitution require states to grant a right to do the impossible? *BYU Journal of Public Law* 12 (2) 309–32.

Selby, David M. 1960. Cruelty as a matrimonial offence. *Sydney Law Review* 1 (2): 237–45.

Sharpe, Andrew N. 2002. *Transgender jurisprudence: Dysphoric bodies of law.* London: Cavendish.

———. 1997. The transsexual and marriage: Law's contradictory desires. *Australasian Gay and Lesbian Law Journal* 7: 1–14.

Siegel, Reva B. 1996. "The rule of love": Wife beating as prerogative and privacy. *Yale Law Journal* 105 (8): 2117–207.

Sinclair, June D. 1996. *The law of marriage.* 5th ed. Cape Town: Juta.

Singer, Samantha L. C. 2004. Bellinger v. Bellinger 2003 2 AC 467. *Journal of Social Welfare and Family Law* 26 (1): 79–87.

Skelly, Stephen J. 1969. Refusal of sexual intercourse and cruelty as a ground for divorce. *Alberta Law Review* 7 (2): 239–46.

Smart, Carol. 1984. *The ties that bind: Law, marriage and the reproduction of patriarchal relations.* London: Routledge and Kegan Paul.

———. 1996. Collusion, collaboration and confession: On moving beyond the heterosexuality debate. In *Theorising heterosexuality: Telling it straight,* ed. Diane Richardson, 161–77. Buckingham and Philadelphia: Open Univ.Press.

Smith, Douglas K. 1971. Comment: Transsexualism, sex reassignment surgery, and the law. *Cornell Law Review* 56 (6): 963–1009.

Smith, Ian. 2002. European divorce: laws, rates, and consequences. In *The Law and Economics of Marriage and Divorce,* eds. Antony W. Dnes and Robert Rowthorn, 212–29. Cambridge: Cambridge Univ. Press.

Sollors, Werner, ed. 2000. *Interracialism: Black-white intermarriage in American history, literature, and law.* New York: Oxford Univ. Press.

Spaht, Katherine Shaw. 1998. Louisiana's covenant marriage: Social analysis and legal implications. *Louisiana Law Review* 59 (1): 63–130

Spender, Dale, ed. 1994. *Weddings and wives.* Ringwood, VIC: Penguin.

Stafford, Rebecca, Elaine Backman, and Pamela Dibona. 1977. The division of labor among cohabiting and married couples. *Journal of Marriage and the Family* 39 (1): 43–57.

Stanton, Elizabeth Cady. 1891. Patriotism and chastity. *Westminster Review* 135 (January): 1–5.

Starnes, Cynthia. 1993. Divorce and the displaced homemaker: A discourse on playing with dolls, partnership buyouts and dissociation under no-fault. *University of Chicago Law Review* 60 (1): 67–140.

Stein, Stuart J. 1969. Common law marriage: Its history and certain contemporary problems. *Journal of Family Law*, 9 (3): 271–99

Stember, Charles Herbert. 1976. *Sexual racism: The emotional barrier to an integrated society.* New York: Elsevier.

Stone, Linda, and R. J. Parkin, eds. 2004. *Kinship and family: An anthropological reader.* Malden, MA: Blackwell.

Stuart, Eileen F. 1994. *Dissolution and annulment of marriage by the Catholic Church.* Sydney: Federation.

Stychin, Carl, and Didi Herman, eds. 2000. *Law and sexuality: The global arena.* Minneapolis: Univ. of Minnesota Press.

Sullivan, Andrew, ed. 1997. *Same-sex marriage: Pro and con, a reader.* New York: Vintage.

Sullivan, Andrew. 1996. *Virtually normal: An argument about homosexuality.* 2nd ed. London: Picador.

Sullivan, Barbara. 1997. *The politics of sex: Prostitution and pornography in Australia since 1945.* New York: Cambridge Univ. Press.

Sundberg, Jacob W. F. 1975. Recent changes in Swedish family law: Experiment repeated. *American Journal of Comparative Law* 23 (1): 34–46.

Swisher, Peter Nash. 2004–5. Marriage and some troubling issues with no-fault divorce. *Regent University Law Review* 17 (2): 243–59.

Tarlo, H. 1963. Intention and insanity in divorce law. *Australian Law Journal* 37 (1): 3–19.

Tatz, Colin. 2001. Confronting Australian genocide. *Aboriginal History* 25 (2001): 16–36.

Teichman, Jenny. 1982. *Illegitimacy: A philosophical examination.* Oxford: Basil Blackwell.

Telfer, E. J. 1939. *Amongst Australian Aborigines: Forty years of missionary work.* Sydney: Fraser and Morphet.

Tucker, Joe A. 1991. Assimilation to the United States: A study of the adjustment of status and the immigration marriage fraud statutes. *Immigration and Nationality Law Review* 13: 26–106.

Turner, Jonathan H. 1997. *The institutional order: Economy, kinship, religion, polity, law, and education in evolutionary and comparative perspective.* New York: Longman.

United Kingdom Law Society, Family Law Sub-Committee. 1979. *A better way out.* London: Law Society.

United States of America. 1996. *Defense of Marriage Act* Pub L 104–99.

VanEvery, Jo. 1996a. Heterosexuality and domestic life. In *Theorising heterosexuality: Telling it straight*, ed. Diane Richardson, 39–54. Buckingham and Philadelphia: Open Univ. Press.

———. 1996b. Sinking into his arms . . . arms in his sink: Heterosexuality and feminism revisited. In *Sexualizing the social: Power and the organisation of sexuality*, eds. Lisa Adkins and Vicki Merchant, 35–54. Basingstoke and London: Macmillan.

Van Tassel, Emily Field. 1995. "Only the law would rule between us": Antimiscegenation, the moral economy of dependency, and the debate over rights after the civil war. *Chicago-Kent Law Review* 70 (3): 873–926.

Vlosky, Denese Ashbaugh, and Pamela A. Monroe. 2002. The effective dates of no-fault divorce laws in the 50 states. *Family Relations* 51 (4): 317–25.

Wade, John (ed.). 1990. Defacto marriage: The legal framework. In *Defacto and ex-nuptial rights, 1–16*. Melbourne: Business Law Education Centre.

Wadlington, Walter. 1966. The *Loving* case: Virginia's anti-miscegenation statute in historical perspective. *Virginia Law Review* 52 (7): 1189–223.

Walby, Sylvia. 1990. *Theorizing patriarchy*. Oxford: Basil Blackwell.

Wallenstein, Peter. 2002. *Tell the court I love my wife: Race, marriage, and law—an American history*. New York: Palgrave Macmillan.

Wardle, Lynn D. 1991. No-fault divorce and the divorce conundrum. *Brigham Young University Law Review* 1991 (1): 79–142.

———. 1998. *Loving v. Virginia* and the constitutional right to marry, 1790–1990. *Howard Law Journal* 41 (2): 289–347.

———. 2003. The bonds of matrimony and the bonds of constitutional democracy. *Hofstra Law Review* 32 (1): 349–78.

Warner, Michael. 1999. Beyond gay marriage. In *The trouble with normal: Sex, politics and the ethics of queer life*. New York: Free Press.

Warnock, G. J. 1973. Some types of performative utterance. In *Essays on J. L. Austin*, ed. Berlin et al., 69–89. London: Oxford at Clarendon.

Wartenberg, Thomas. 1994. "But would you want your daughter to marry one?" The representation of race and racism in *Guess Who's Coming to Dinner? Journal of Social Philosophy* 28: 99–130.

Webb, P. R. H. 1959. "Shot-gun" marriages and the conflict of laws. *Modern Law Review* 22 (2): 198–204.

Webb, P. R. H., and H. K. Bevan. 1964. *Source book of family law*. London: Butterworths.

Weedon, Chris. 1999. *Feminism, theory and the politics of difference*. Oxford: Blackwell.

Weitzman, Lenore J. 1985. *The divorce revolution: The unexpected social and economic consequences for women and children in America*. New York: Free Press.

West, Cornel. 1993. *Race matters.* New York: Vintage.

Westermarck, Edward Alexander. 1922. *The history of human marriage.* 5th ed. New York: Allerton.

Weston, Kath. 1991. *Families we choose: Lesbians, gays, kinship.* New York: Columbia Univ. Press.

Wheeler, Michael. 1974. *No-fault divorce.* Boston: Beacon.

Wicks, Erik V. 2000. Fault-based divorce "reforms," archaic survivals, and ancient lessons. *Wayne Law Review* 46 (3): 1565–601.

Willmott, Lindy. 1996. *De facto relationships law.* North Ryde: LBC Information Services.

Wilson, Carol. 2005. Wedding cake: A slice of history. *Gastronomica* 5 (2): 69–72.

Wilson, James Q. 1997. Against homosexual marriage. In *Same-sex marriage: The moral and legal debate,* eds. Robert M. Baird and Stuart E. Rosenbaum, 137–45. Amherst, NY: Prometheus.

Wilson, Midge, and Kathy Russell. 1996. *Divided sisters: Bridging the gap between black women and white women.* New York: Anchor Books/Doubleday.

Wintemute, Robert, and Mads Andenæs, eds. 2001. *Legal recognition of same-sex partnerships: A study of national, European and international law.* Oxford and Portland: Hart.

Winton, F. R., and L. E. Bayliss. 1949. *Human physiology.* 3rd ed. London: J. and A. Churchill.

Witte, John, Jr. 1997. *From sacrament to contract: Marriage, religion, and law in the western tradition.* Louisville, KY: Westminster John Knox.

Wolf, Naomi. 1993. Radical heterosexuality: Or, how to love a man and save your feminist soul. In *Transforming a rape culture,* eds. Emilie Buchwald, Pamela Fletcher, and Martha Roth, 359–68. Minneapolis: Milkweek Editions.

Wolfram, Sybil. 1987. *In-laws and outlaws: Kinship and marriage in England.* New York: St. Martins.

———. 1990. "Husband and wife are one person: The husband" (Nineteenth-century English aphorism.) In *Women's rights and the rights of man,* eds. Andre-Jean Arnaud and Elizabeth Kingdom, 158–71. Aberdeen: Aberdeen Univ. Press.

Wolfson, Evan. 2004. *Why marriage matters: America, equality, and gay people's right to marry.* New York: Simon and Schuster.

———. 1997. Why we should fight for the freedom to marry. In *Same-sex marriage: Pro and con: A reader,* ed. Andrew Sullivan, 128–132. New York: Vintage.

———. 1994. Crossing the threshold: Equal marriage rights for lesbians and gay men and the intra-community critique. *New York University Review of Law and Social Change,* 21 (3): 567–615.

Wollstonecraft, Mary. 1985. *Vindication of the rights of woman.* Ed. Miriam Brody. London: Penguin.

Woodhouse, Barbara Bennett. 1994. Sex, lies and dissipation: The discourse of fault in a no-fault era. *Georgetown Law Journal* 82 (7): 2525–68.

Yalom, Marilyn. 2001. *A history of the wife.* New York: HarperCollins.

Notes

Chapter 1

1. Many of my younger students have a different understanding, believing that "Ms." signifies a divorcee.
2. Interested readers should see Constable 2003.

Chapter 2

1. Levi-Strauss (1969); McLennan (1970); Stone and Parkin (2004), *inter alia*.
2. Osborne (1994); Gilbert (1991); Rousseau (1974); Russell (1958); Deming (1995); Reynolds (1994); Elliott (1993), *inter alia*.
3. Aries and Duby (1987–1991); Westermarck (1922); Quale (1988); Outhwaite (1981); Coontz (1992); Hudson and Jacot (1995); Collier (1995); Chapman (1968); Eekelaar and Maclean (1994); Gillis (1985); Hartog (2000); Cott (2000); Coontz (2005); *inter alia*.
4. Collins (1985); Everett (1997); Carmichael (1988); Landis and Landis (1952); Wolfram (1987); Browning and Miller (1999), *inter alia*.
5. Hafner (1993); Freeman (1990); Bockus (1993); Brehm (1992); *inter alia*.
6. In fact, Bernard's work—like many of the texts under discussion in this chapter—bridges the categories being posited. There are degrees of

overlap in nearly all of the works surveyed here, but the distinctions I have drawn are conceptually useful nonetheless.

7. See, for example, Lois Banner's reference to "what we used to call patriarchy" (2000, 258) in an essay reviewing three feminist texts.

8. My exploration of new ways to theories marriage should in no way be understood as a hasty or disrespectful rejection of existing critiques. Rather, I am suggesting ways to continue, augment, and extend existing feminist scholarship.

9. Naomi Wolf (1993) and Dale Spender (1994) do come perilously close, however.

10. In Australia, for example, the crude marriage rate has been in decline since the 1970s (Australian Bureau of Statistics [ABS] 2007).

11. Some radical feminists expressed precisely this hope in the 1970s. Sheila Cronan (1973, 213) cites Kathie Sarachild, "When male supremacy is completely eliminated, marriage, like the state, will wither away." Despite declining crude marriage rates (noted above), marriage remains popular.

12. See Okin (1989), *inter alia*.

13. Mainstream institutional analysts identify several different categories of institution. Roy and Sideras, for example, differentiate economic, political, legal, and social institutions (2006, 5). Marriage arguably spans all four categories of institution, yet tends not to rate much attention in any but the most specifically feminist analyses. By contrast, in the volume edited by Moira Gatens and Alison Mackinnon (1998), marriage features not so much as a standalone institution as a kind of mega-institution informing all others. Nowhere is this more delightfully apparent than in the editors' acknowledgements (xx), for example.

14. I am not sure that it is possible, in the case of marriage, to maintain the conceptual distinction advocated by Foucault. As is so often the case, the problem is much easier to identify than to avoid.

15. Nielsen (1990); essays in Baird and Rosenbaum (1996); Stychin and Herman (2000); and A. Sullivan (1997); *inter alia*.

16. Such strategies include "opt-in" regulations usually described as "domestic partnerships" legislation, presumptive regulations such as broadening the definitional scope of de facto relationships, and calls for the legalization of same-sex marriage (see Brook 2000).

17. For convenience, I do not distinguish the strategies listed above but refer to them collectively under the rubric of "same-sex marriage," except where specified.

18. I have borrowed this phrase for the title of Chapter 7 of this book.

19. Frazer and Lacey (1993, 45); Grimshaw (1986, ch. 6); Pateman (1989 passim, but especially chapter 2).

20. More precisely, it is a particular, idealized version of the masculine body, which operates as the liberal norm.

21. Although Butler does not cite French thinker Jean Baudrillard, her work has a thematic consonance with his, at least in respect of her treatment of iterative mimicry and his work on simulacra (see Chapter 7 of this volume).

CHAPTER 3

1. See (inter alia) Foster 1999; Hegy and Martos 2000; Stuart 1994.
2. For present purposes, the terms "annulment" and "nullity" are interchangeable.
3. For this reason, the discussion of various elements and conditions that may invalidate a marriage will be discussed wherever possible in general terms.
4. The case was ruled under British law—Jagger is English, Hall is American. The result is very likely to have been similar had it been judged in the United States (Oldham 2000, 1409). One wonders, in their case, whether this ground for annulment was always being held in reserve, so to speak, in order to avoid any state interference in the couple's financial arrangements in the event of their breaking up. As it turned out, the pair was reported to have come to a private settlement regarding the divestment of their "marital" property (BBC News Online, 1999).
5. See Clark 1968, 100–14.
6. If the shotgun were real rather than metaphorical, the story would be different. In the American case *Lee v. Lee* (1928), a marriage in which "if there had not been a wedding there would have been a funeral" was deemed void (Cretney and Masson 1997, 63).
7. If the principle it polices is that legitimate issue must be the sons and daughters of a marriage, bigamy might be expected to be an offense on the part of a wife, but not a husband. After all, ambiguity as to paternity may arise, but in the absence of surrogacy or similar arrangements, maternity is generally self-evident.
8. See Vikki Bell 1993; Bratt 1984.
9. Of course King Henry VIII's matrimonial history—with all its causes and consequences—is much more complicated than this. Whether anyone apart from the King could or ever did seek an annulment of marriage on the same grounds is highly unlikely. Though Finlay's example speaks more of monarchical power than matrimonial law, his illustration is nonetheless telling.
10. For a thorough and excellent analysis of illegitimacy, see Reekie 1998.
11. In the United States, blood tests form part of some marriage license requirements (Krause 1983, 39).

12. Historically (and even into the 1960s), epilepsy was sometimes considered a disqualification for marriage (Clark 1968, 87).

13. Nevertheless, the sometimes procreative aspect of heterosexual marriage is repeatedly generalized and invoked as a defense against homosexual marriage.

14. Evidence presented to the court was to the effect that the wife had been artificially inseminated with the husband's sperm.

15. I adopt Katrina Roen's definition of the term "transsexuality" as "a [psychiatrically defined] state of being that assumes the preexistence of two sexes between which one may transition" (Roen 2002, 501–2). I use this term rather than the arguably more inclusive term "transgender" because in matrimonial law, sex and not gender is the more significant site of anxiety and debate. One of the key assumptions to be borne in mind in relation to this definition is that the transsexual person wants to "pass full time as a woman or as a man" (502) with all that attends such passing. For present purposes, when I refer to a transsexual person's (or indeed any person's) *true* sex, I mean to indicate self-identified sex. In this chapter, self-identified sex is almost inevitably a highly gender-conformist identification.

16. This is not to insist that transsexual people are inevitably heterosexual, but to note the distinction drawn between anxieties over corporeal sex/gender coherence and homophobia. This conceptual separation is routinely professed. While I acknowledge the usefulness of the distinction, like Andrew Sharpe (1997), I believe that these anxieties are in fact intimately related.

17. Exactly what constitutes the "social order" that refuses the truth of transsexuality is, of course, subject to debate in itself. Certainly some elements of even the most "progressive" thinking (queer theory, feminist theory) as well as the more conservative traditions of law and medicine have been unable to accommodate transsexual people's realities—i.e., that despite having been born "male," a person might really be "female."

18. One cannot help wondering what Ormrod would have had to say had Ashley decided that she really was homosexual (that is, a lesbian) and sought to marry a (natally) female lover. Given that by Ormrod's logic the marriage would be between a "male" and a "female," he would presumably not object.

19. Note, however, that where a married person elects to undergo surgical transition, they are usually required to divorce their spouse prior to proceeding. Where surgical reassignment is not contemplated, of course, there would be no impediment to the marriage continuing so long as neither spouse objects.

20. Small wonder, then, that queer responses to this positioning are sometimes interpreted as contradictory or confused. On this, see Currah 2003.

Chapter 4

1. Blackstone's words are: "By marriage, the husband and wife are one person in law: that is, the very being or legal existence of the woman is suspended during the marriage, or at least is incorporated and consolidated into that of the husband" (Blackstone 1773; as cited by Parker et al. 1994, 308). See also Blackstone's predecessor, Hale (1713) on marriage.

2. This was apparently a rare and scandalous occurrence (Menefee 1981). The best-known example is fictional, in the opening chapter of Thomas Hardy's *The Mayor of Casterbridge* (1939).

3. Scholars engaging with feminist thought provide numerous exceptions, particularly in relation to domestic violence (see Marcus 1994, 22, for example). See also Robert Chapman, who says, "The abolition of coverture, although begun before the [American] Civil War, was still in progress well into the latter half of the twentieth century" (Chapman 2000, n. 26).

4. See, for example, Norma Basch's analysis of American divorce trial pamphlets of the eighteenth and nineteenth centuries (Basch 1999, especially chapter 6).

5. See, for example, the Australian *Matrimonial Causes Act* (1959), §60–64.

6. In *White v. White* (1948), the judge found that a husband's preference for coitus interruptus constituted cruelty not insofar as it frustrated his wife *sexually*, but in that it frustrated her desire for children. For elaboration and discussion, see Skelly (1969).

7. There is also a great deal of overlap—in various times and places—between "criminal conversation" and "alienation of affections." Roderick Phillips, for example, describes civil actions for criminal conversation in eighteenth-century England, which resemble "alienation of affections" more than "criminal conversation" as such (1988, 228). While the meaning of each term shifts across time and space, they are by no means interchangeable.

8. It is not immediately obvious why the term "conversation" is apposite, but it is probably not merely a quaint euphemism. The word derives from the Latin contraction of *contra*, "against," with *vertere*, "to turn." The roots of the everyday meaning of the word "conversation" are similar but not identical. In the to and fro-ing of dialogue, conversation's *con* implies "with" rather than "against," and pairs with *versare*, "to keep turning." In any case, the assonant vocabulary of speech acts and sex acts is intriguing.

9. As if matters were not already complex enough, adultery has also figured as a criminal or misdemeanor offense in a number of jurisdictions (Green, Long, and Murawski 1986, 17; Perkins 1972, 224–25). Prosecutions, however, are rare (Jones 1998, 65; Friedman 2000, 1523).

10. Roderick Phillips (1988, 228) likens the availability of suits open only to husbands against their wife's lover to a kind of trespass, after Davidoff (1974).

11. See Chapter 6.

12. See, for example, Tony Honoré, who says that adultery has been prohibited and penalized because it "leads to the danger that the children of strangers will be accepted as members of an adulterous wife's family" (1978, 28). O. R. McGregor's views are similar (1957, 20-21). The sexual double standard operating in a belief such as this is startling. From a mother's perspective, any child born to oneself must (by definition) ordinarily be understood as one's child, and a member of one's family.

13. This case prompted New Zealand to include, in its *Matrimonial Proceedings Act* 1963, a stipulation that artificial insemination occurring without the husband's knowledge and using the semen of a man other than the husband constituted a matrimonial offense (Phillips 1988, 45).

14. The reasoning behind the higher standard of certainty in criminal law is that the offender's liberty is at stake in criminal trials, but not in civil actions. Standards have differed, of course, across time and jurisdiction.

15. "Manual satisfaction," in this context, means masturbation of the man by the woman.

16. See too, however, the more expansive definition of "marital rights" outlined in an *American Law Reports* annotation, where "sympathies and confidences" are referred to along with enjoyment of each other's company, sharing meals, and so on (1953, 153–54). These elements seem to come into play only where a wife claims that her "condoning" sex with her husband in fact occurred under duress.

17. That a single act of intercourse constitutes condonation seems to hold more as a bar or defense against grounds of adultery, and is somewhat less likely to succeed where one act of intercourse is held to have condoned cruelty and similar offenses. In some jurisdictions, even in cases not brought on grounds of adultery, "a single act of intercourse is *evidence of* condonation," (*American Law Reports* 1953, my emphasis) even though it may not be sufficient in itself. In others, a single occasion of intercourse has been held to condone cruelty.

18. There are exceptions to this rule, but these have been idiosyncratic and strongly contested. In a 1950 case, the Supreme Court of Nebraska ruled that "Sexual intercourse is not an indispensable element of condonation" (*Wright v. Wright* 1950, 424). The court also stated, however, that cohabitation implies sexual intercourse, and forgiveness can be inferred from sexual intercourse.

19. See *Henderson v. Henderson* 1944, where it was accepted that the wife induced intercourse fraudulently.

CHAPTER 5

1. See, for example, Allen (2000); Brown (1996); Cott (2000); Hodes (1999); Kennedy (2003); Moran (2001); Newbeck (2004); Romano (2003); Saks (2000); Sollors (2000); and Wallenstein (2002).

2. See, for example, most of the works listed in the previous note, along with Pascoe (1991, 1996); Ellinghaus (2001); Grimshaw (2002); Higginbotham and Kopytoft (2000); McGrath (1987); Van Tassel (1995); Robinson (2003); Goodale (1971); Ganter (2005); inter alia.

3. Brinig (1998); Carter (1998); Coolidge (1998); Destro (1997); Kennedy (1997); Nolan (1998); Pratt (1998); Sekulow and Tuskey (1997). See also Andreasen (2004); Koppelman (1997); Marcosson (1992), and especially Ross (2002).

4. The relationship of no-fault divorce and rising divorce rates is subject to contestation, and will be considered in Chapter 6.

5. On the effects of "Aboriginalism" and its terminologies, see Attwood and Arnold (1992); Moreton-Robinson (2000, 73–77).

6. Richard Dyer's (1997) work on representations of whiteness and Celia Daileader's (2005) book exploring representations of interracial couples are especially interesting. Martha Nussbaum's (1997) essay on *Loving v. Virginia* and the literary imagination is also particularly pertinent, as is Susan Courtney's (2005) book.

7. See, for example, Gordon (1964); Alibhai-Brown and Montague (1992); Owen (2002); McNamara et al. (1999); Root (2001); Rosenblatt et al. (1995).

8. Membership of the categories "white" and "non-white" varied according to time and place, and was often ambiguous. Generally, the category "white" was unmarked or only vaguely defined. Thirty-eight states have had bans on interracial marriage in place at various times. The states that prohibited interracial marriage until the Virginian legislation was overturned were Alabama, Arkansas, Delaware, Florida, Georgia, Kentucky, Louisiana, Mississippi, Missouri, North Carolina, Oklahoma, South Carolina, Tennessee, Texas, Virginia, and West Virginia.

9. Perhaps this is characteristic of people in highly mobile, highly migratory societies like my own. A qualification, then: people of my acquaintance are rarely able to name their great-grandparents.

10. In an absorbing and astute critique, Shane Phelan (1997) discusses sexual corollaries to hypo-descent. She considers, for example, whether a single episode of male-to-male sex makes a man (inevitably, irrevocably, fundamentally) homosexual. Her comparison is provocative and compelling, and will be considered again later in this book (Chapter 8).

11. The fears held by Powell and his followers were possibly based on white supremacist interpretations of Mexican experience. We can surmise that

miscegenation—and not the invasion, dispossession, massacre, rape, and cultural denudation of Indigenous people by colonising forces—was held responsible for the generation of Mexico's mostly *mestizo* population. That such miscegenation occurred, in the first place, largely as a result of the rape of Indigenous Indian women (Mörner 1967, 36; Gutiérrez 1995, 166) by the Spanish colonisers would probably not have figured in Powell's thinking.

12. And other anti-racist feminists, of course, including the influential contributions of Patricia Hill Collins (1990), Angela Davis (1998), Ruth Frankenberg (1993), and Aileen Moreton-Robinson (2000).

13. In Australia, non-Indigenous people can expect to live nearly twenty years longer than Indigenous people. This situation is mirrored by a raft of disadvantages accruing to Indigenous men and women in every aspect of individual and social well being.

14. In Australia, missionaries shifted this familiar logic to garner sympathy for the idea that Indigenous infants—and especially infant girls—should be removed from cultures practicing infant betrothal. For more on this, see below.

15. For a more complete account of Indigenous Australian women's experience as drovers and drovers' wives, see Ann McGrath's celebrated *Born In The Cattle* (1987).

16. Paul Lombardo notes that the architects of Virginia's *Racial Integrity Act of 1924* (on which the proscription of the Lovings' marriage rested) made similar claims: the white supremacist Anglo-Saxon Clubs of America organization insisted that it was "definitely and explicitly opposed to . . . racial prejudice" (Lombardo 1988, 429). Across both continents, then, we see what Peggy Pascoe (1996, 68) calls "an Alice-in-Wonderland interpretation of racism in which even those who argue for racially oppressive policies can adamantly deny being racists."

17. The divisive effects of wardship and exemptions from wardship are noted in Brock (1995), Baldini (1995), and Mattingley (1988, 48–52), inter alia.

18. Wallenstein notes in an appendix that Nazi Germany and South Africa under apartheid proscribed interracial marriage, but does not mention Australia (Wallenstein 2002, 255–56). Herma Hill Kay asserts that laws forbidding mixed race marriage "never existed in England or Australia" (Kay 1991, 71). Newbeck is the exception, noting that Australia (along with a number of other nations) has prohibited mixed race marriage, but her point is to emphasize that the United States was "virtually unique" in its rejection of mixed marriage (Newbeck 2004, 25).

19. Debating the justification for this clause (c) in the Northern Territory Legislative Council, the Government Secretary said:

> My experience suggests to me that the offences of the kind I am describing are most likely to be committed during the night hours

than during the daylight hours. If therefore it is made an offence for persons to be in company between the hours of sunset and sunrise, attempted offences of the kind that I have mentioned will be more easily detected. What is aimed at in this clause is not the actual association between those hours but the prevention of the offence that I have mentioned by making it an offence to be in association at all. (As cited in Hughes 1965, 303–4)

20. For a competing view, see Stember (1976, 5), who argues that "the term 'intermarriage,' among the bigoted, . . . is merely a euphemism for *any* sexual activity: though they may use the word 'marriage,' they simply mean 'sex'" (Ross 2002, 257).
21. Indeed, white cultural fears built on the assumption that black peoples would prefer white marriage partners if such partners were available to them attests to the ridiculous cultural-sexual vanity of whiteness.
22. For an interesting discussion of the recognition of customary marriage in post-apartheid South Africa, see Mamashela (2004).
23. As Perry and Sutton note, "the myth of a lascivious, rapacious, and insatiable black sexuality is perhaps one of the most enduring themes in Western racialized cultures" (2006, 891–92). See also Cornel West (1993, 119).
24. For an interesting treatment of the contrast and its relationship to liberal humanism in particular, see Povinelli (2006, chap. 3); see also Cott "Consent, the American Way" (2000, chap. 6).
25. Archived records were eventually made available under the thirty-year rule.
26. As Romano observes, "Dating a white girl could be a status symbol for a black boy, but dating a black girl conferred no status on a white boy" (Romano 2003, 237).
27. For example, historian Patricia Grimshaw suggests that Indigenous women in colonial times become the sexual partners of white men out of "desperat[ion] for food" or as victims of rape (2002, 20). (This is not the sum of her argument, which is more astute than this note suggests.) For a different view, see Cowlishaw (1999, 68); McGrath (1987, 82).
28. Romano cites two sets of figures, the higher of which puts the percentage of "interracial" American marriages at just over four percent in 2000 (Romano 2003, 3). Though substantially higher than Wilson and Russell's figure, the percentage is small nonetheless.

CHAPTER 6

1. For comparative studies, see Day (1964); Marwick (1969); Goode (1993); Smith (2002); and especially Glendon (1989).

2. Similarly, if in a cross-petition *neither* spouse were found to have committed an offense, the divorce sought by the parties must be denied. In *Le Brocq v. Le Brocq* (1964), for example, the husband and wife were found to be merely (though completely) incompatible with each other—insufficient grounds for divorce.

3. This attitude was not limited to "new" nations like Australia: Deborah Field notes almost identical discourses in the Russian Khrushchev era. At this time, she says, "Moralists and party propagandists emphasized that divorce was selfish, and they urged married people to control their passions for the sake of . . . the country's future" (Field 1998, 599). See also Lynn Wardle's (2003) treatment of similar issues.

4. Josephine Ross notes that in the early 1960s, every U.S. state had laws against sodomy (Ross 2002, 262n32).

5. Unfortunately, Lord Justice Fenton Atkinson did not cite those cases.

6. When these cases were heard in England, "unnatural offenses" were not in themselves grounds for divorce there. It would seem that the justness of allowing divorce in these circumstances but their inexact conformity to (existing) grounds of "cruelty" led to their inclusion as separate grounds.

7. The possibility that a woman might be a rapist or that a man might be raped seems not to have been countenanced.

8. The "elasticity" of cruelty is not consistent over time and space. For an interesting elaboration of the operations of cruelty as a ground for divorce in more recent times, see Clute (1991).

9. For an interesting consideration of related issues, see *Williams v. Williams* (1964). In this case, the wife alleged cruelty on the part of her certifiably schizophrenic husband. The husband defended the petition, arguing that the "cruelty" of which he was accused was entirely the result of his illness. The court had to decide whether mental illness could be considered a defense against a divorce petition relying on grounds of cruelty. The majority decision was that it could not. Thus, the wife's petition and appeals were allowed.

10. Consider this telling exchange in Margaret Atwood's brilliant 1969 novel *The Edible Woman* (1978, 275):

> "Maybe I should see a psychiatrist," she said gloomily.
>
> "Oh no, don't do that. They'd only want to adjust you."
>
> "But I want to be adjusted, that's just it. I don't see any point in being unstable."

11. Isabel Marcus (1994) describes her experience lecturing on women's rights in India. She says that whenever she discussed the incidence of domestic violence, men would retort, "But what about the shamefully

high divorce rate in your country [the United States]?" (1994, 13–14). Marcus describes the men's response as a *non-sequitur*, but in many ways the connection is quite clear.

12. Producer Tracey Riddiford is researching a "what if?" mockumentary exploring the consequences of a (mythical) statute that would allow women to shoot male partners with virtual impunity. If a presumption of self-defense were mobilized every time a woman shot a man, what social consequences would ensue? (2005).

13. It is worth noting the additional delays experienced by some divorcing couples when appeals to decisions were heard. Lord Justice Harman, for example, notes in a 1964 court of appeals case that the case was brought two years previously, and concerned events which had occurred some ten years previously (*Le Brocq v. Le Brocq* 1964).

14. For the effective dates of no-fault divorce laws in the United States, see Vlosky and Monroe (2002).

15. For an interesting discussion of similar issues, see Wardle (2003).

16. Swisher (2005); Hanschu and Kisthardt (2003); Hasson (2003); Dnes and Rowthorn (2002); Wicks (2000); Ellman (1997); Schimmerling (1997); Starnes (1993); Wardle (1991).

17. Swisher (2005); Smith (2002); Vlosky and Monroe (2002); but *cf* Biondi (1999, 618); Marvell (1989, 543, 547); Ellman (1997).

18. I am not suggesting that the debate is limited to politically conservative thinkers; see Swisher (2005) for a guide to relevant sources and arguments. For examples of the politically conservative claim that "easy" divorce causes more marriages to break down, see Schoenfeld (1996).

19. As Ellman argues, "Fans of fault often make the mistake of thinking that fault laws protect the innocent. They do not. They protect the person who does not care about delaying the divorce, at the expense of the person who does—and who may have very good reasons for wanting out" (Ellman 1997, 224).

20. In Australia, for example, where separation has served as the *only* relevant evidence of marital breakdown since 1975, any return to fault is utterly inconceivable. Similarly, I suspect that any "marriage movement" of the kind endorsed by the Bush administration would be unlikely to flourish in many places beyond the United States.

21. Flory (2000) notes that one year after "covenant" marriage was introduced in Louisiana, only one percent of couples had opted for it.

CHAPTER 7

1. This is interesting in itself and possibly reflects the inferior political status of cohabitation relative to marriage.

2. These are words and phrases used in official terminology; there are even more in colloquial use.
3. The same logic informs the criminalization of prostitution, of course—a connection long acknowledged and explored in feminist scholarship (see B. Sullivan 1997, Pateman 1988 for relevant examples).
4. See, for example, Foreman and O'Ryan (1983, 29) on the United Kingdom; Carney (2006, 185–88) on Australia; Douthwaite (1979, 49–55 on the United States.
5. Cohabitative relationships have been (historically) and still are (usually) restricted to heterosexual couples, though some places have moved to extend the scope of laws to cover gay and lesbian couples. This will be discussed in more detail in the following chapter.
6. Except, perhaps, where women are welfare recipients. In this case, the state is very interested. We might speculate that where women are social security recipients, the state often stands as a surrogate husband. To extend this formulation, the (welfare) state will stand neither bigamy nor cuckolding.
7. Since this issue is strongly articulated to debates on same-sex marriage, I will explore it in more depth later in the book.
8. Coolidge and Duncan (2001) inevitably place quote marks around "marriage" when they discuss same-sex relationships. They do this to indicate their view that same-sex relationships can never be *real* marriages, whatever the law might say.
9. See Rose and Wood's (2005) discussion of authenticity and reality television.

CHAPTER 8

1. See, for example, Amadiume (1987); Callender and Kochems (1983); Blackwood (1986); Oboler (1980). I would not go as far as Eskridge (1996) does in claiming certain arrangements as "same-sex marriage" or even "unions," since some do not involve any kind of sexual relationship at all (Lubin and Duncan 1998).
2. For discussion of "The Berdache Wars," see Califia (1997).
3. For references to *Loving* versus *Virginia*, see Hunter (1995, 110–11); Eskridge (1996, 153–82); Wolfson (1997, 130–32); Posner (1997, 187–89); Kay (1991); Koppelman (1997, 2001); Baird and Rosenbaum (1997, 12); Pierce (1997, 170); Hawaii, Commission on Sexual Orientation and the Law (1997, 213); A. Sullivan (1997, 238–39); Richards (2001, 29); Feldblum (2001, 70–71).
4. A raft of alternative terms, including "civil union," "domestic partnership," "domestic relationship," and "registered partnership" has been

suggested in lieu of "marriage" for same-sex spouses. These terminologies and the different forms of conjugality they assume will be discussed toward the end of this chapter.

5. See for example Sheila Jeffreys's (2004) commentary on *Feminism & Psychology's* special double issue on marriage; Saalfield (1993); Card (1996); Colker (1991).

6. One might argue that the technical detail of *copula vera* requires the symbolic "man" to be incorporated into the symbolic "woman." That is, the penis is enveloped by the vagina. Those versed in psychoanalysis might read into this a source of corporeal-psychic anxiety animating marital misogyny.

INDEX

cruelty, 127–29, 134–39, 244n8.
See also domestic violence;
matrimonial offenses
Currie, Dawn H., 167

Daly, Mick, 106–14, 116–19
Davis, Angela, 104
de facto marriage. *See* cohabitation
Deech, Ruth, 158–60
defense of marriage, 6, 33, 179,
180, 189
definitional anxieties, 185–86,
196–97, 200–201
Delphy, Christine, 21, 26, 34, 155
democracy and marriage, 50–51
dependence, economic, 10, 17, 19,
24, 34, 158, 164–65, 170–71
desertion, 76, 129–31
desexualization, 160–61, 182–84,
193, 195–96, 202–4
dissolution of marriage. *See*
annulment; divorce
divorce, 7, 10, 18, 24, 28, 121–22;
adversarial, 123–39; bars to,
131–34; as "death," 141, 149;
"easy," 136, 148, 245n18;
grounds for, 123; no-fault,
139–51, 195, 245n14. *See also*
collusion; condonation;
connivance; consent; divorce;
matrimonial offenses;
separation
domestic labor, 16, 18, 19, 21, 24,
26, 27–28, 155
domestic relationships. *See* civil
unions; same-sex marriage
domestic violence, 7, 19, 20, 24,
28–29, 123, 129, 134–39,
245n11. *See also* cruelty;
violence
double standards. *See* inequality,
spousal
drunkenness, as ground for divorce,
124

duress, 48–49, 91, 240n16
Dworkin, Andrea, 157–58
Dyer, Richard, 98

"easy" divorce, 136, 148, 245n18.
See also no-fault divorce
Ecclesiastical law, 9
ejaculation, 53, 54
eligibility to marry, 44, 49–53
Ellis, J. *See Otahuhu Family Court,
Attorney-General v.*
Ellman, Ira Mark, 245n19
embodiment. *See* corporeality
Engels, Friedrich, 4, 85
epilepsy, 238n12
epistemology, 17, 31
equality, spousal. *See* inequality,
spousal
Eskridge, William, 64, 181–82,
188, 246n1
Ettelbrick, Paula, 30, 188–89, 191
Evans v. Evans, 79–80

family, 50, 109–10
"family values," 179
Fatal Attraction, 84–85
fathers. *See* paternity
feminism, 10, 151, 155; and
cohabitation, 157–59; and
marriage, 14–40; and racism,
103–6, 184; and same-sex
marriage, 189–92
feminist critiques of marriage, 3,
11, 15, 155, 179–80, 188; as
patriarchal, 19–22; as sexist,
16–19
feminist theory, 13–40
Field, Deborah, 244n3
Fineman, Martha, 22
forgiveness; forgiving sex. *See*
condonation

LaVergne, TN USA
14 December 2009
166938LV00003B/34/P